CHLOE & CO

First published 2016

Amberley Publishing
The Hill, Stroud
Gloucestershire, GL5 4EP

www.amberley-books.com

Copyright © Gray Jolliffe, 2016

The right of Gray Jolliffe to be identified as the Author
of this work has been asserted in accordance with the
Copyrights, Designs and Patents Act 1988.

ISBN 978 1 4456 6298 5 (paperback)
ISBN 978 1 4456 6299 2 (ebook)

British Library Cataloguing in Publication Data.
A catalogue record for this book is available from the British
Library.

CHLOE & CO

IF I OFFERED YOU A GRAND A WEEK AS MY PERSONAL ASSISTANT WOULD YOU SAY YES?
YOU BET
TWICE A DAY IF NECESSARY

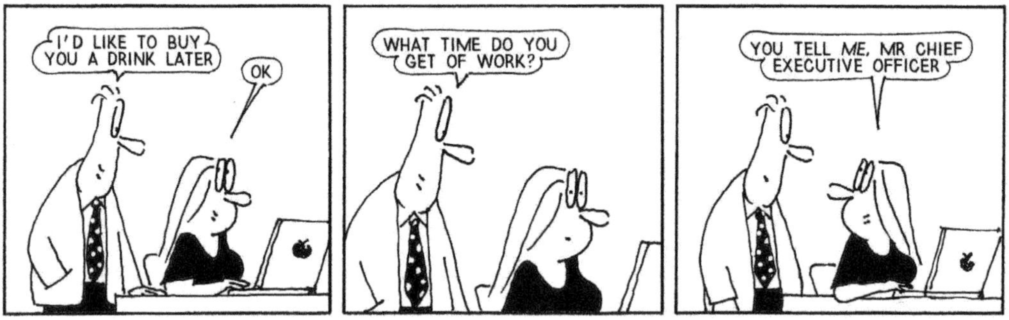
I'D LIKE TO BUY YOU A DRINK LATER
OK
WHAT TIME DO YOU GET OF WORK?
YOU TELL *ME,* MR CHIEF EXECUTIVE OFFICER

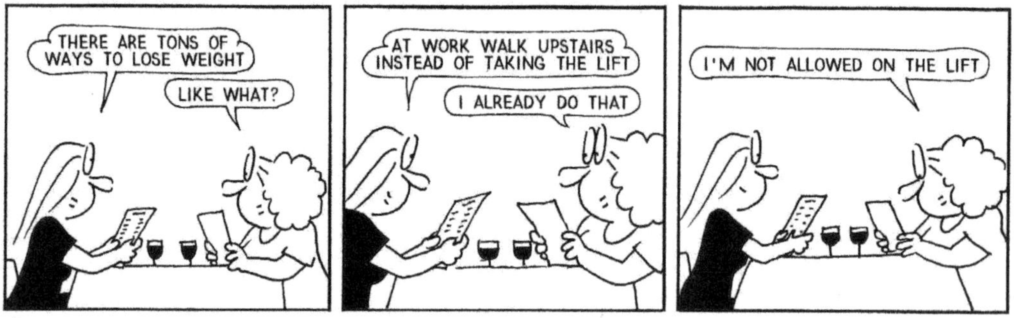
THERE ARE TONS OF WAYS TO LOSE WEIGHT
LIKE WHAT?
AT WORK WALK UPSTAIRS INSTEAD OF TAKING THE LIFT
I ALREADY DO THAT
I'M NOT ALLOWED ON THE LIFT

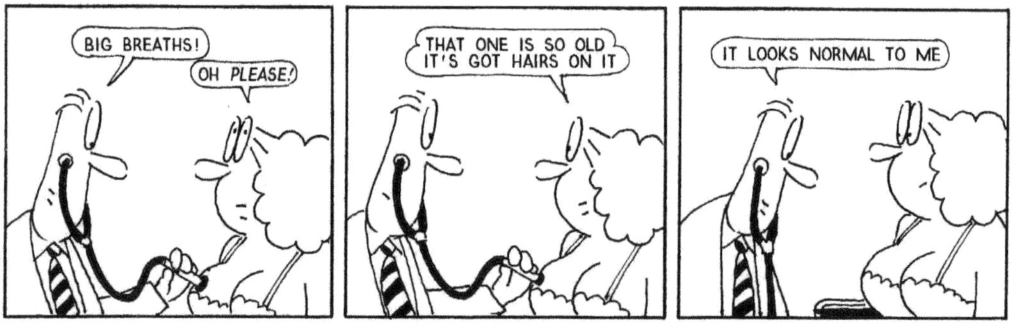
BIG BREATHS!
OH *PLEASE!*
THAT ONE IS SO OLD IT'S GOT HAIRS ON IT
IT LOOKS NORMAL TO ME

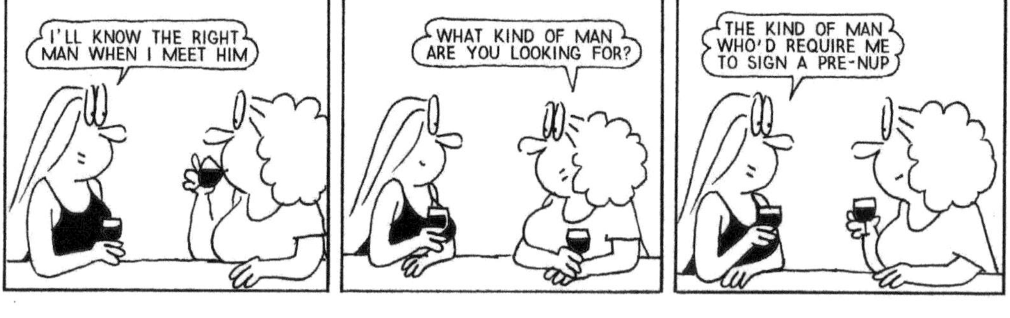
I'LL KNOW THE RIGHT MAN WHEN I MEET HIM
WHAT KIND OF MAN ARE YOU LOOKING FOR?
THE KIND OF MAN WHO'D REQUIRE ME TO SIGN A PRE-NUP

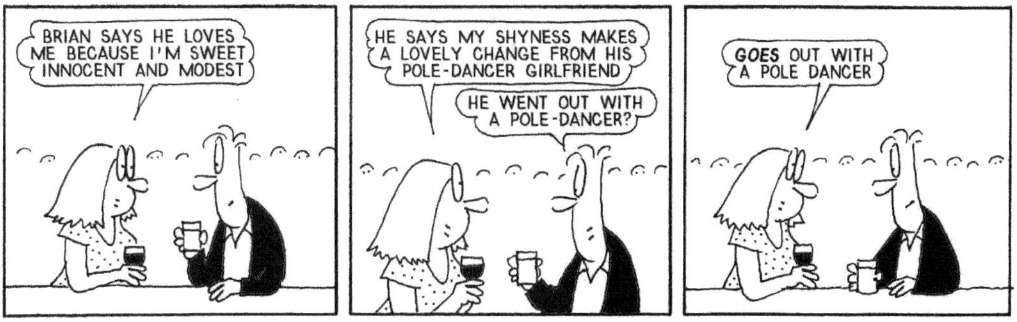
BRIAN SAYS HE LOVES ME BECAUSE I'M SWEET INNOCENT AND MODEST
HE SAYS MY SHYNESS MAKES A LOVELY CHANGE FROM HIS POLE-DANCER GIRLFRIEND
HE WENT OUT WITH A POLE-DANCER?
GOES OUT WITH A POLE DANCER

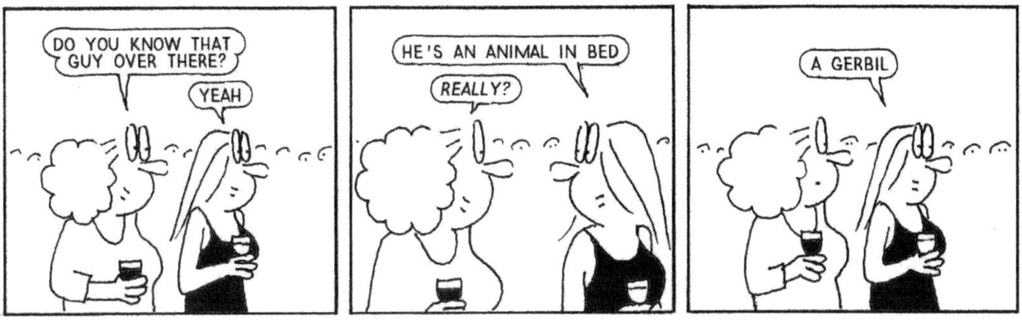
DO YOU KNOW THAT GUY OVER THERE?
YEAH
HE'S AN ANIMAL IN BED
REALLY?
A GERBIL

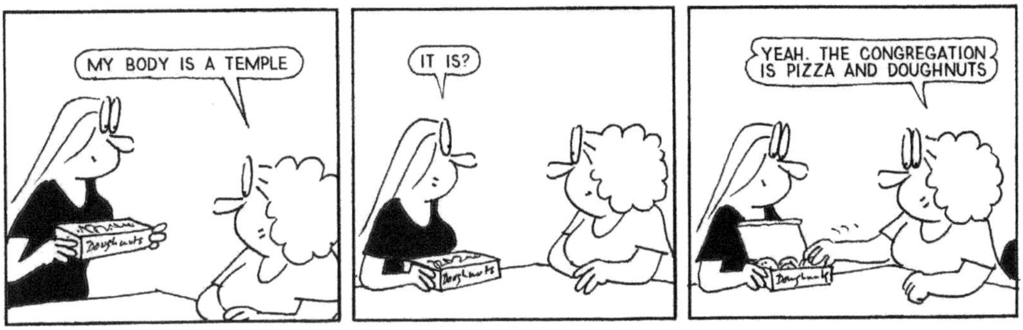
MY BODY IS A TEMPLE
IT IS?
YEAH. THE CONGREGATION IS PIZZA AND DOUGHNUTS

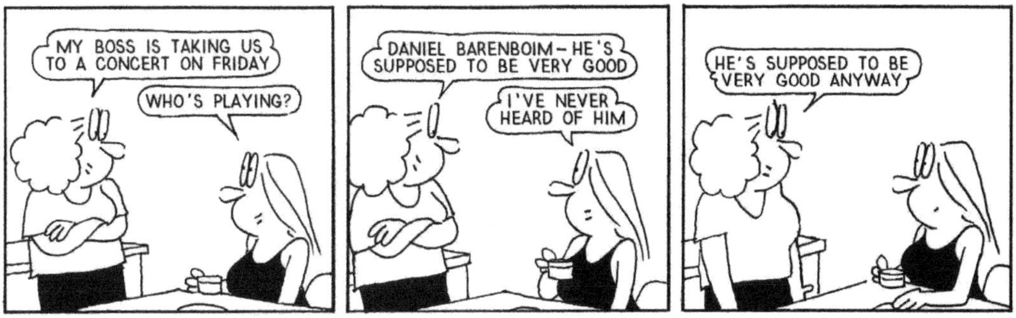
MY BOSS IS TAKING US TO A CONCERT ON FRIDAY
WHO'S PLAYING?
DANIEL BARENBOIM - HE'S SUPPOSED TO BE VERY GOOD
I'VE NEVER HEARD OF HIM
HE'S SUPPOSED TO BE VERY GOOD ANYWAY

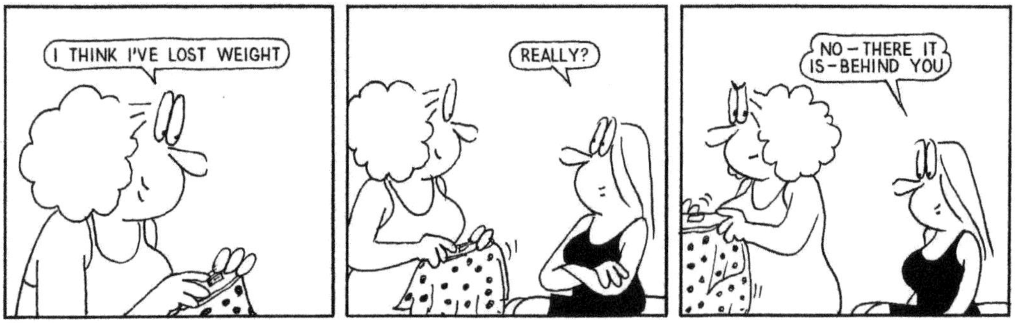
I THINK I'VE LOST WEIGHT
REALLY?
NO – THERE IT IS – BEHIND YOU

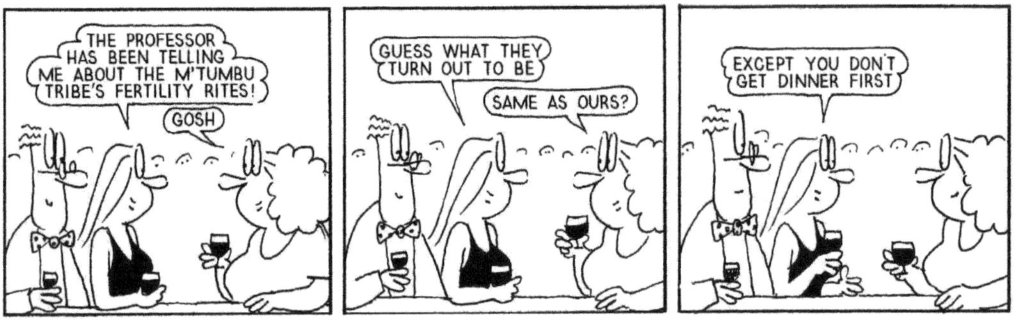
THE PROFESSOR HAS BEEN TELLING ME ABOUT THE M'TUMBU TRIBE'S FERTILITY RITES!
GOSH
GUESS WHAT THEY TURN OUT TO BE
SAME AS OURS?
EXCEPT YOU DON'T GET DINNER FIRST

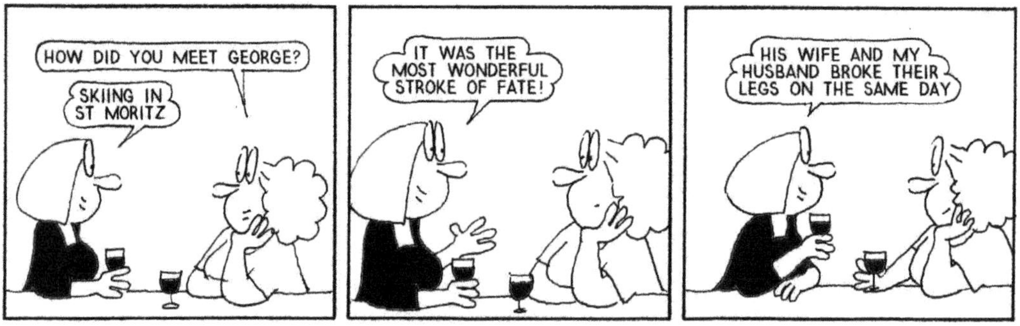
HOW DID YOU MEET GEORGE?
SKIING IN ST MORITZ
IT WAS THE MOST WONDERFUL STROKE OF FATE!
HIS WIFE AND MY HUSBAND BROKE THEIR LEGS ON THE SAME DAY

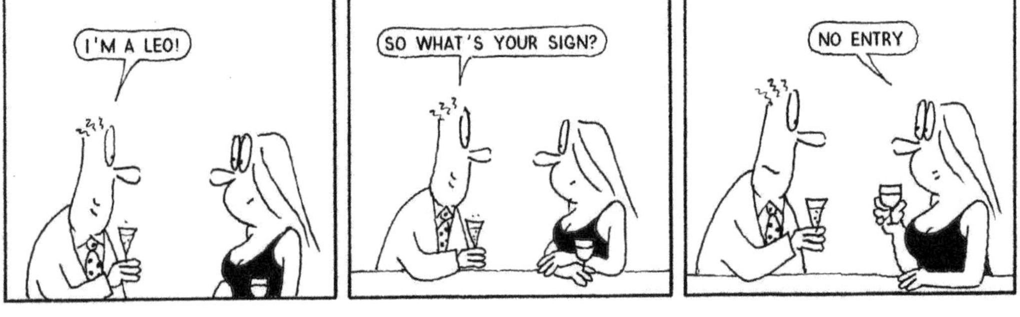
I'M A LEO!
SO WHAT'S YOUR SIGN?
NO ENTRY

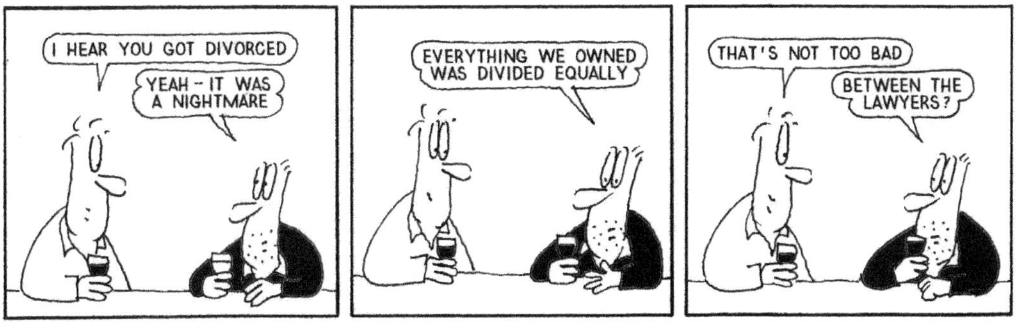
I HEAR YOU GOT DIVORCED
YEAH - IT WAS A NIGHTMARE
EVERYTHING WE OWNED WAS DIVIDED EQUALLY
THAT'S NOT TOO BAD
BETWEEN THE LAWYERS?

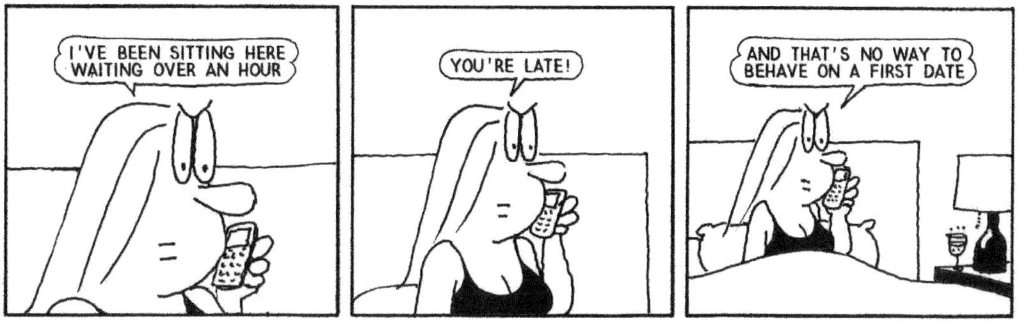
I'VE BEEN SITTING HERE WAITING OVER AN HOUR
YOU'RE LATE!
AND THAT'S NO WAY TO BEHAVE ON A FIRST DATE

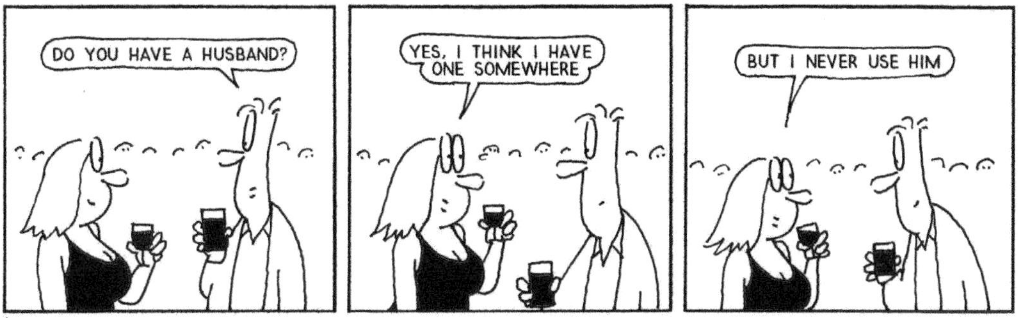
DO YOU HAVE A HUSBAND?
YES, I THINK I HAVE ONE SOMEWHERE
BUT I NEVER USE HIM

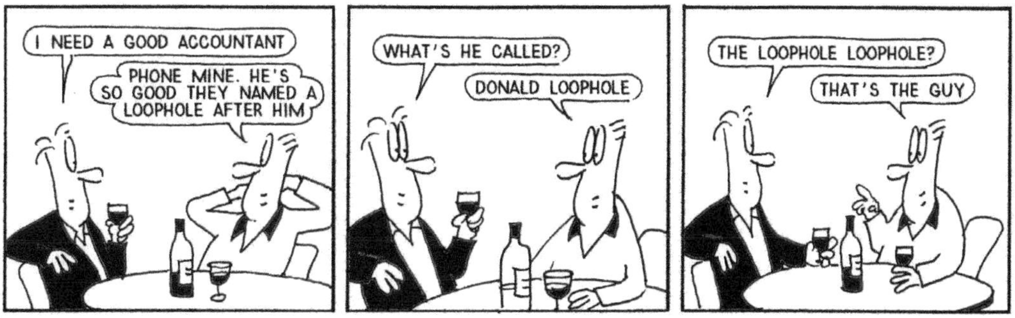
I NEED A GOOD ACCOUNTANT
PHONE MINE. HE'S SO GOOD THEY NAMED A LOOPHOLE AFTER HIM
WHAT'S HE CALLED?
DONALD LOOPHOLE
THE LOOPHOLE LOOPHOLE?
THAT'S THE GUY

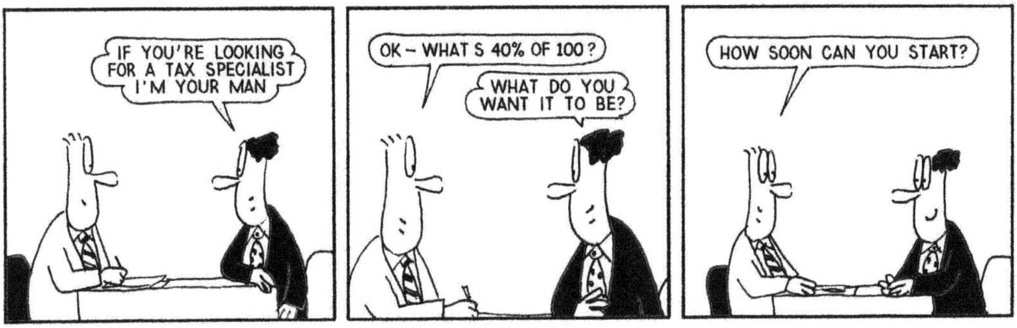
IF YOU'RE LOOKING FOR A TAX SPECIALIST I'M YOUR MAN
OK – WHAT S 40% OF 100?
WHAT DO YOU WANT IT TO BE?
HOW SOON CAN YOU START?

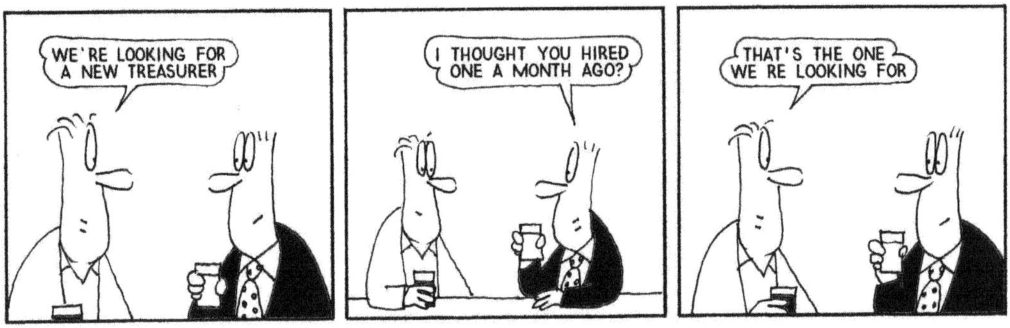
WE'RE LOOKING FOR A NEW TREASURER
I THOUGHT YOU HIRED ONE A MONTH AGO?
THAT'S THE ONE WE RE LOOKING FOR

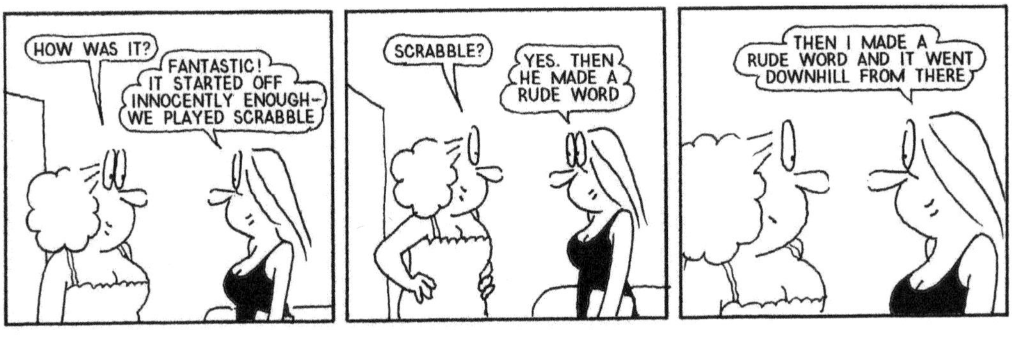
HOW WAS IT?
FANTASTIC! IT STARTED OFF INNOCENTLY ENOUGH– WE PLAYED SCRABBLE
SCRABBLE?
YES. THEN HE MADE A RUDE WORD
THEN I MADE A RUDE WORD AND IT WENT DOWNHILL FROM THERE

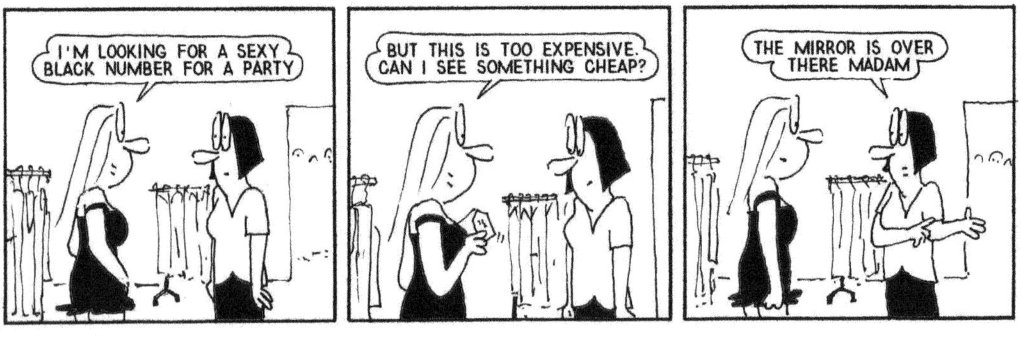
I'M LOOKING FOR A SEXY BLACK NUMBER FOR A PARTY
BUT THIS IS TOO EXPENSIVE. CAN I SEE SOMETHING CHEAP?
THE MIRROR IS OVER THERE MADAM

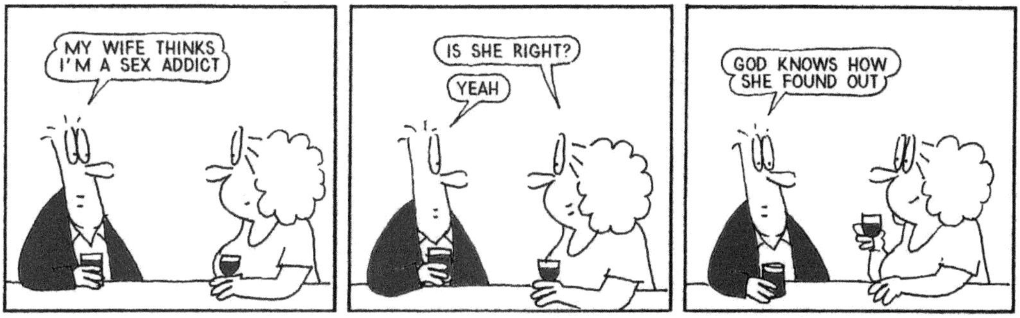
MY WIFE THINKS I'M A SEX ADDICT
IS SHE RIGHT?
YEAH
GOD KNOWS HOW SHE FOUND OUT

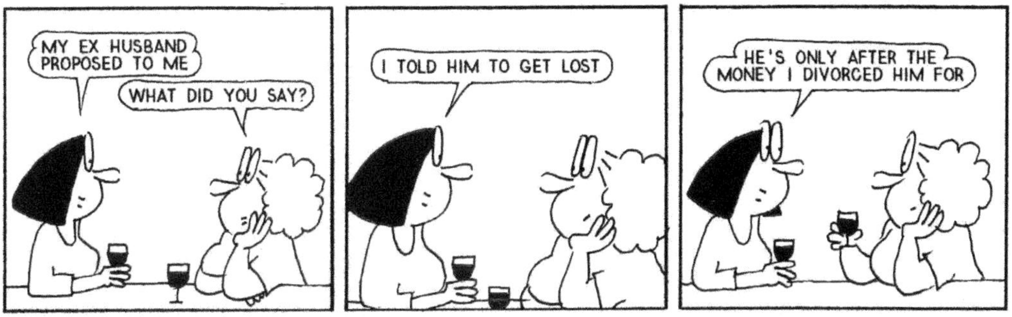
MY EX HUSBAND PROPOSED TO ME
WHAT DID YOU SAY?
I TOLD HIM TO GET LOST
HE'S ONLY AFTER THE MONEY I DIVORCED HIM FOR

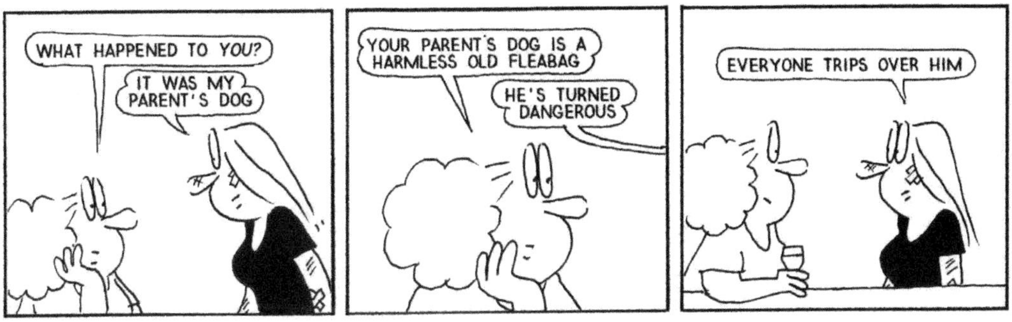
WHAT HAPPENED TO *YOU?*
IT WAS MY PARENT'S DOG
YOUR PARENT'S DOG IS A HARMLESS OLD FLEABAG
HE'S TURNED DANGEROUS
EVERYONE TRIPS OVER HIM

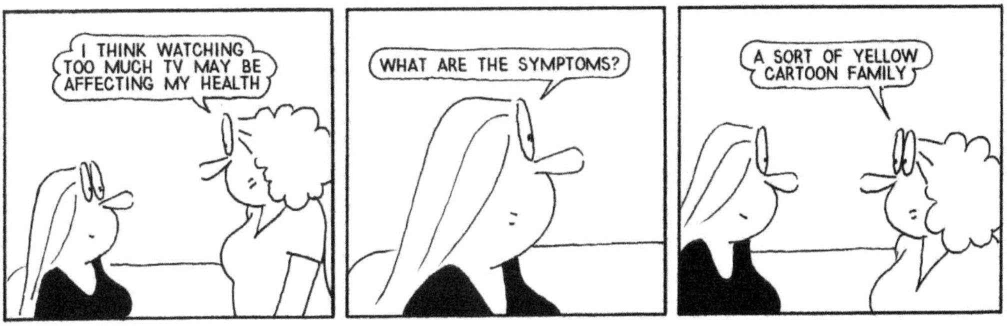
I THINK WATCHING TOO MUCH TV MAY BE AFFECTING MY HEALTH
WHAT ARE THE SYMPTOMS?
A SORT OF YELLOW CARTOON FAMILY

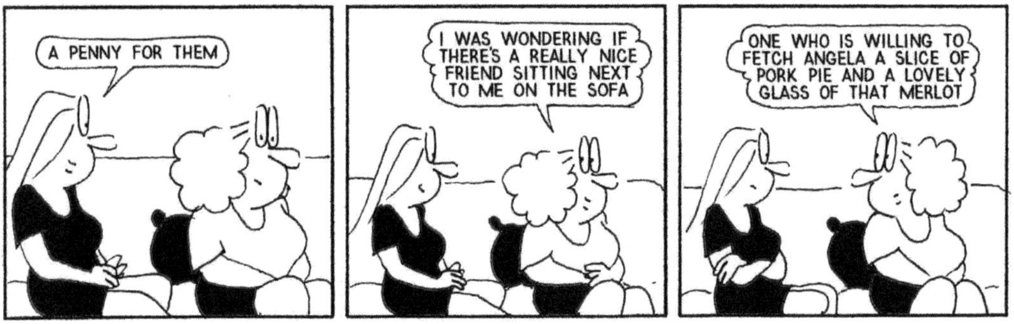
A PENNY FOR THEM
I WAS WONDERING IF THERE'S A REALLY NICE FRIEND SITTING NEXT TO ME ON THE SOFA
ONE WHO IS WILLING TO FETCH ANGELA A SLICE OF PORK PIE AND A LOVELY GLASS OF THAT MERLOT

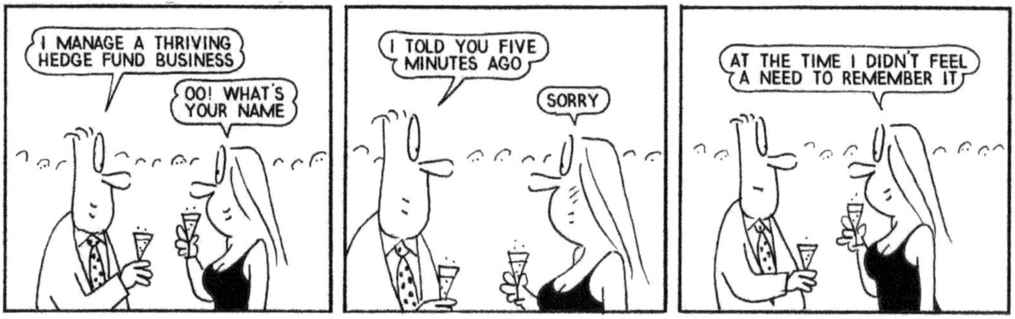
I MANAGE A THRIVING HEDGE FUND BUSINESS
OO! WHAT'S YOUR NAME
I TOLD YOU FIVE MINUTES AGO
SORRY
AT THE TIME I DIDN'T FEEL A NEED TO REMEMBER IT

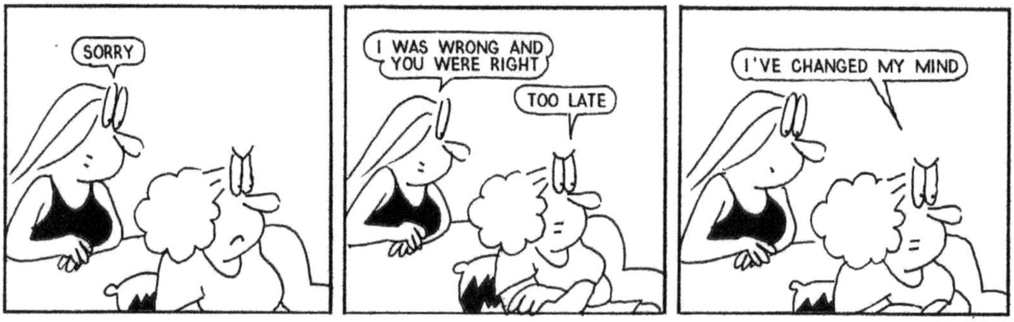
SORRY
I WAS WRONG AND YOU WERE RIGHT
TOO LATE
I'VE CHANGED MY MIND

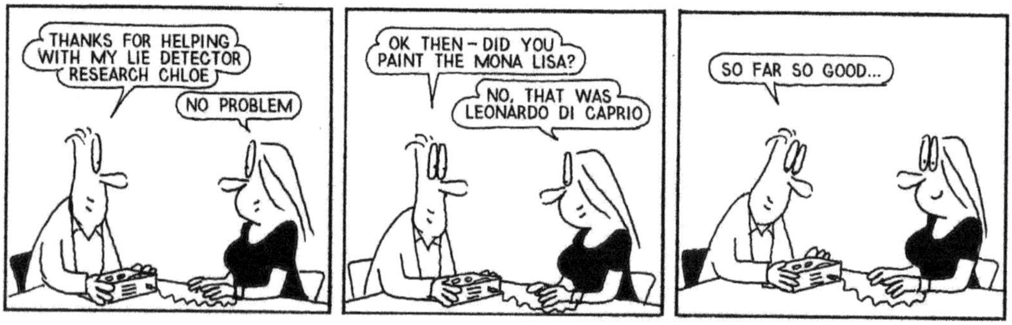
THANKS FOR HELPING WITH MY LIE DETECTOR RESEARCH CHLOE
NO PROBLEM
OK THEN – DID YOU PAINT THE MONA LISA?
NO, THAT WAS LEONARDO DI CAPRIO
SO FAR SO GOOD...

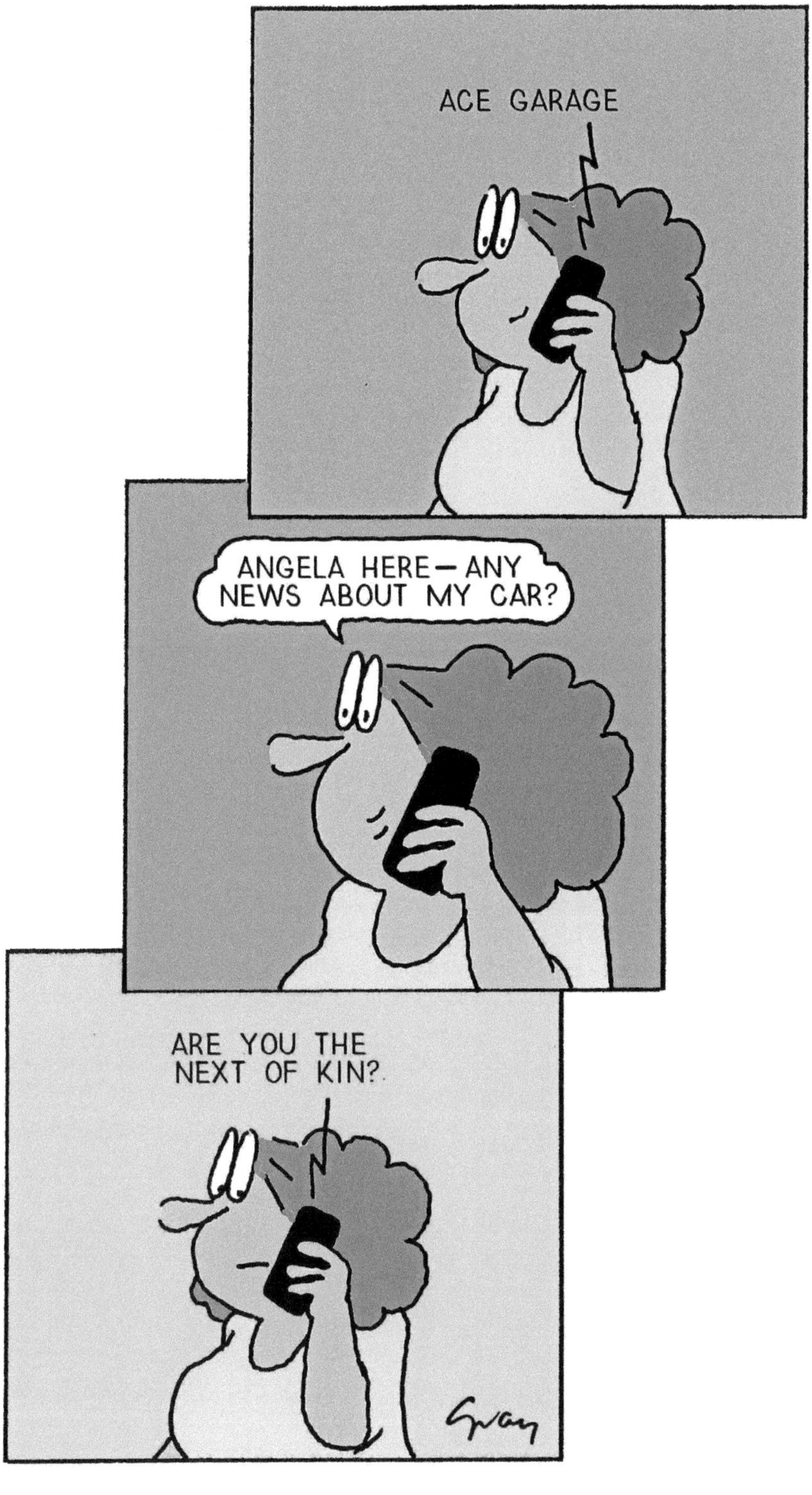
ACE GARAGE
ANGELA HERE—ANY NEWS ABOUT MY CAR?
ARE YOU THE NEXT OF KIN?

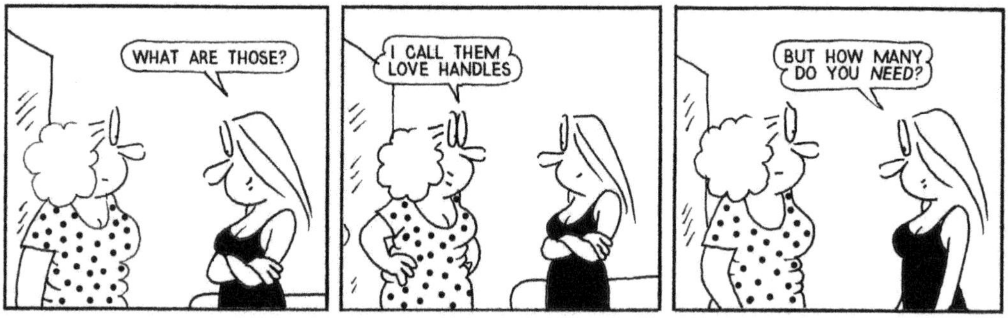
WHAT ARE THOSE?
I CALL THEM LOVE HANDLES
BUT HOW MANY DO YOU *NEED?*

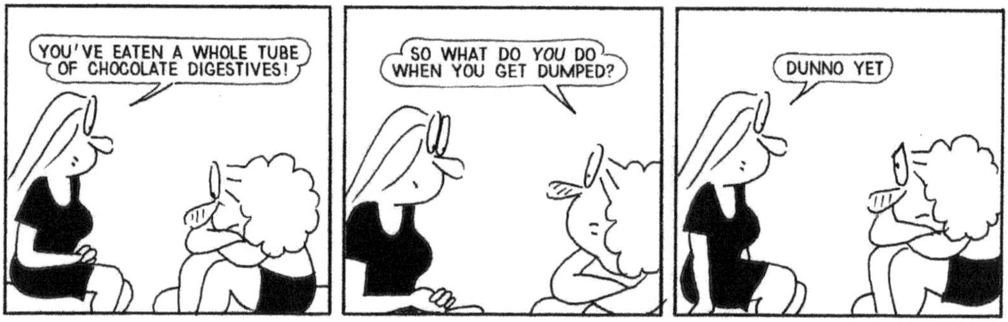
YOU'VE EATEN A WHOLE TUBE OF CHOCOLATE DIGESTIVES!
SO WHAT DO *YOU* DO WHEN YOU GET DUMPED?
DUNNO YET

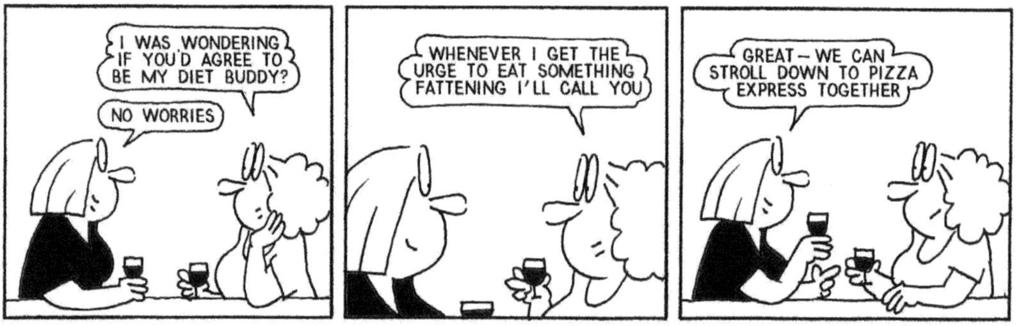
I WAS WONDERING IF YOU'D AGREE TO BE MY DIET BUDDY?
NO WORRIES
WHENEVER I GET THE URGE TO EAT SOMETHING FATTENING I'LL CALL YOU
GREAT – WE CAN STROLL DOWN TO PIZZA EXPRESS TOGETHER

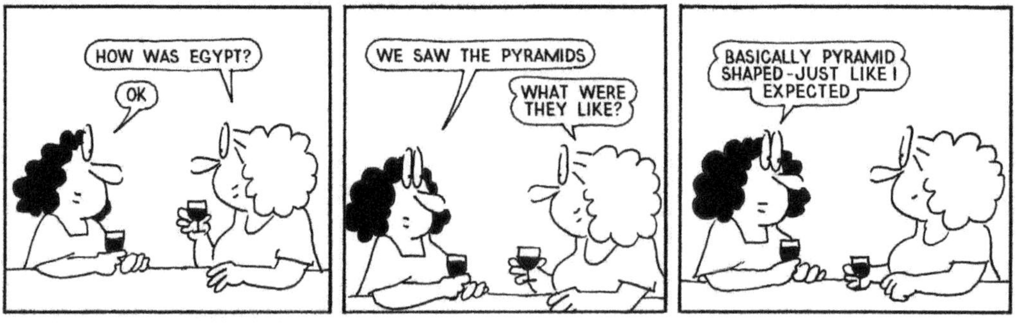
HOW WAS EGYPT?
OK
WE SAW THE PYRAMIDS
WHAT WERE THEY LIKE?
BASICALLY PYRAMID SHAPED-JUST LIKE I EXPECTED

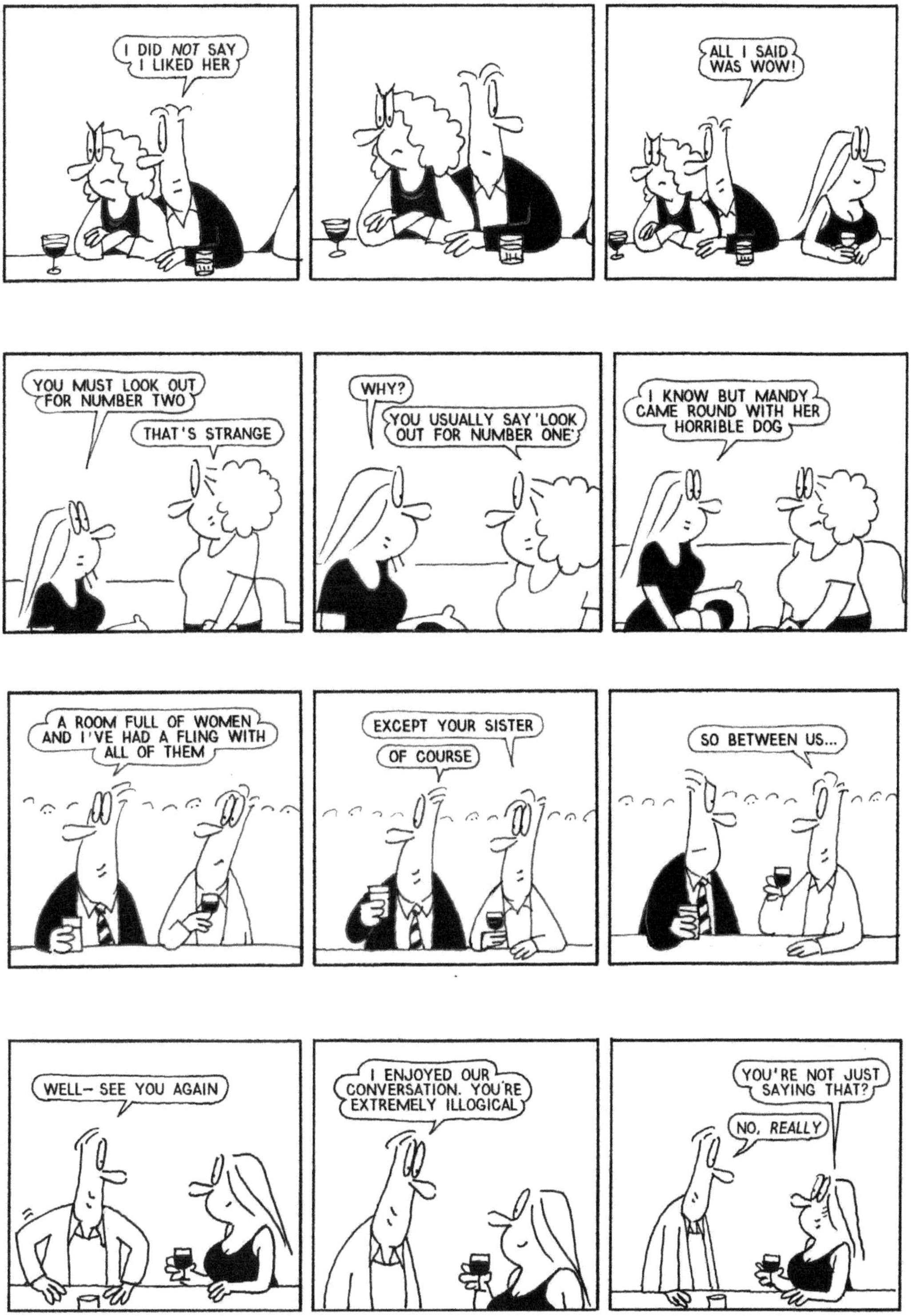
I DID *NOT* SAY I LIKED HER
ALL I SAID WAS WOW!
YOU MUST LOOK OUT FOR NUMBER TWO
THAT'S STRANGE
WHY?
YOU USUALLY SAY 'LOOK OUT FOR NUMBER ONE'
I KNOW BUT MANDY CAME ROUND WITH HER HORRIBLE DOG
A ROOM FULL OF WOMEN AND I'VE HAD A FLING WITH ALL OF THEM
EXCEPT YOUR SISTER
OF COURSE
SO BETWEEN US...
WELL- SEE YOU AGAIN
I ENJOYED OUR CONVERSATION. YOU'RE EXTREMELY ILLOGICAL
YOU'RE NOT JUST SAYING THAT?
NO, *REALLY*

TEN YEARS AGO WE LIVED IN A RUN - DOWN, POOR NEIGHBOURHOOD
NOW WE LIVE IN A FASHIONABLE, EXPENSIVE NEIGHBOURHOOD
WHEN DID YOU MOVE?
MOVE?

TELL YOU WHAT
INSTEAD OF PERSECUTING MOTORISTS YOU COULD BE OUT THERE CHASING CRIMINALS
CRIME DOESN'T PAY, MISS

I THINK IT'S A DISGRACE THE WAY YOU MADE YOUR MILLIONS
AND I ALWAYS THOUGHT CRIME DOESN'T PAY
IT DOESN'T AT YOUR LEVEL

YOU HAVE NO INTEGRITY JIM
YOU WANT INTEGRITY? SO I'LL GIVE YOU INTEGRITY
NOT TOO MUCH TO START WITH

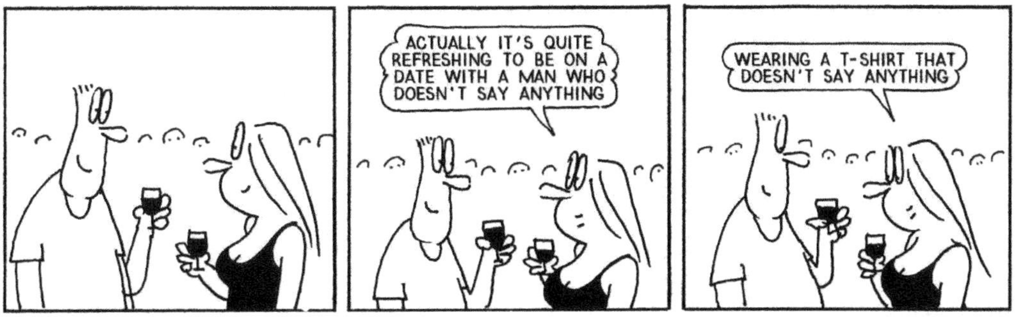
ACTUALLY IT'S QUITE REFRESHING TO BE ON A DATE WITH A MAN WHO DOESN'T SAY ANYTHING
WEARING A T-SHIRT THAT DOESN'T SAY ANYTHING

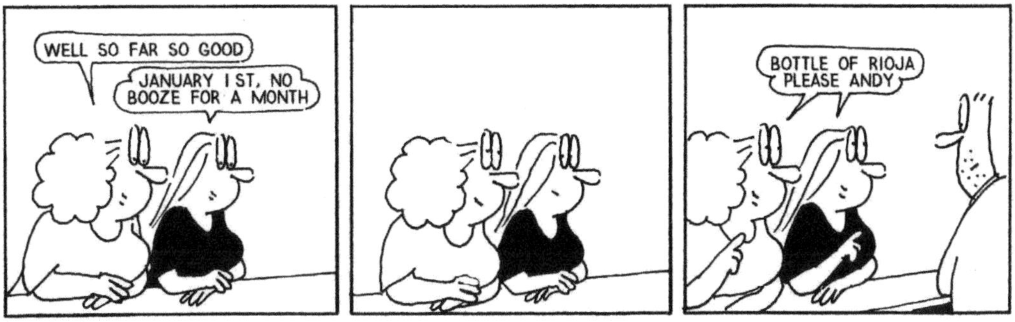
WELL SO FAR SO GOOD
JANUARY 1ST, NO BOOZE FOR A MONTH
BOTTLE OF RIOJA PLEASE ANDY

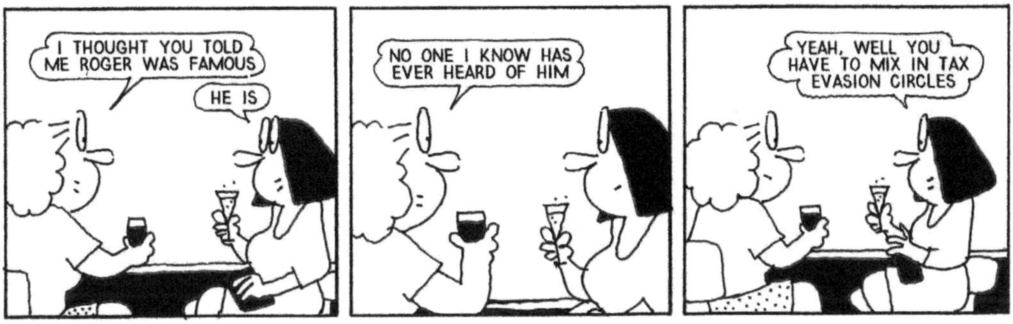
I THOUGHT YOU TOLD ME ROGER WAS FAMOUS
HE IS
NO ONE I KNOW HAS EVER HEARD OF HIM
YEAH, WELL YOU HAVE TO MIX IN TAX EVASION CIRCLES

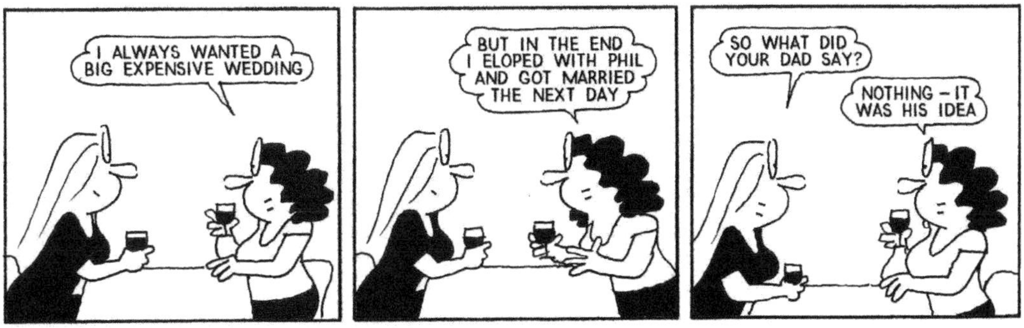
I ALWAYS WANTED A BIG EXPENSIVE WEDDING
BUT IN THE END I ELOPED WITH PHIL AND GOT MARRIED THE NEXT DAY
SO WHAT DID YOUR DAD SAY?
NOTHING – IT WAS HIS IDEA

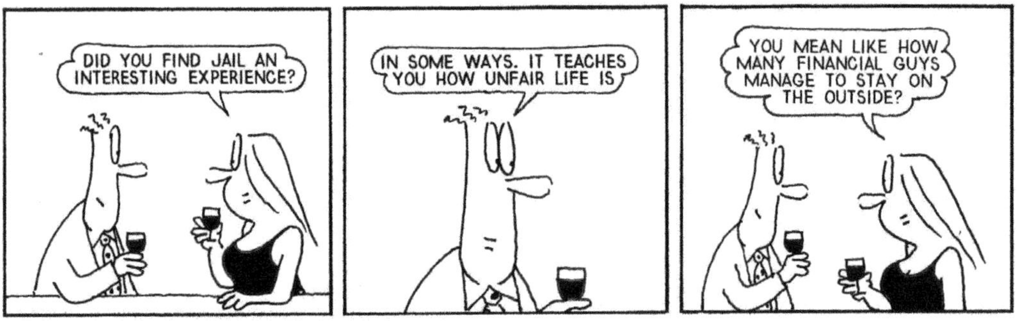
DID YOU FIND JAIL AN INTERESTING EXPERIENCE?
IN SOME WAYS. IT TEACHES YOU HOW UNFAIR LIFE IS
YOU MEAN LIKE HOW MANY FINANCIAL GUYS MANAGE TO STAY ON THE OUTSIDE?

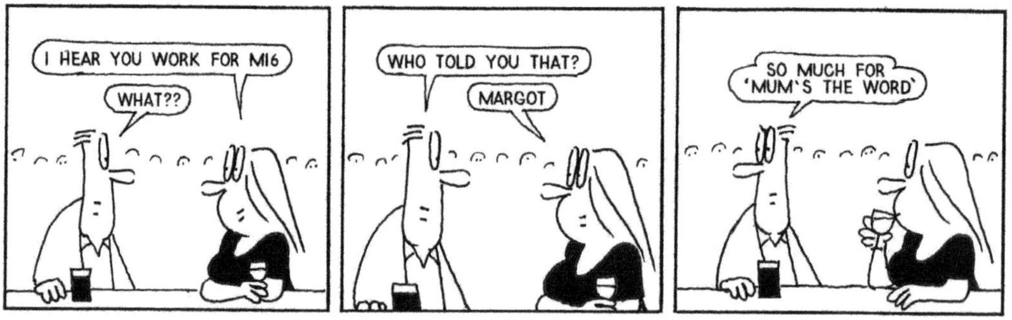
I HEAR YOU WORK FOR MI6
WHAT??
WHO TOLD YOU THAT?
MARGOT
SO MUCH FOR 'MUM'S THE WORD'

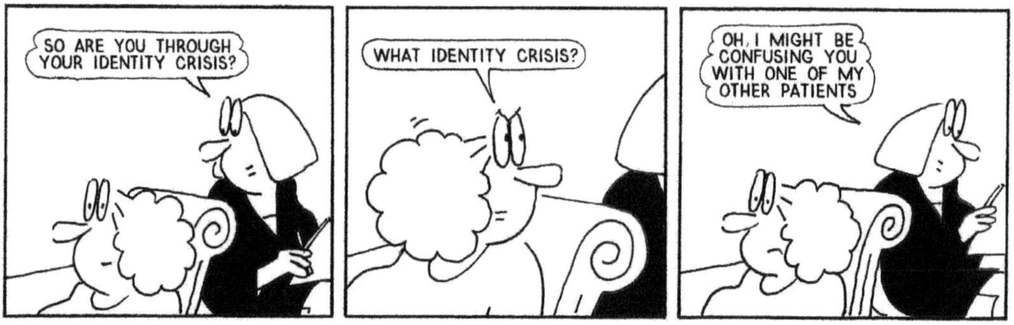
SO ARE YOU THROUGH YOUR IDENTITY CRISIS?
WHAT IDENTITY CRISIS?
OH, I MIGHT BE CONFUSING YOU WITH ONE OF MY OTHER PATIENTS

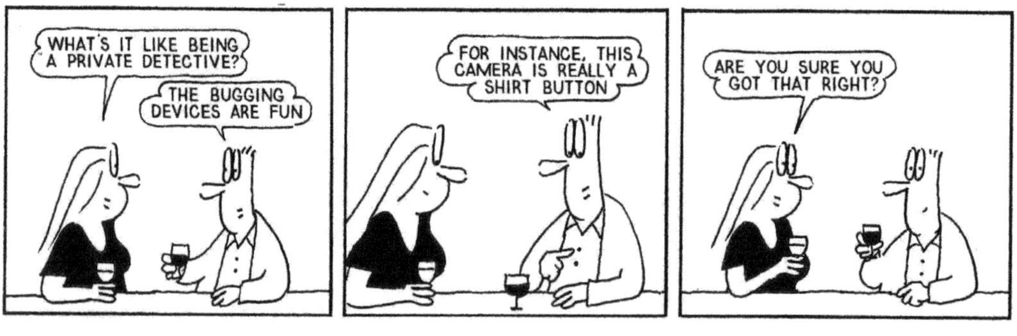
WHAT'S IT LIKE BEING A PRIVATE DETECTIVE?
THE BUGGING DEVICES ARE FUN
FOR INSTANCE, THIS CAMERA IS REALLY A SHIRT BUTTON
ARE YOU SURE YOU GOT THAT RIGHT?

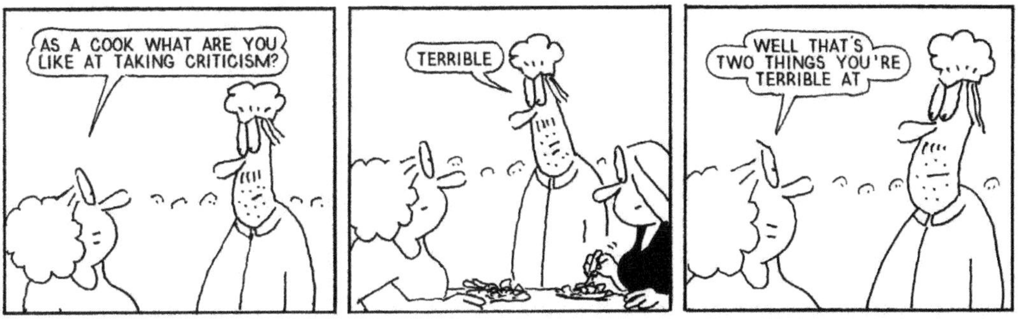
AS A COOK WHAT ARE YOU LIKE AT TAKING CRITICISM?
TERRIBLE
WELL THAT'S TWO THINGS YOU'RE TERRIBLE AT

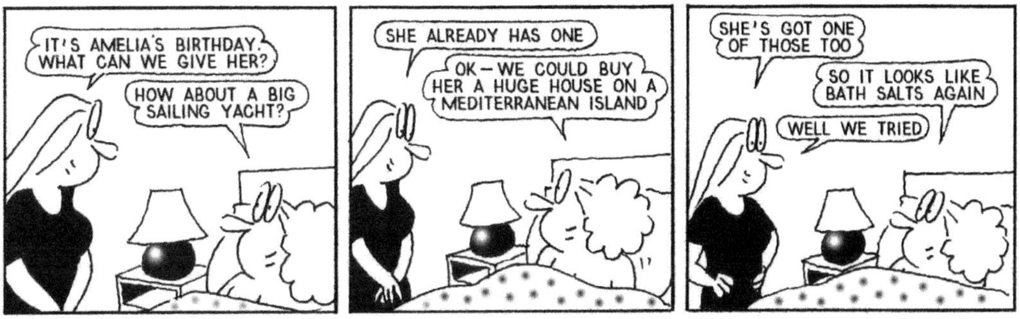
IT'S AMELIA'S BIRTHDAY. WHAT CAN WE GIVE HER?
HOW ABOUT A BIG SAILING YACHT?
SHE ALREADY HAS ONE
OK – WE COULD BUY HER A HUGE HOUSE ON A MEDITERRANEAN ISLAND
SHE'S GOT ONE OF THOSE TOO
SO IT LOOKS LIKE BATH SALTS AGAIN
WELL WE TRIED

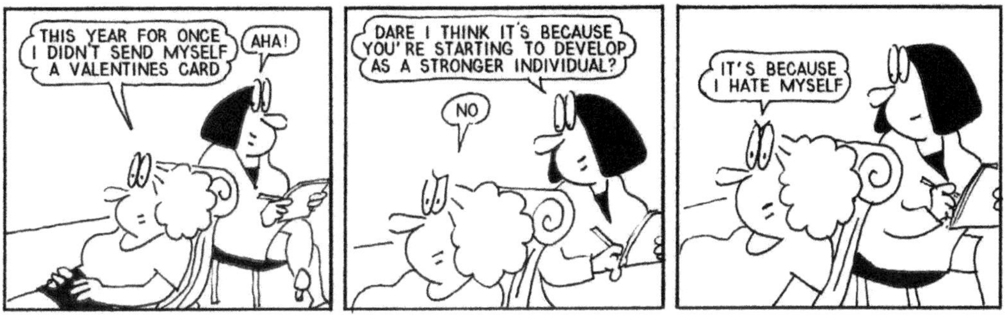
THIS YEAR FOR ONCE I DIDN'T SEND MYSELF A VALENTINES CARD
AHA!
DARE I THINK IT'S BECAUSE YOU'RE STARTING TO DEVELOP AS A STRONGER INDIVIDUAL?
NO
IT'S BECAUSE I HATE MYSELF

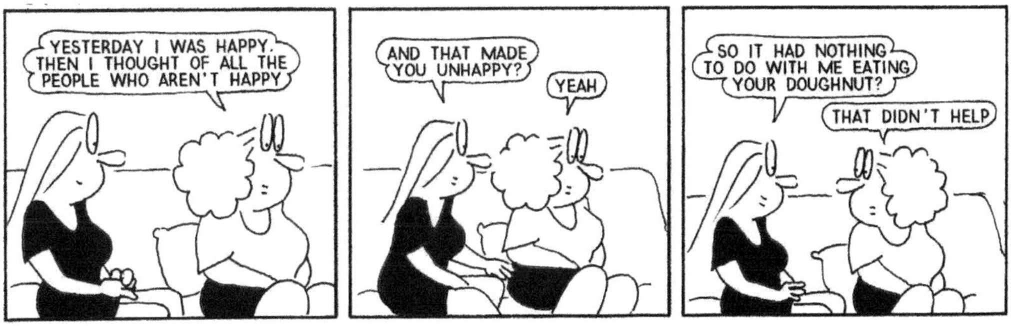
YESTERDAY I WAS HAPPY. THEN I THOUGHT OF ALL THE PEOPLE WHO AREN'T HAPPY
AND THAT MADE YOU UNHAPPY?
YEAH
SO IT HAD NOTHING TO DO WITH ME EATING YOUR DOUGHNUT?
THAT DIDN'T HELP

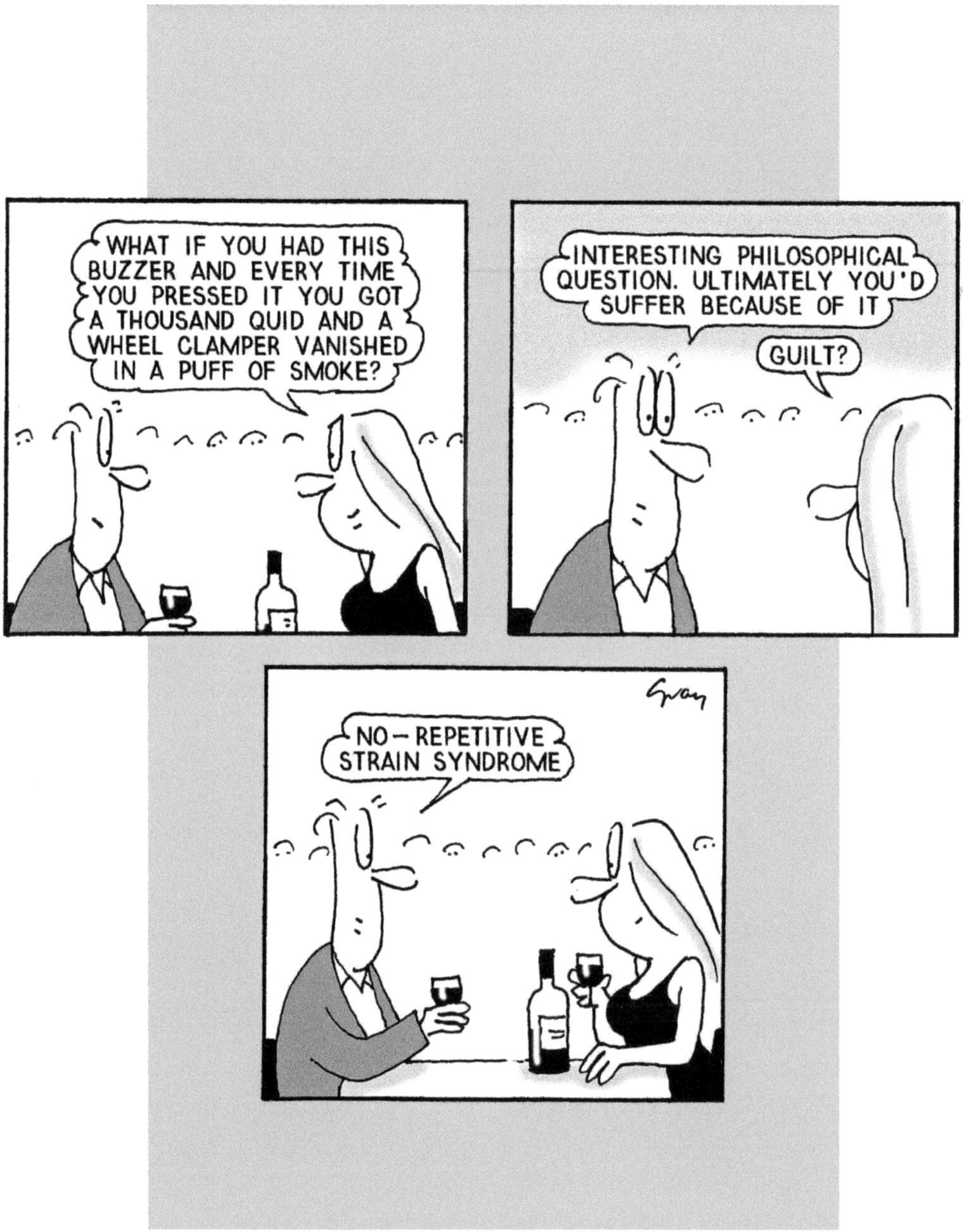
WHAT IF YOU HAD THIS BUZZER AND EVERY TIME YOU PRESSED IT YOU GOT A THOUSAND QUID AND A WHEEL CLAMPER VANISHED IN A PUFF OF SMOKE?
INTERESTING PHILOSOPHICAL QUESTION. ULTIMATELY YOU'D SUFFER BECAUSE OF IT
GUILT?
NO – REPETITIVE STRAIN SYNDROME

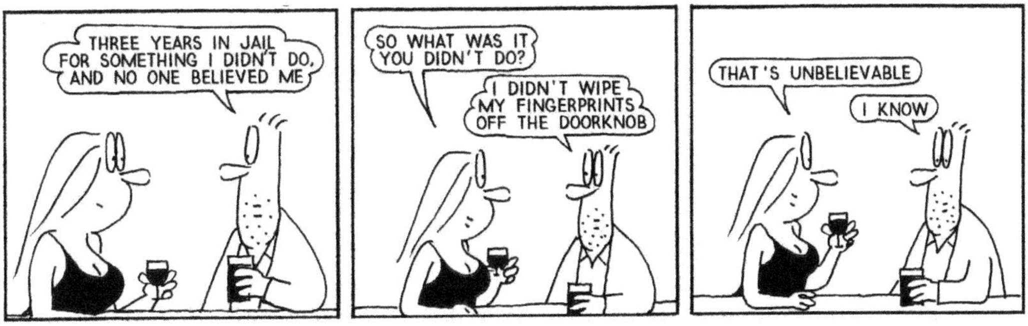
THREE YEARS IN JAIL FOR SOMETHING I DIDN'T DO, AND NO ONE BELIEVED ME
SO WHAT WAS IT YOU DIDN'T DO?
I DIDN'T WIPE MY FINGERPRINTS OFF THE DOORKNOB
THAT'S UNBELIEVABLE
I KNOW

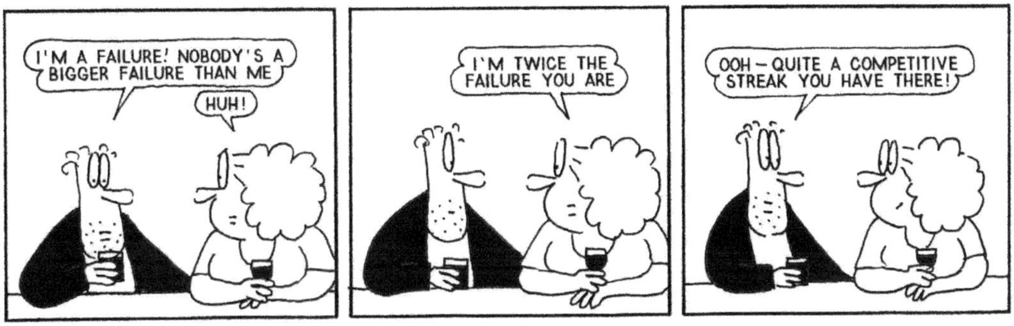
I'M A FAILURE! NOBODY'S A BIGGER FAILURE THAN ME
HUH!
I'M TWICE THE FAILURE YOU ARE
OOH – QUITE A COMPETITIVE STREAK YOU HAVE THERE!

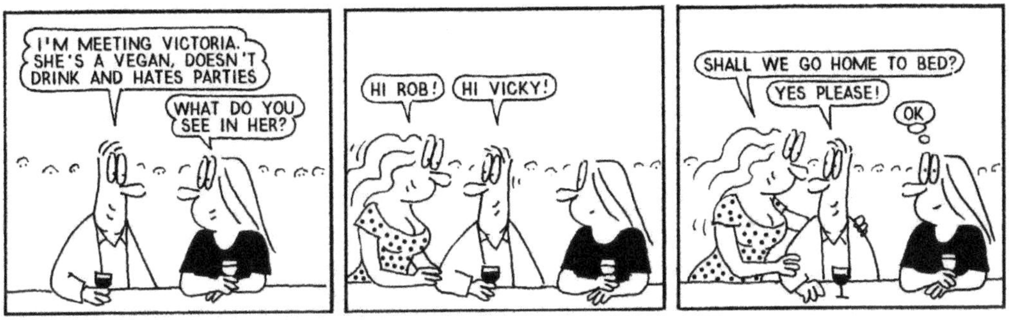
I'M MEETING VICTORIA. SHE'S A VEGAN, DOESN'T DRINK AND HATES PARTIES
WHAT DO YOU SEE IN HER?
HI ROB!
HI VICKY!
SHALL WE GO HOME TO BED?
YES PLEASE!
OK

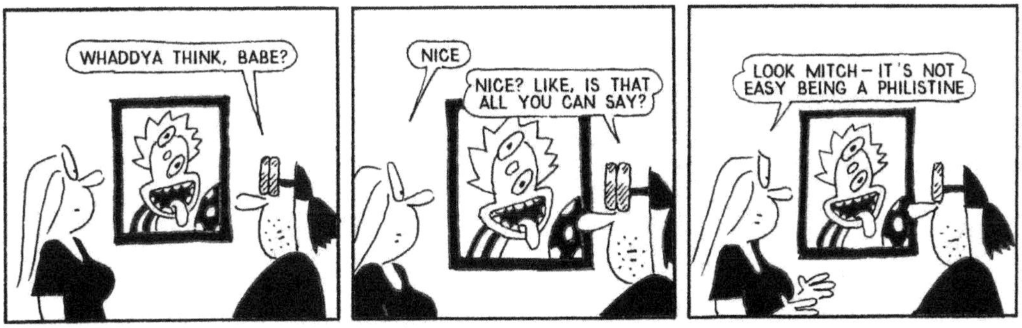
WHADDYA THINK, BABE?
NICE
NICE? LIKE, IS THAT ALL YOU CAN SAY?
LOOK MITCH – IT'S NOT EASY BEING A PHILISTINE

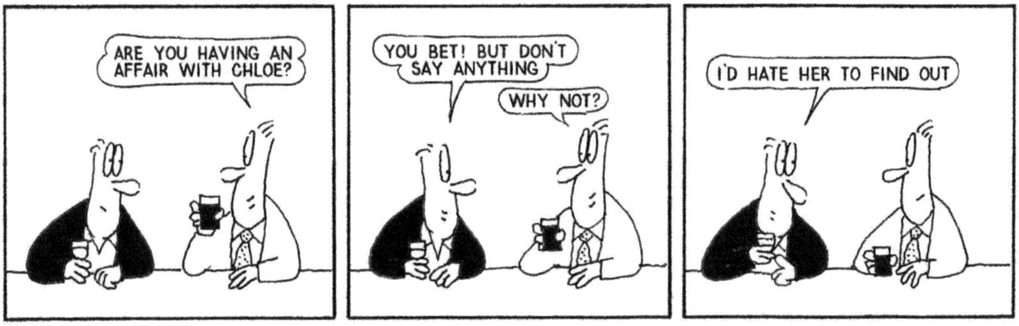
ARE YOU HAVING AN AFFAIR WITH CHLOE?
YOU BET! BUT DON'T SAY ANYTHING
WHY NOT?
I'D HATE HER TO FIND OUT

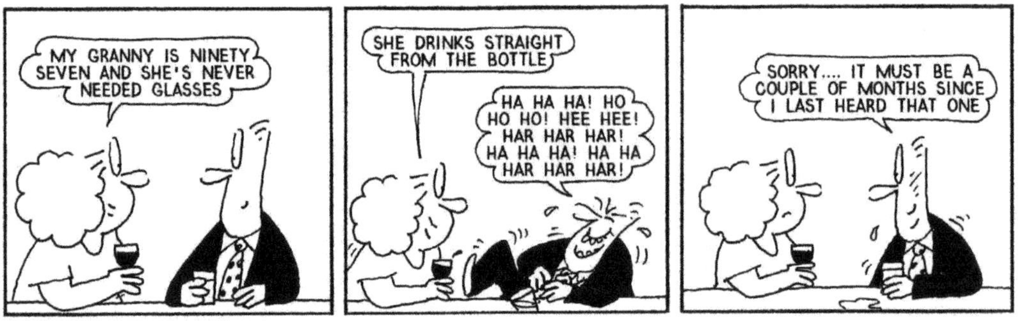
MY GRANNY IS NINETY SEVEN AND SHE'S NEVER NEEDED GLASSES
SHE DRINKS STRAIGHT FROM THE BOTTLE
HA HA HA! HO HO HO! HEE HEE! HAR HAR HAR! HA HA HA! HA HA HAR HAR HAR!
SORRY.... IT MUST BE A COUPLE OF MONTHS SINCE I LAST HEARD THAT ONE

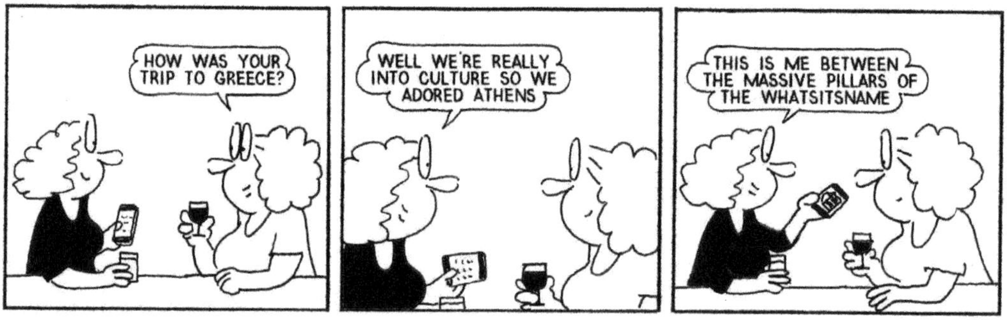
HOW WAS YOUR TRIP TO GREECE?
WELL WE'RE REALLY INTO CULTURE SO WE ADORED ATHENS
THIS IS ME BETWEEN THE MASSIVE PILLARS OF THE WHATSITSNAME

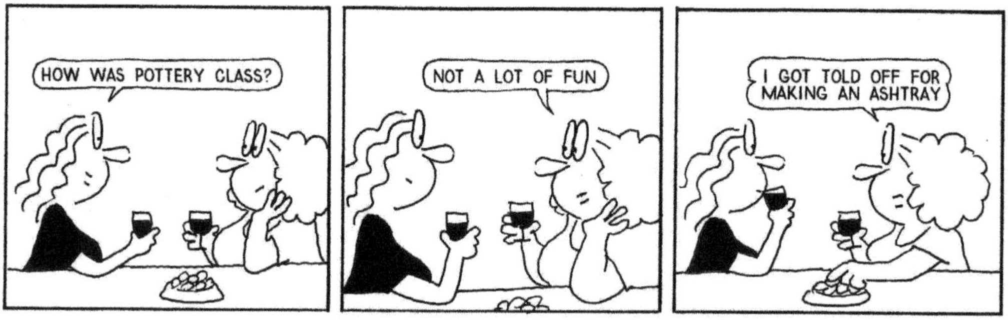
HOW WAS POTTERY CLASS?
NOT A LOT OF FUN
I GOT TOLD OFF FOR MAKING AN ASHTRAY

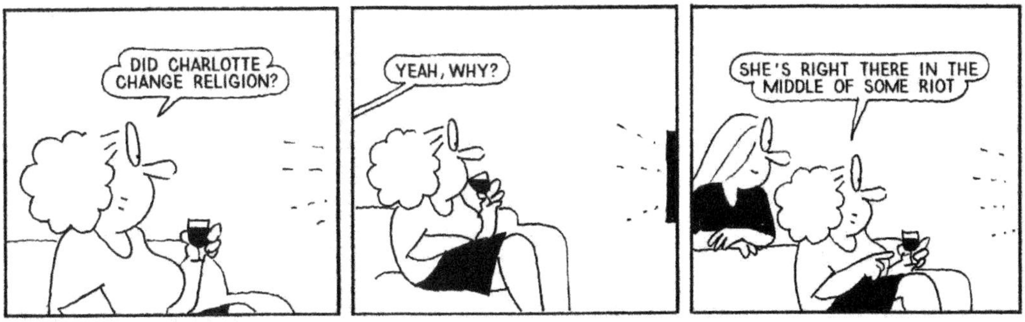
DID CHARLOTTE CHANGE RELIGION?
YEAH, WHY?
SHE'S RIGHT THERE IN THE MIDDLE OF SOME RIOT

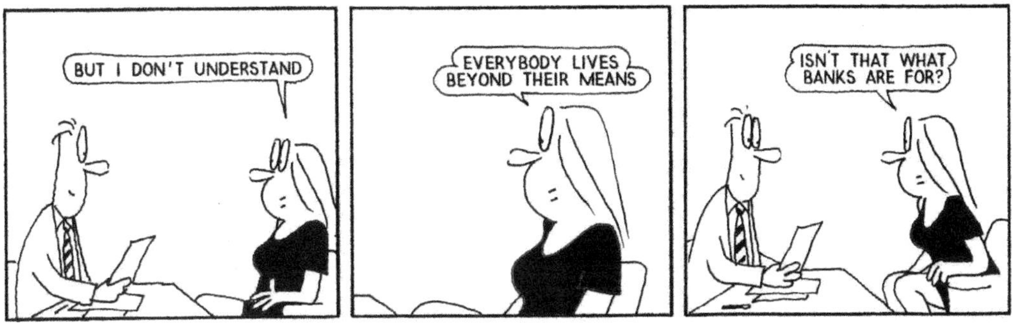
BUT I DON'T UNDERSTAND
EVERYBODY LIVES BEYOND THEIR MEANS
ISN'T THAT WHAT BANKS ARE FOR?

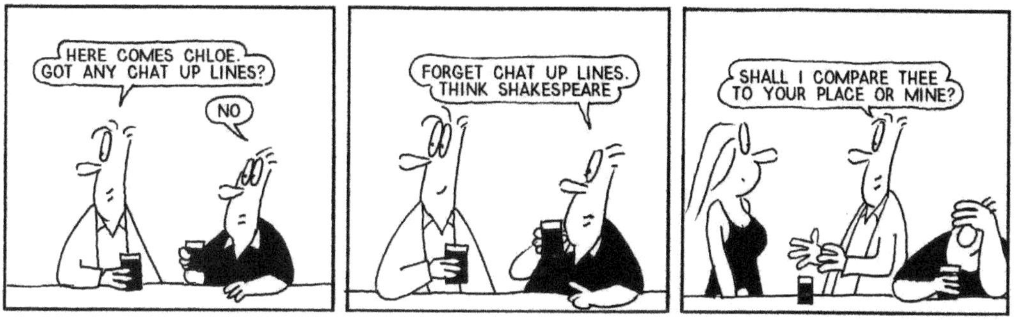
HERE COMES CHLOE. GOT ANY CHAT UP LINES?
NO
FORGET CHAT UP LINES. THINK SHAKESPEARE
SHALL I COMPARE THEE TO YOUR PLACE OR MINE?

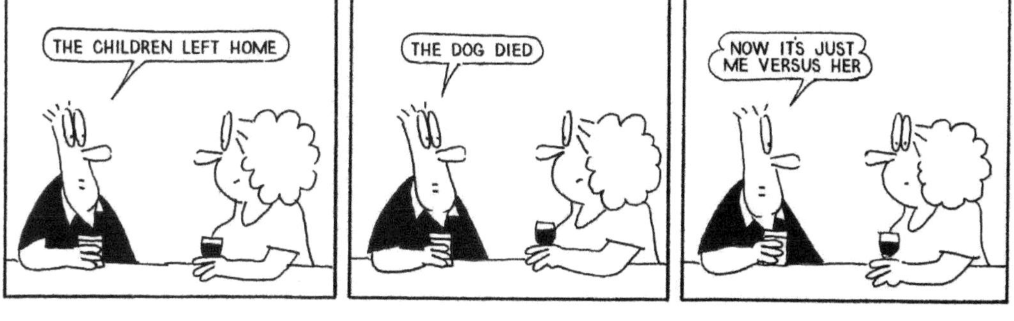
THE CHILDREN LEFT HOME
THE DOG DIED
NOW IT'S JUST ME VERSUS HER

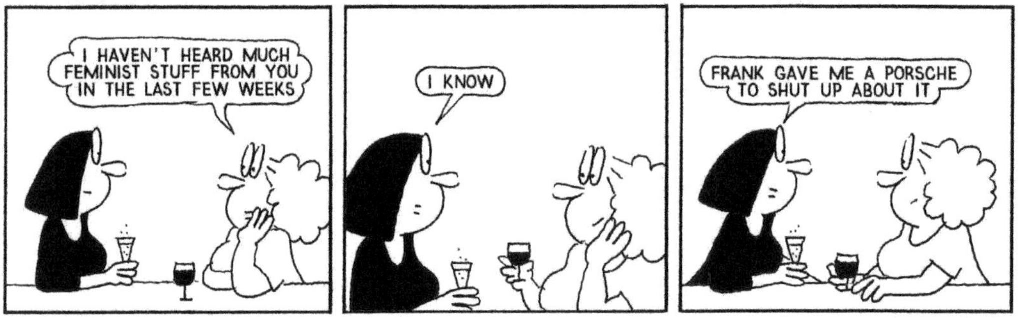
I HAVEN'T HEARD MUCH FEMINIST STUFF FROM YOU IN THE LAST FEW WEEKS
I KNOW
FRANK GAVE ME A PORSCHE TO SHUT UP ABOUT IT

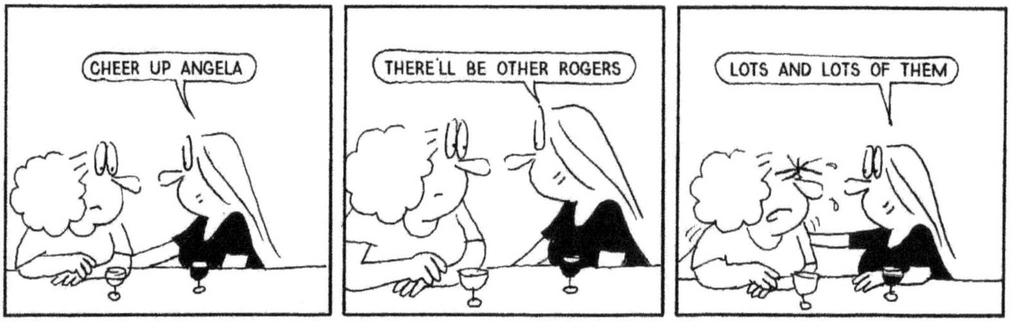
CHEER UP ANGELA
THERE'LL BE OTHER ROGERS
LOTS AND LOTS OF THEM

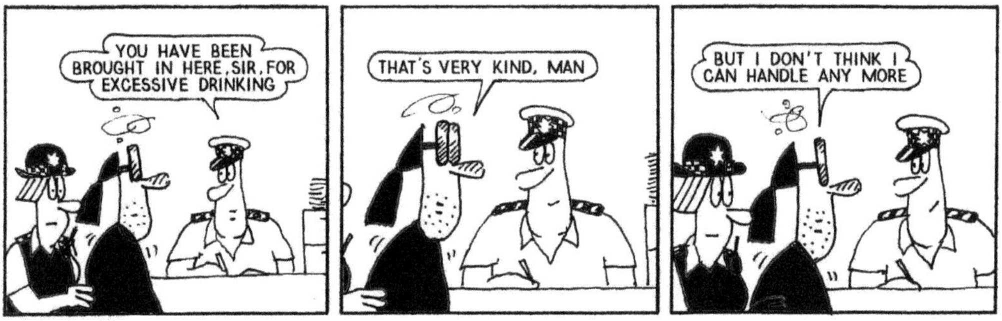
YOU HAVE BEEN BROUGHT IN HERE, SIR, FOR EXCESSIVE DRINKING
THAT'S VERY KIND, MAN
BUT I DON'T THINK I CAN HANDLE ANY MORE

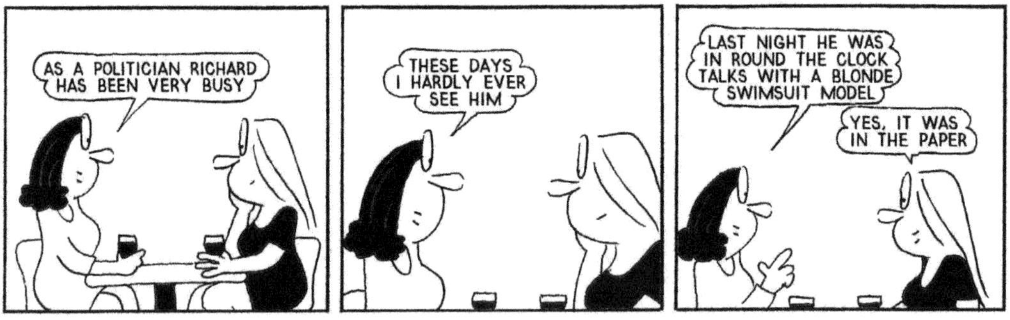
AS A POLITICIAN RICHARD HAS BEEN VERY BUSY
THESE DAYS I HARDLY EVER SEE HIM
LAST NIGHT HE WAS IN ROUND THE CLOCK TALKS WITH A BLONDE SWIMSUIT MODEL
YES, IT WAS IN THE PAPER

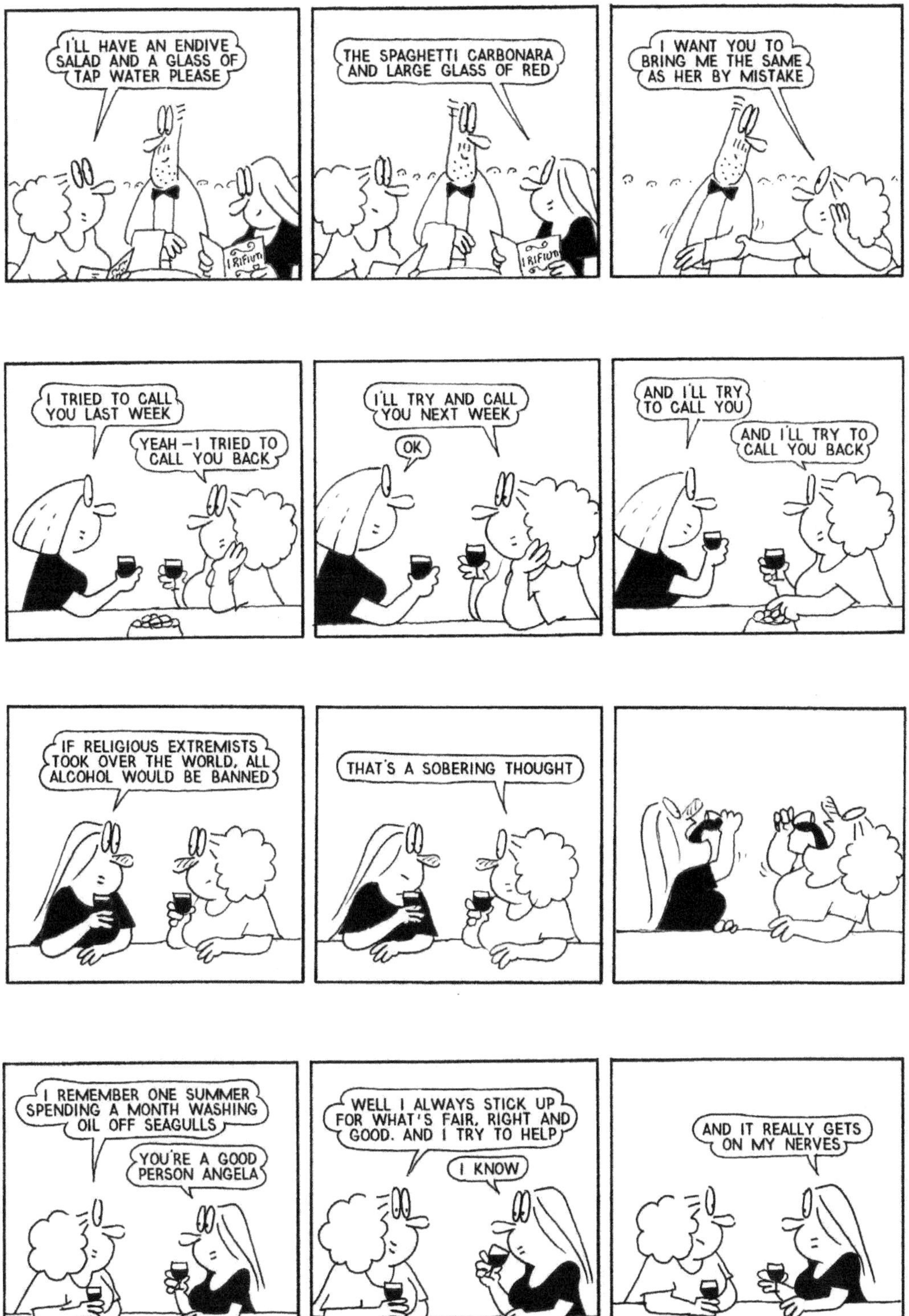
I'LL HAVE AN ENDIVE SALAD AND A GLASS OF TAP WATER PLEASE
I RIFIUTI
THE SPAGHETTI CARBONARA AND LARGE GLASS OF RED
I RIFIUTI
I WANT YOU TO BRING ME THE SAME AS HER BY MISTAKE
I TRIED TO CALL YOU LAST WEEK
YEAH — I TRIED TO CALL YOU BACK
I'LL TRY AND CALL YOU NEXT WEEK
OK
AND I'LL TRY TO CALL YOU
AND I'LL TRY TO CALL YOU BACK
IF RELIGIOUS EXTREMISTS TOOK OVER THE WORLD, ALL ALCOHOL WOULD BE BANNED
THAT'S A SOBERING THOUGHT
I REMEMBER ONE SUMMER SPENDING A MONTH WASHING OIL OFF SEAGULLS
YOU'RE A GOOD PERSON ANGELA
WELL I ALWAYS STICK UP FOR WHAT'S FAIR, RIGHT AND GOOD. AND I TRY TO HELP
I KNOW
AND IT REALLY GETS ON MY NERVES

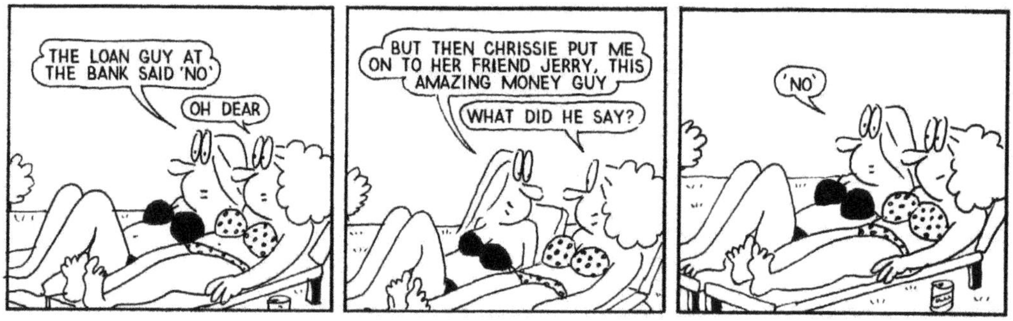
THE LOAN GUY AT THE BANK SAID 'NO'
OH DEAR
BUT THEN CHRISSIE PUT ME ON TO HER FRIEND JERRY, THIS AMAZING MONEY GUY
WHAT DID HE SAY?
'NO'

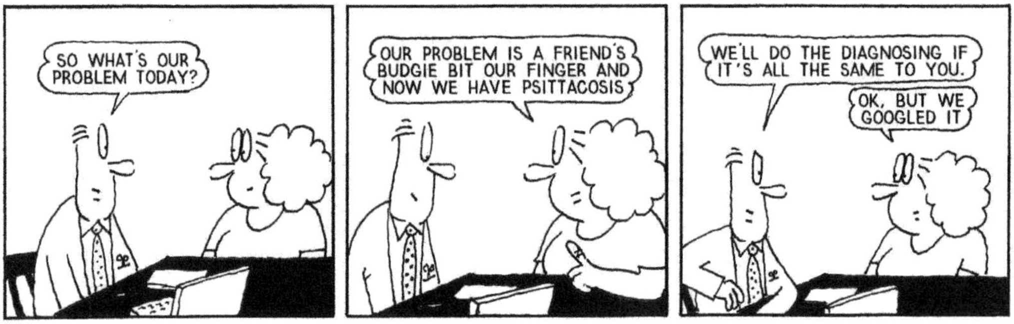
SO WHAT'S OUR PROBLEM TODAY?
OUR PROBLEM IS A FRIEND'S BUDGIE BIT OUR FINGER AND NOW WE HAVE PSITTACOSIS
WE'LL DO THE DIAGNOSING IF IT'S ALL THE SAME TO YOU.
OK, BUT WE GOOGLED IT

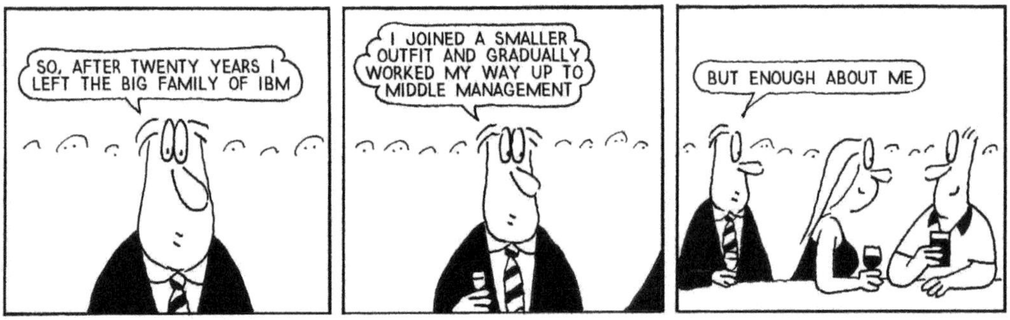
SO, AFTER TWENTY YEARS I LEFT THE BIG FAMILY OF IBM
I JOINED A SMALLER OUTFIT AND GRADUALLY WORKED MY WAY UP TO MIDDLE MANAGEMENT
BUT ENOUGH ABOUT ME

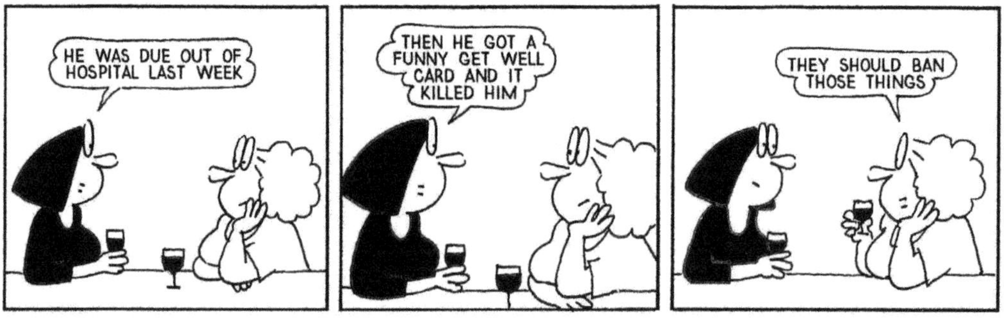
HE WAS DUE OUT OF HOSPITAL LAST WEEK
THEN HE GOT A FUNNY GET WELL CARD AND IT KILLED HIM
THEY SHOULD BAN THOSE THINGS

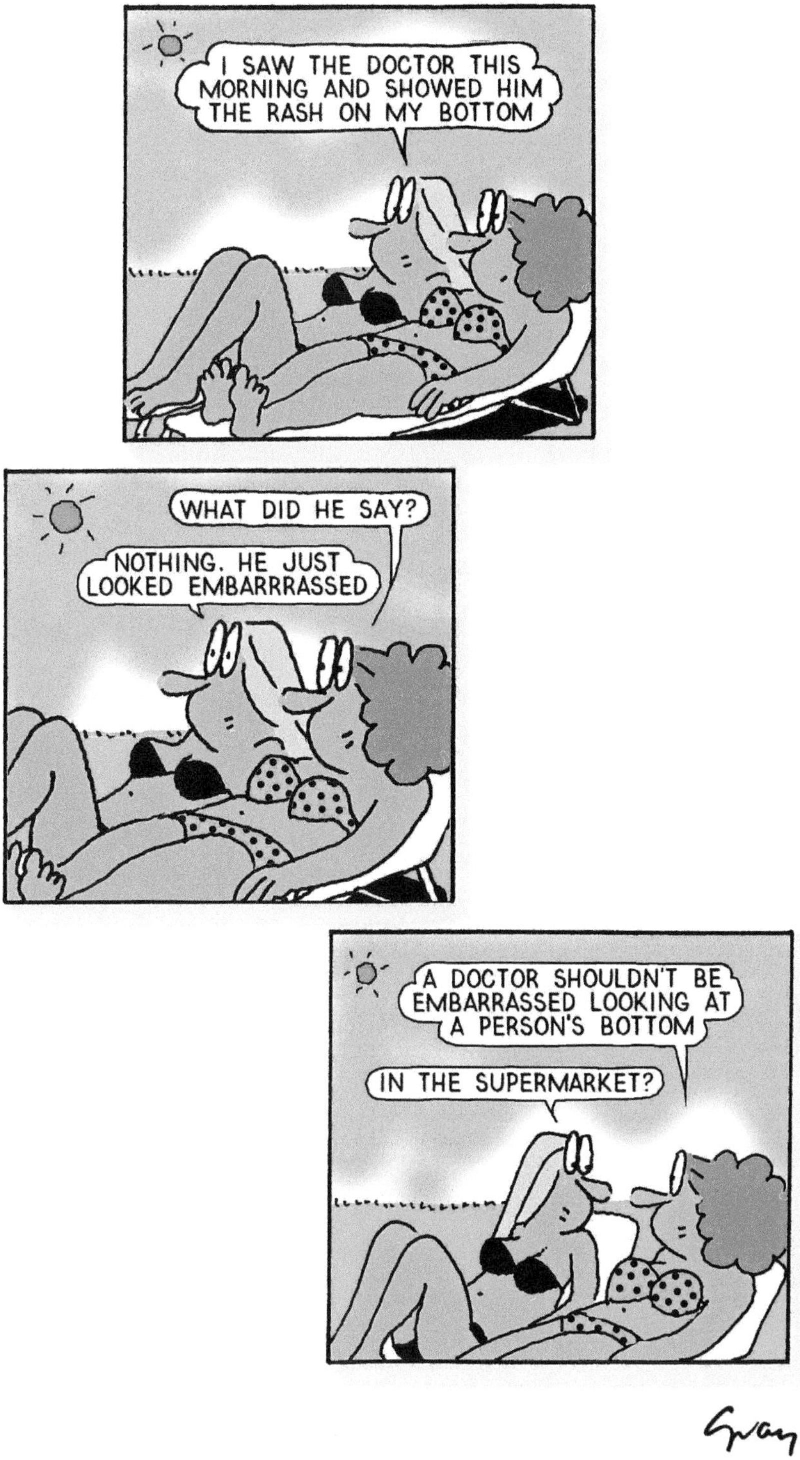
I SAW THE DOCTOR THIS MORNING AND SHOWED HIM THE RASH ON MY BOTTOM
WHAT DID HE SAY?
NOTHING. HE JUST LOOKED EMBARRRASSED
A DOCTOR SHOULDN'T BE EMBARRASSED LOOKING AT A PERSON'S BOTTOM
IN THE SUPERMARKET?

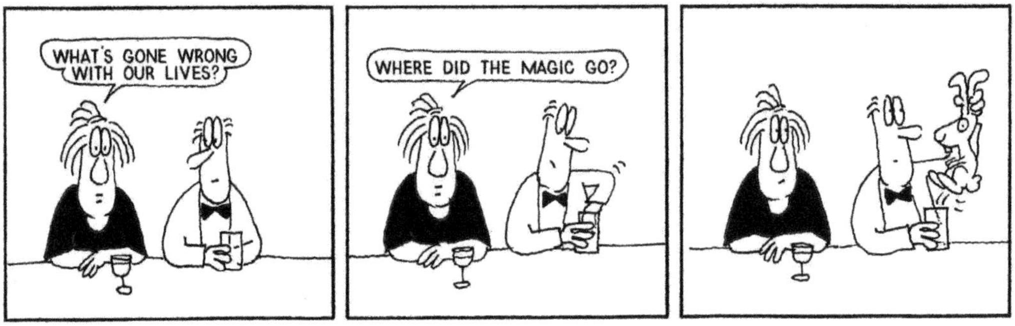
WHAT'S GONE WRONG WITH OUR LIVES?
WHERE DID THE MAGIC GO?

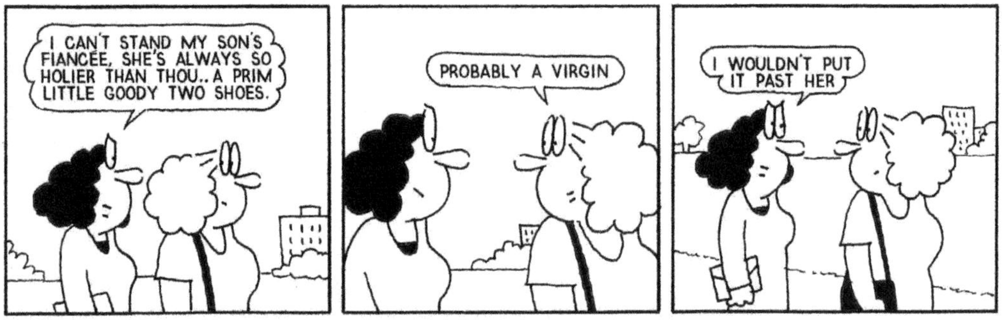
I CAN'T STAND MY SON'S FIANCÉE, SHE'S ALWAYS SO HOLIER THAN THOU.. A PRIM LITTLE GOODY TWO SHOES.
PROBABLY A VIRGIN
I WOULDN'T PUT IT PAST HER

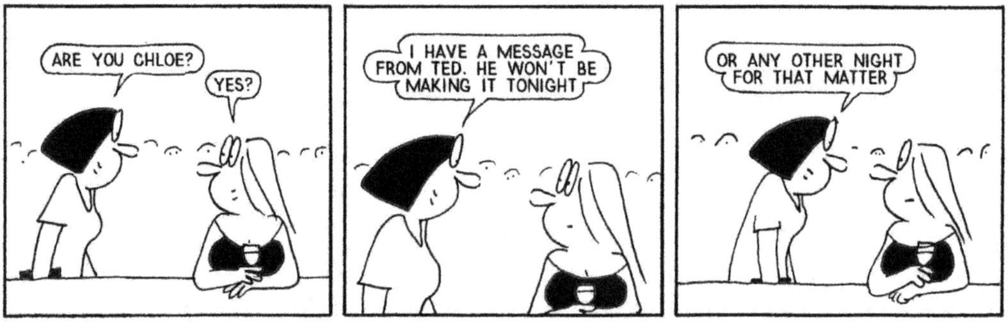
ARE YOU CHLOE?
YES?
I HAVE A MESSAGE FROM TED. HE WON'T BE MAKING IT TONIGHT
OR ANY OTHER NIGHT FOR THAT MATTER

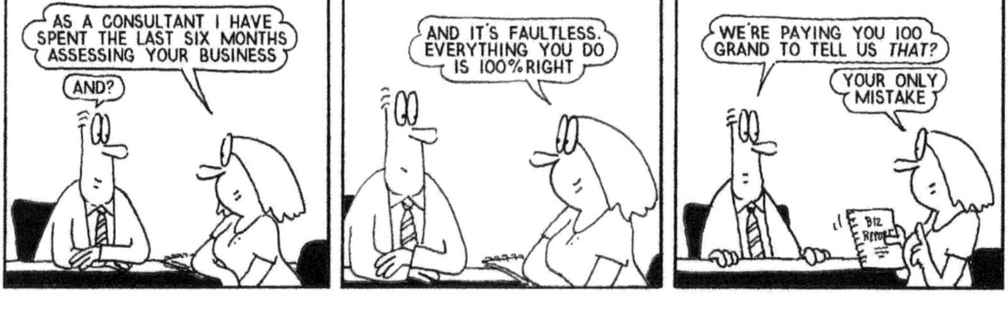
AS A CONSULTANT I HAVE SPENT THE LAST SIX MONTHS ASSESSING YOUR BUSINESS
AND?
AND IT'S FAULTLESS. EVERYTHING YOU DO IS 100% RIGHT
WE'RE PAYING YOU 100 GRAND TO TELL US *THAT?*
YOUR ONLY MISTAKE
BIZ REPORT

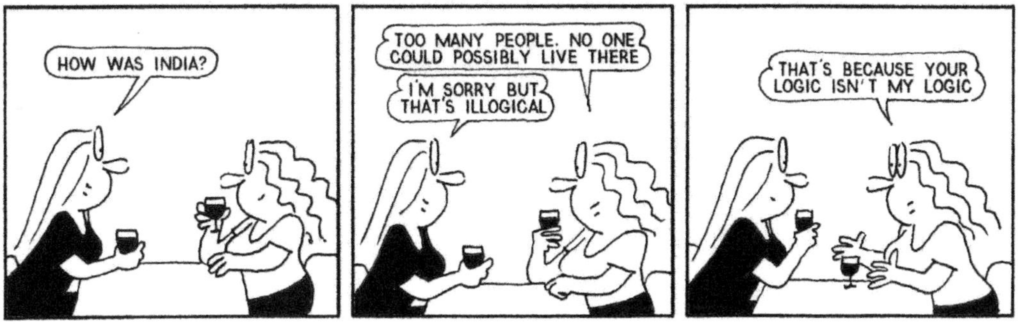
HOW WAS INDIA?
TOO MANY PEOPLE. NO ONE COULD POSSIBLY LIVE THERE
I'M SORRY BUT THAT'S ILLOGICAL
THAT'S BECAUSE YOUR LOGIC ISN'T MY LOGIC

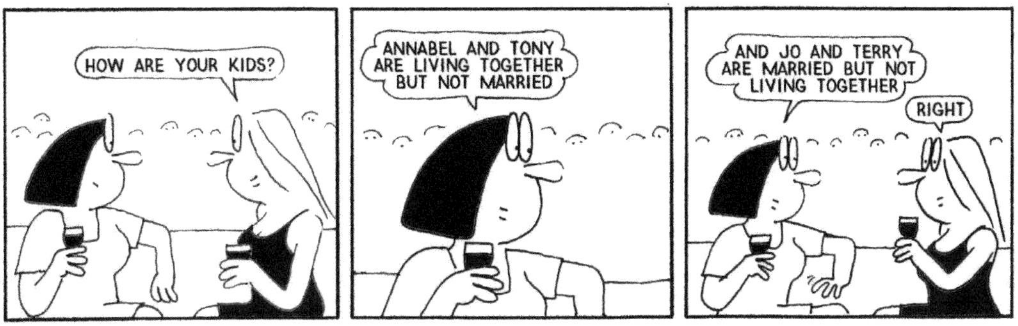
HOW ARE YOUR KIDS?
ANNABEL AND TONY ARE LIVING TOGETHER BUT NOT MARRIED
AND JO AND TERRY ARE MARRIED BUT NOT LIVING TOGETHER
RIGHT

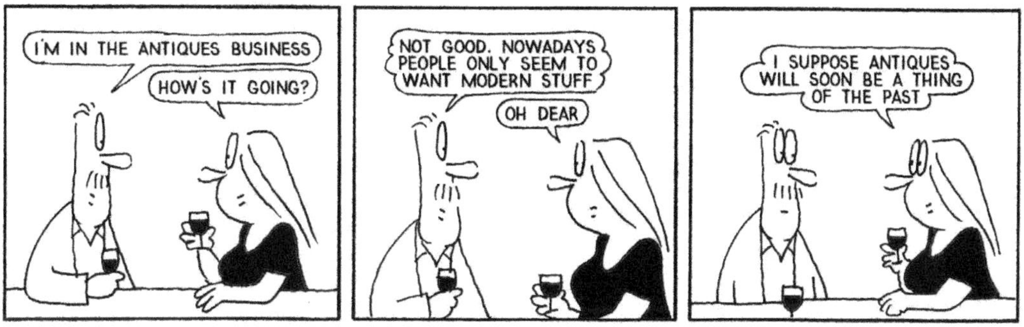
I'M IN THE ANTIQUES BUSINESS
HOW'S IT GOING?
NOT GOOD. NOWADAYS PEOPLE ONLY SEEM TO WANT MODERN STUFF
OH DEAR
I SUPPOSE ANTIQUES WILL SOON BE A THING OF THE PAST

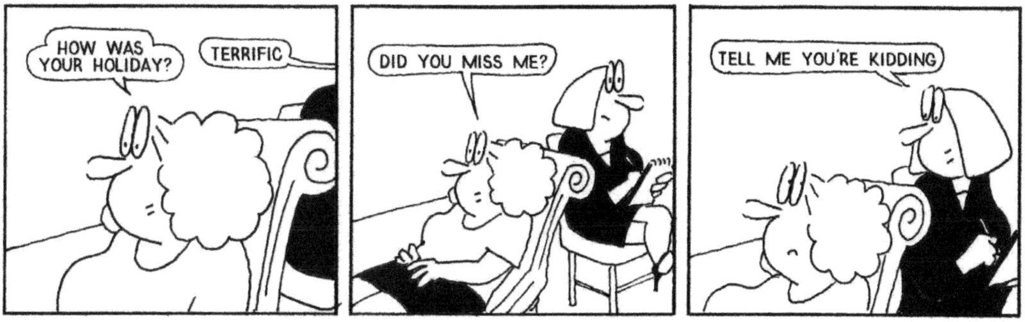
HOW WAS YOUR HOLIDAY?
TERRIFIC
DID YOU MISS ME?
TELL ME YOU'RE KIDDING

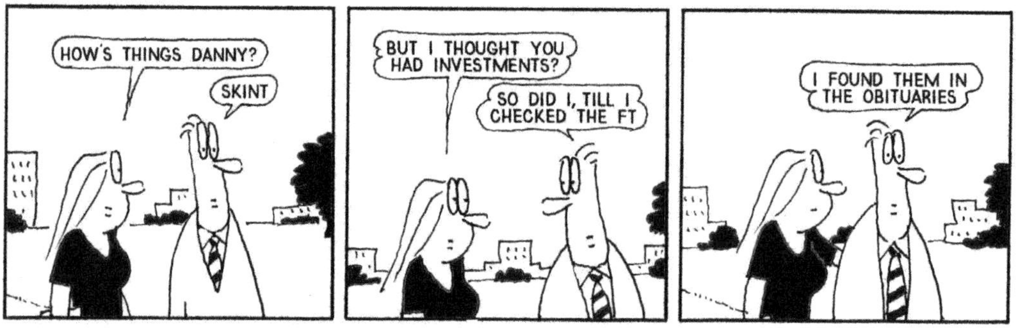
HOW'S THINGS DANNY?
SKINT
BUT I THOUGHT YOU HAD INVESTMENTS?
SO DID I, TILL I CHECKED THE FT
I FOUND THEM IN THE OBITUARIES

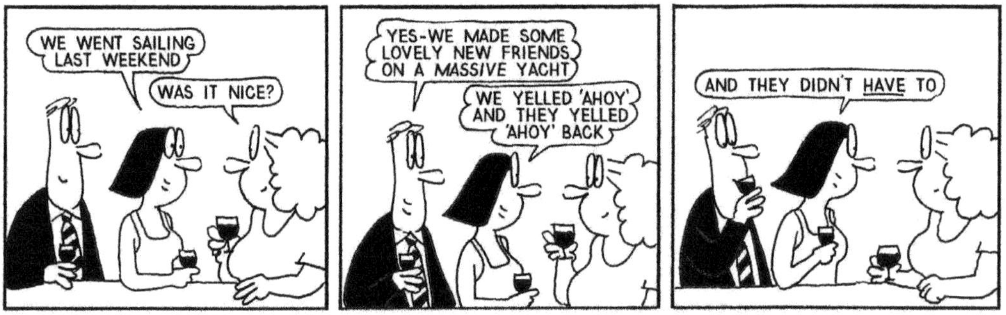
WE WENT SAILING LAST WEEKEND
WAS IT NICE?
YES-WE MADE SOME LOVELY NEW FRIENDS ON A *MASSIVE* YACHT
WE YELLED 'AHOY' AND THEY YELLED 'AHOY' BACK
AND THEY DIDN'T HAVE TO

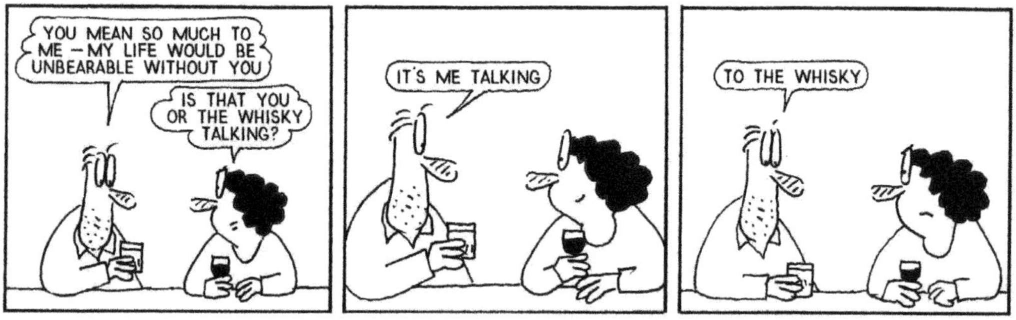
YOU MEAN SO MUCH TO ME – MY LIFE WOULD BE UNBEARABLE WITHOUT YOU
IS THAT YOU OR THE WHISKY TALKING?
IT'S ME TALKING
TO THE WHISKY

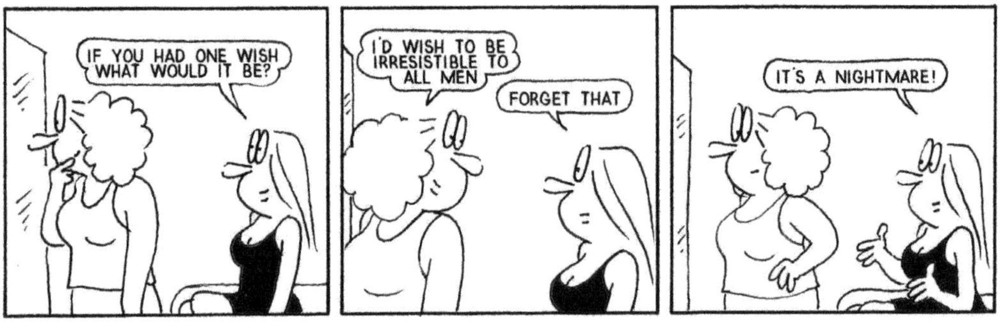
IF YOU HAD ONE WISH WHAT WOULD IT BE?
I'D WISH TO BE IRRESISTIBLE TO ALL MEN
FORGET THAT
IT'S A NIGHTMARE!

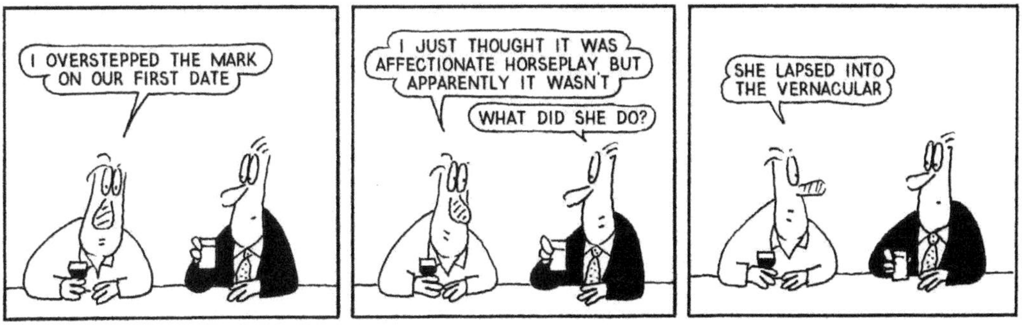
I OVERSTEPPED THE MARK ON OUR FIRST DATE
I JUST THOUGHT IT WAS AFFECTIONATE HORSEPLAY BUT APPARENTLY IT WASN'T
WHAT DID SHE DO?
SHE LAPSED INTO THE VERNACULAR

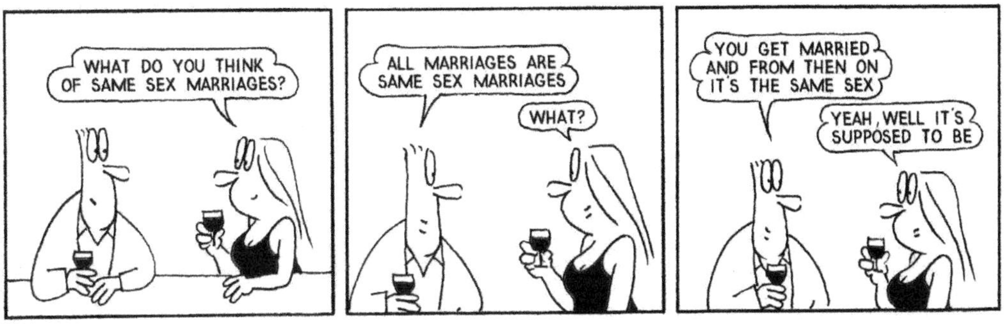
WHAT DO YOU THINK OF SAME SEX MARRIAGES?
ALL MARRIAGES ARE SAME SEX MARRIAGES
WHAT?
YOU GET MARRIED AND FROM THEN ON IT'S THE SAME SEX
YEAH, WELL IT'S SUPPOSED TO BE

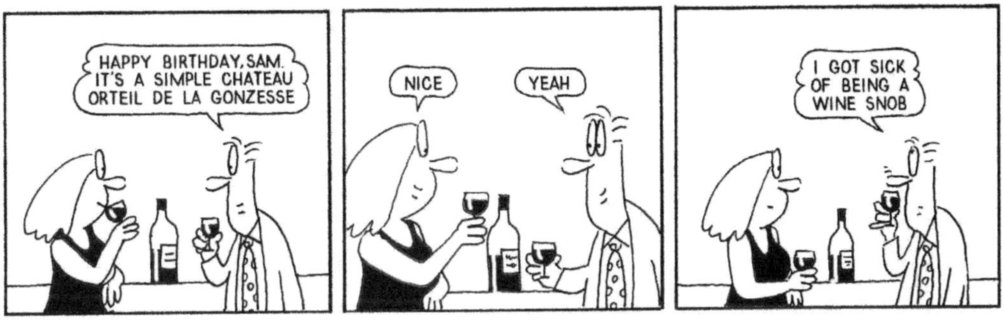
HAPPY BIRTHDAY, SAM. IT'S A SIMPLE CHATEAU ORTEIL DE LA GONZESSE
NICE
YEAH
I GOT SICK OF BEING A WINE SNOB

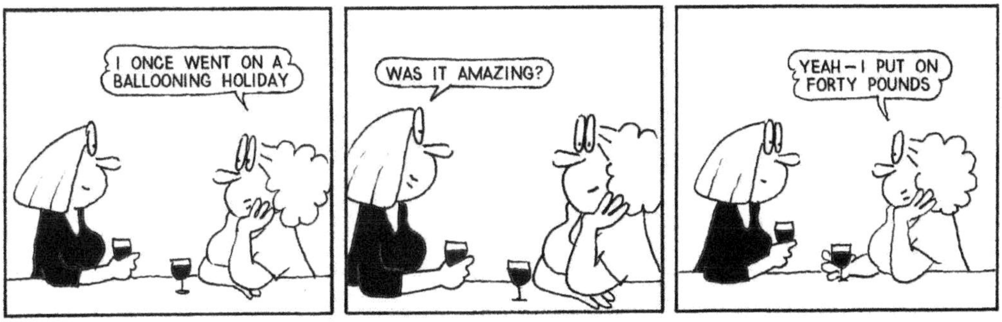
I ONCE WENT ON A BALLOONING HOLIDAY
WAS IT AMAZING?
YEAH — I PUT ON FORTY POUNDS

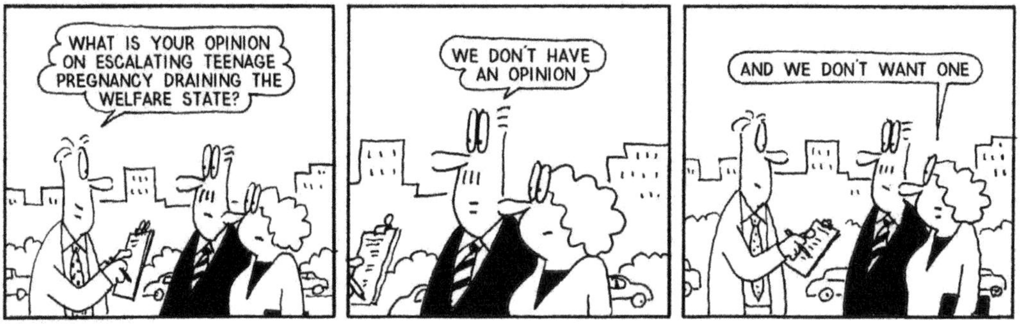
WHAT IS YOUR OPINION ON ESCALATING TEENAGE PREGNANCY DRAINING THE WELFARE STATE?
WE DON'T HAVE AN OPINION
AND WE DON'T WANT ONE

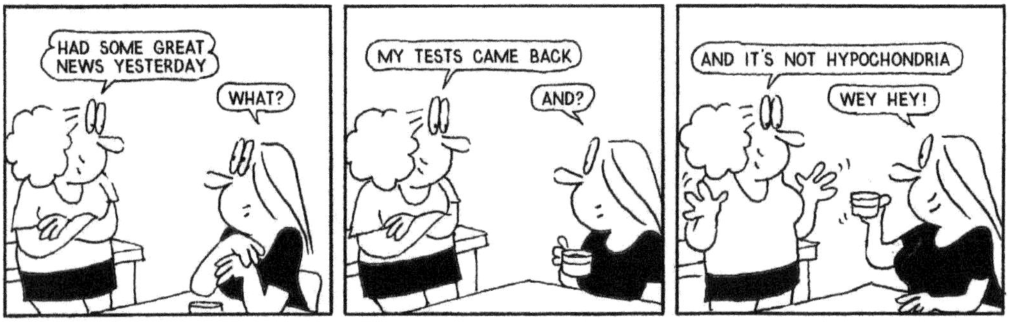
HAD SOME GREAT NEWS YESTERDAY
WHAT?
MY TESTS CAME BACK
AND?
AND IT'S NOT HYPOCHONDRIA
WEY HEY!

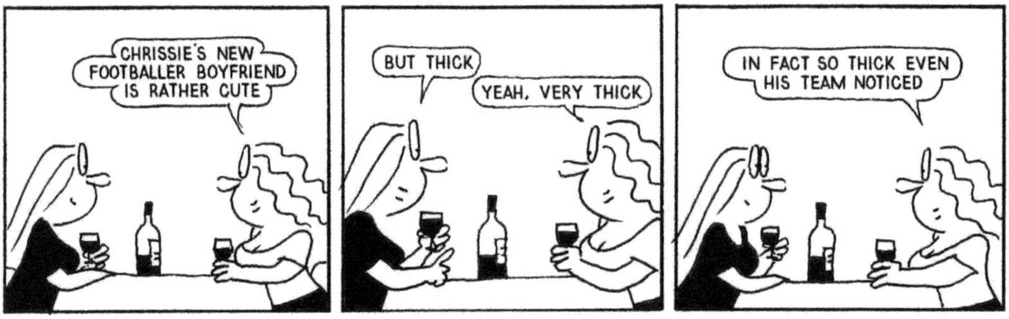
CHRISSIE'S NEW FOOTBALLER BOYFRIEND IS RATHER CUTE
BUT THICK
YEAH, VERY THICK
IN FACT SO THICK EVEN HIS TEAM NOTICED

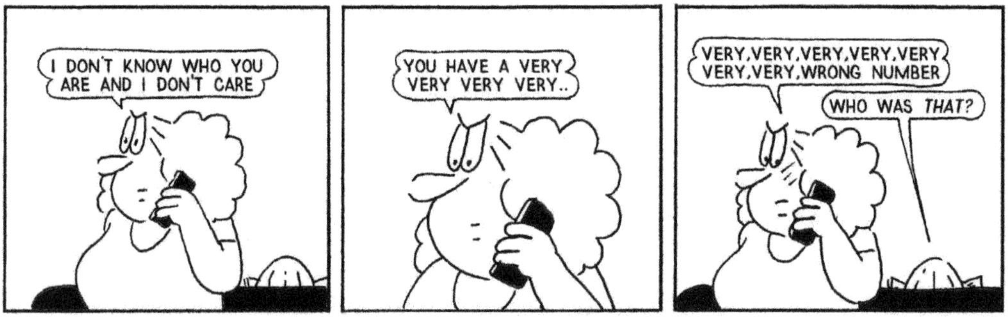
I DON'T KNOW WHO YOU ARE AND I DON'T CARE
YOU HAVE A VERY VERY VERY VERY..
VERY,VERY,VERY,VERY,VERY VERY,VERY,WRONG NUMBER
WHO WAS *THAT?*

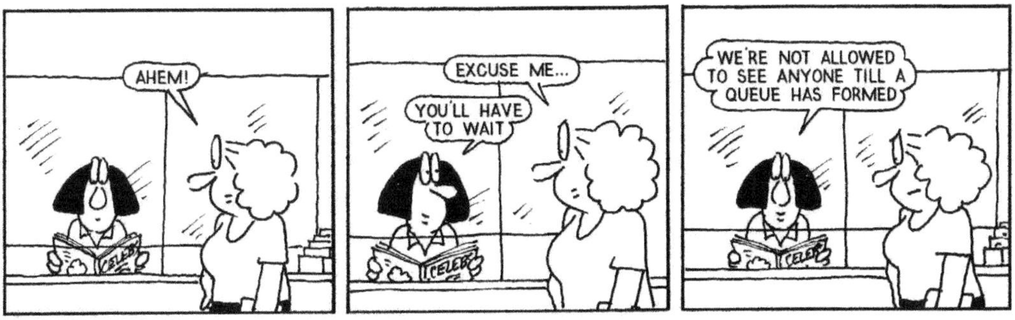
AHEM!
EXCUSE ME...
YOU'LL HAVE TO WAIT
WE'RE NOT ALLOWED TO SEE ANYONE TILL A QUEUE HAS FORMED
CELEB

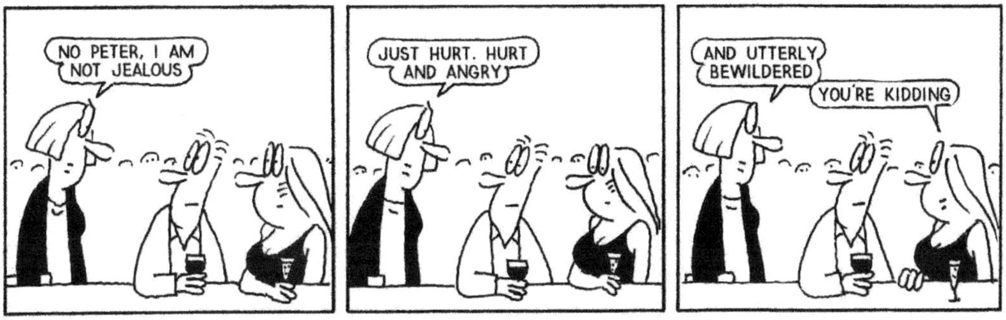
NO PETER, I AM NOT JEALOUS
JUST HURT. HURT AND ANGRY
AND UTTERLY BEWILDERED
YOU'RE KIDDING

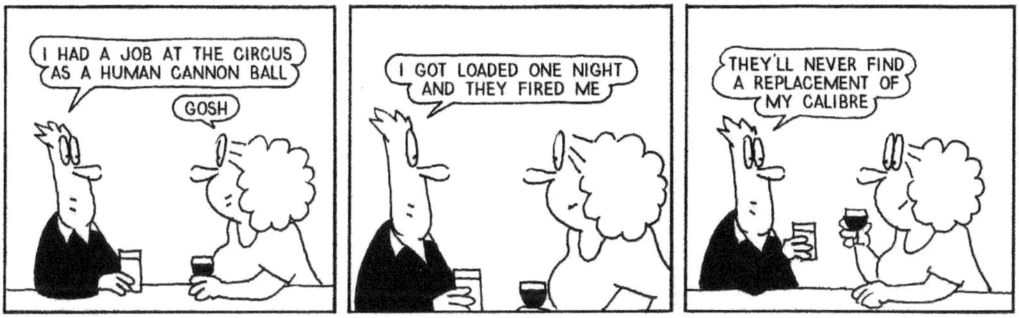
I HAD A JOB AT THE CIRCUS AS A HUMAN CANNON BALL
GOSH
I GOT LOADED ONE NIGHT AND THEY FIRED ME
THEY'LL NEVER FIND A REPLACEMENT OF MY CALIBRE

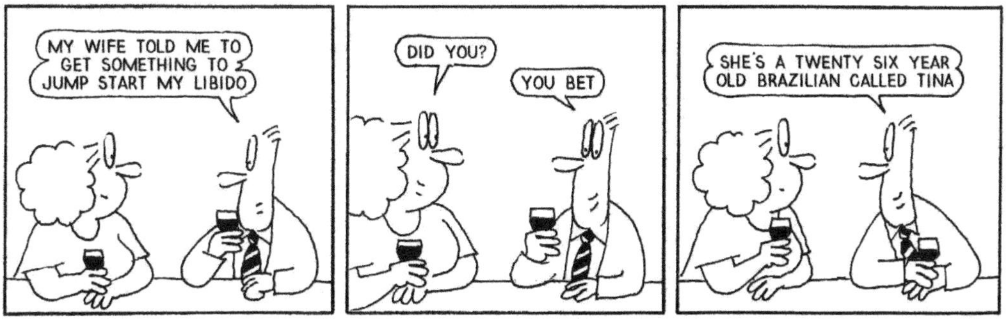
MY WIFE TOLD ME TO GET SOMETHING TO JUMP START MY LIBIDO
DID YOU?
YOU BET
SHE'S A TWENTY SIX YEAR OLD BRAZILIAN CALLED TINA

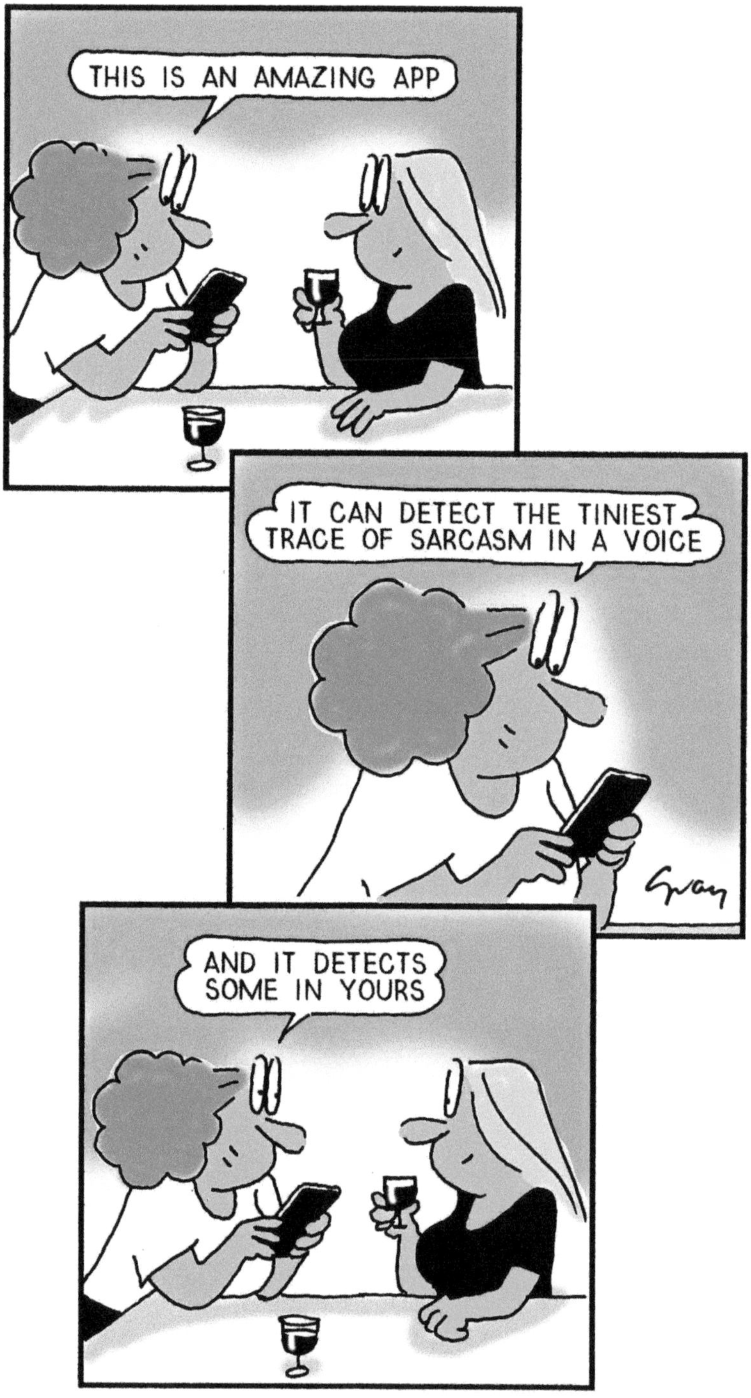
THIS IS AN AMAZING APP
IT CAN DETECT THE TINIEST TRACE OF SARCASM IN A VOICE
AND IT DETECTS SOME IN YOURS

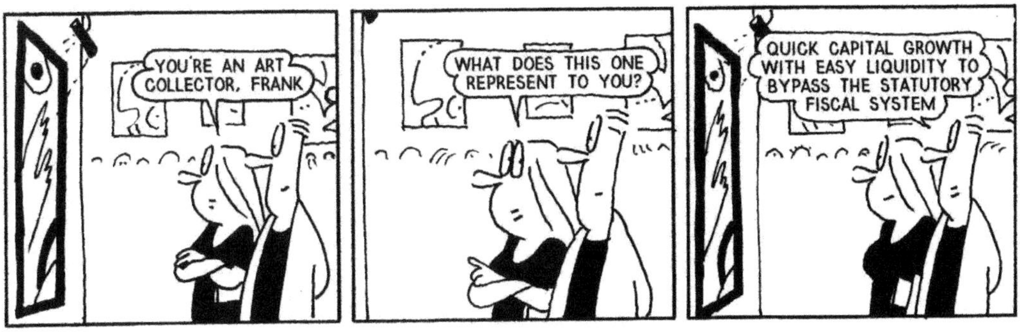
YOU'RE AN ART COLLECTOR, FRANK
WHAT DOES THIS ONE REPRESENT TO YOU?
QUICK CAPITAL GROWTH WITH EASY LIQUIDITY TO BYPASS THE STATUTORY FISCAL SYSTEM

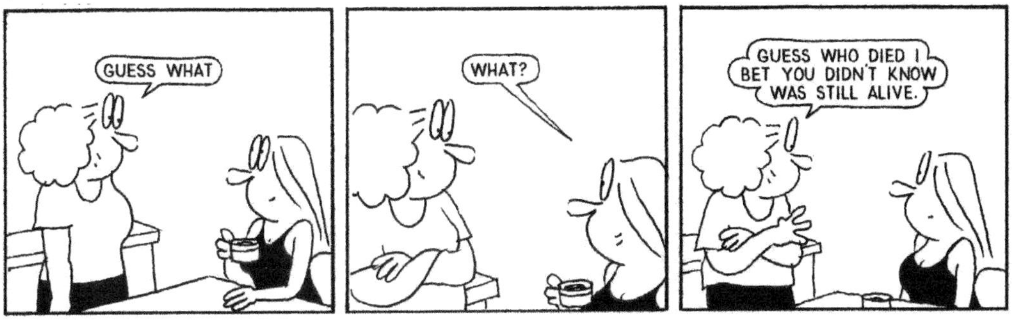
GUESS WHAT
WHAT?
GUESS WHO DIED I BET YOU DIDN'T KNOW WAS STILL ALIVE.

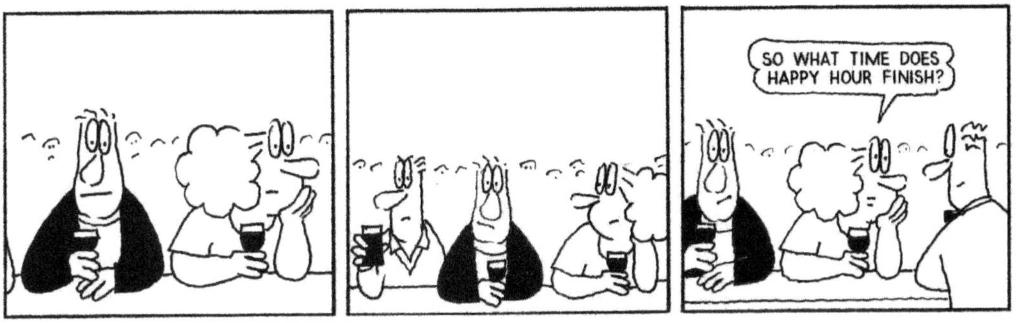
SO WHAT TIME DOES HAPPY HOUR FINISH?

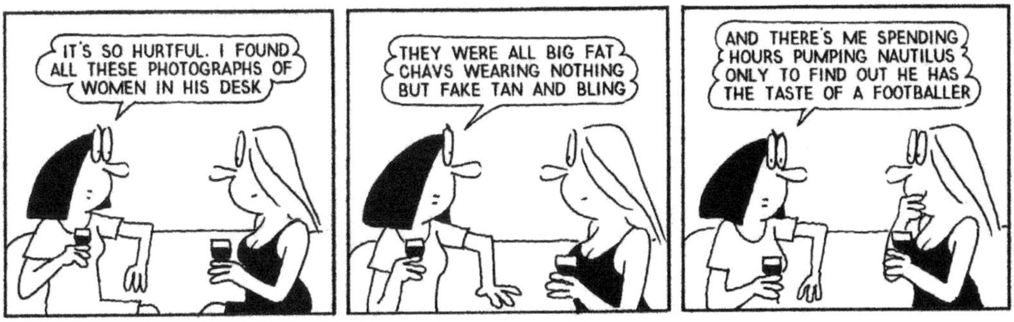
IT'S SO HURTFUL. I FOUND ALL THESE PHOTOGRAPHS OF WOMEN IN HIS DESK
THEY WERE ALL BIG FAT CHAVS WEARING NOTHING BUT FAKE TAN AND BLING
AND THERE'S ME SPENDING HOURS PUMPING NAUTILUS ONLY TO FIND OUT HE HAS THE TASTE OF A FOOTBALLER

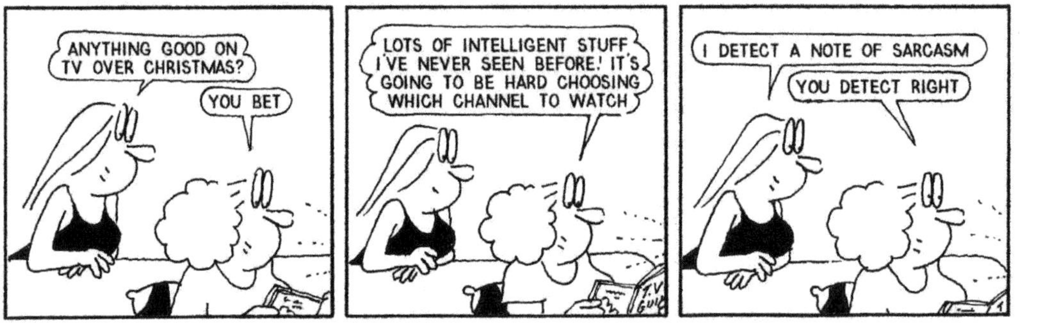
ANYTHING GOOD ON TV OVER CHRISTMAS?
YOU BET
LOTS OF INTELLIGENT STUFF I'VE NEVER SEEN BEFORE! IT'S GOING TO BE HARD CHOOSING WHICH CHANNEL TO WATCH
I DETECT A NOTE OF SARCASM
YOU DETECT RIGHT

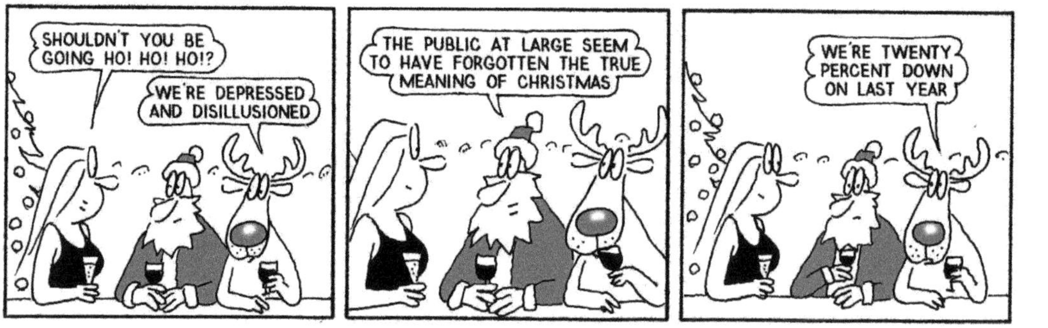
SHOULDN'T YOU BE GOING HO! HO! HO!?
WE'RE DEPRESSED AND DISILLUSIONED
THE PUBLIC AT LARGE SEEM TO HAVE FORGOTTEN THE TRUE MEANING OF CHRISTMAS
WE'RE TWENTY PERCENT DOWN ON LAST YEAR

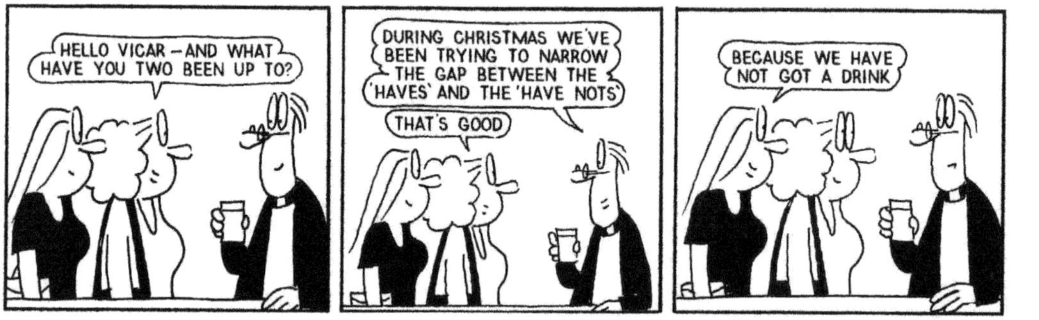
HELLO VICAR – AND WHAT HAVE YOU TWO BEEN UP TO?
DURING CHRISTMAS WE'VE BEEN TRYING TO NARROW THE GAP BETWEEN THE 'HAVES' AND THE 'HAVE NOTS'
THAT'S GOOD
BECAUSE WE HAVE NOT GOT A DRINK

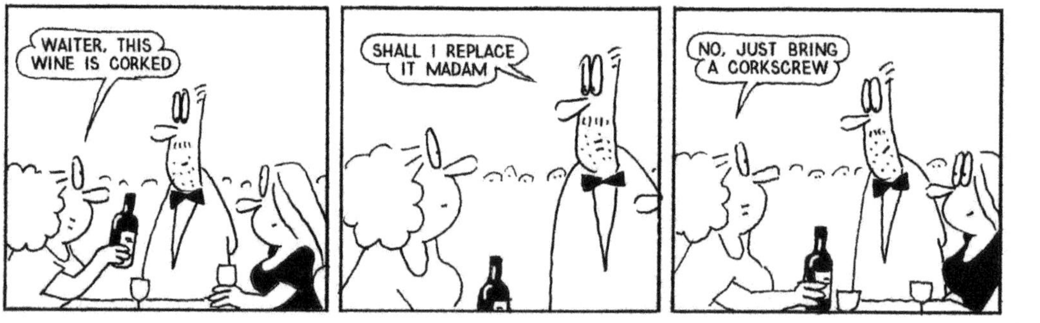
WAITER, THIS WINE IS CORKED
SHALL I REPLACE IT MADAM
NO, JUST BRING A CORKSCREW

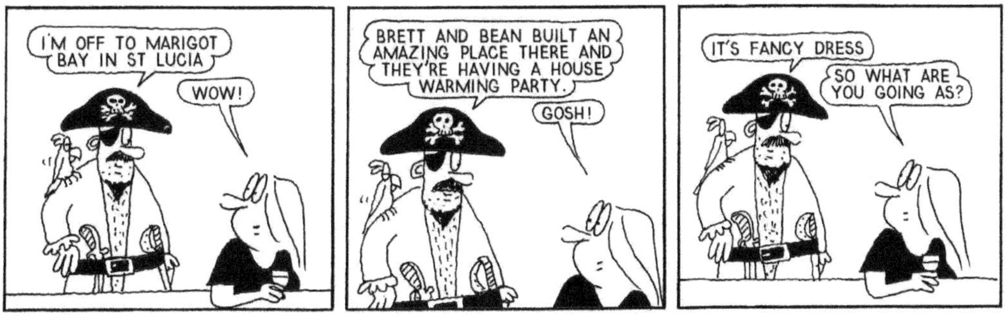
I'M OFF TO MARIGOT BAY IN ST LUCIA
WOW!
BRETT AND BEAN BUILT AN AMAZING PLACE THERE AND THEY'RE HAVING A HOUSE WARMING PARTY.
GOSH!
IT'S FANCY DRESS
SO WHAT ARE YOU GOING AS?

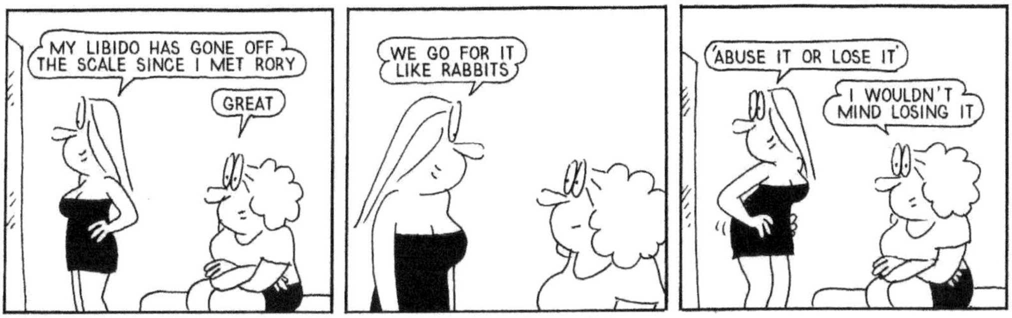
MY LIBIDO HAS GONE OFF THE SCALE SINCE I MET RORY
GREAT
WE GO FOR IT LIKE RABBITS
'ABUSE IT OR LOSE IT'
I WOULDN'T MIND LOSING IT

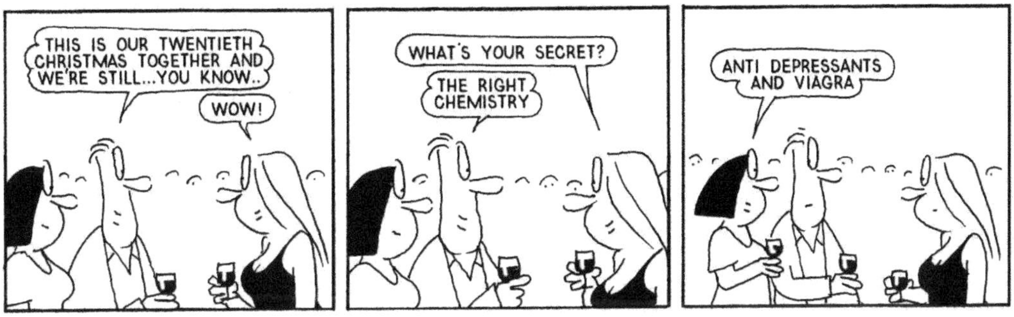
THIS IS OUR TWENTIETH CHRISTMAS TOGETHER AND WE'RE STILL...YOU KNOW..
WOW!
WHAT'S YOUR SECRET?
THE RIGHT CHEMISTRY
ANTI DEPRESSANTS AND VIAGRA

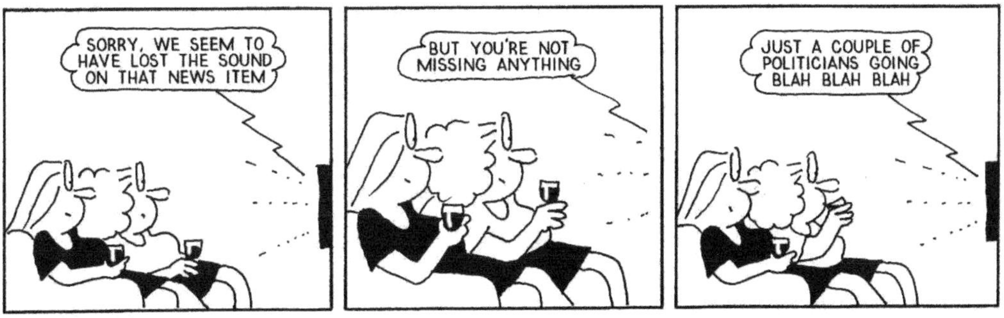
SORRY, WE SEEM TO HAVE LOST THE SOUND ON THAT NEWS ITEM
BUT YOU'RE NOT MISSING ANYTHING
JUST A COUPLE OF POLITICIANS GOING BLAH BLAH BLAH

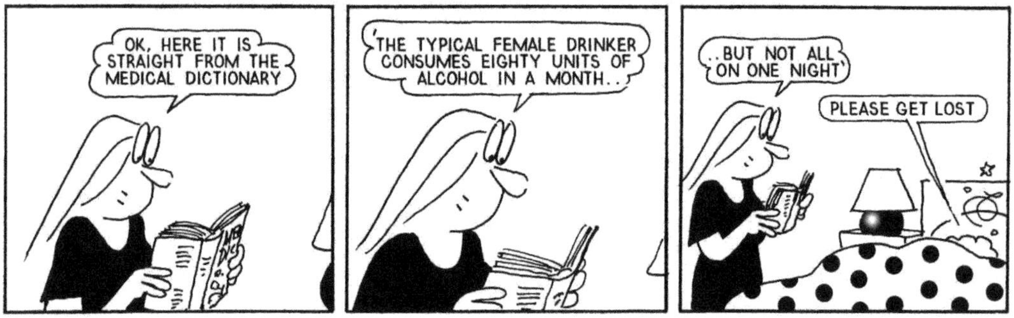
OK, HERE IT IS STRAIGHT FROM THE MEDICAL DICTIONARY
'THE TYPICAL FEMALE DRINKER CONSUMES EIGHTY UNITS OF ALCOHOL IN A MONTH..
..BUT NOT ALL ON ONE NIGHT'
PLEASE GET LOST

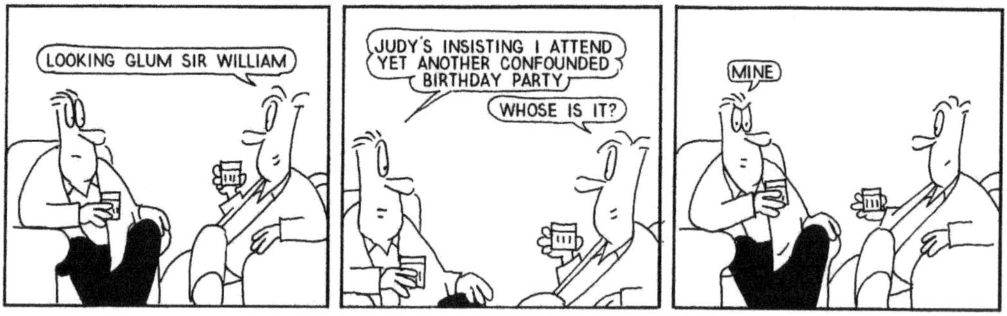
LOOKING GLUM SIR WILLIAM
JUDY'S INSISTING I ATTEND YET ANOTHER CONFOUNDED BIRTHDAY PARTY
WHOSE IS IT?
MINE

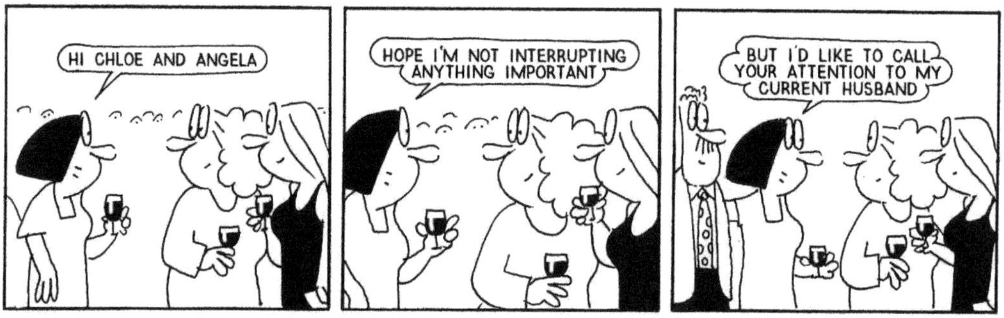
HI CHLOE AND ANGELA
HOPE I'M NOT INTERRUPTING ANYTHING IMPORTANT
BUT I'D LIKE TO CALL YOUR ATTENTION TO MY CURRENT HUSBAND

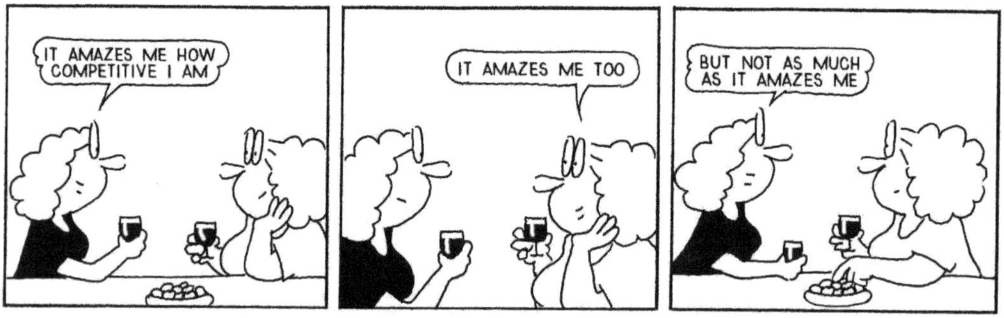
IT AMAZES ME HOW COMPETITIVE I AM
IT AMAZES ME TOO
BUT NOT AS MUCH AS IT AMAZES ME

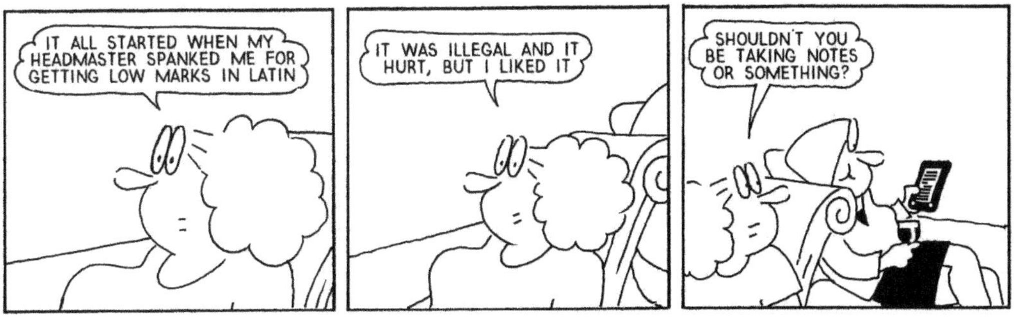
IT ALL STARTED WHEN MY HEADMASTER SPANKED ME FOR GETTING LOW MARKS IN LATIN
IT WAS ILLEGAL AND IT HURT, BUT I LIKED IT
SHOULDN'T YOU BE TAKING NOTES OR SOMETHING?

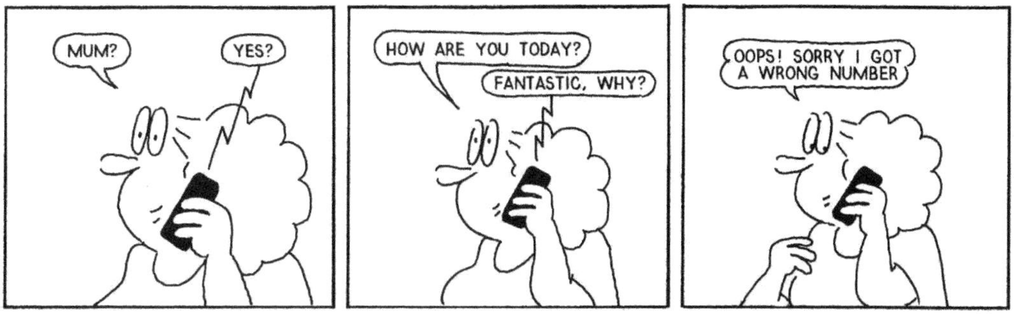
MUM?
YES?
HOW ARE YOU TODAY?
FANTASTIC, WHY?
OOPS! SORRY I GOT A WRONG NUMBER

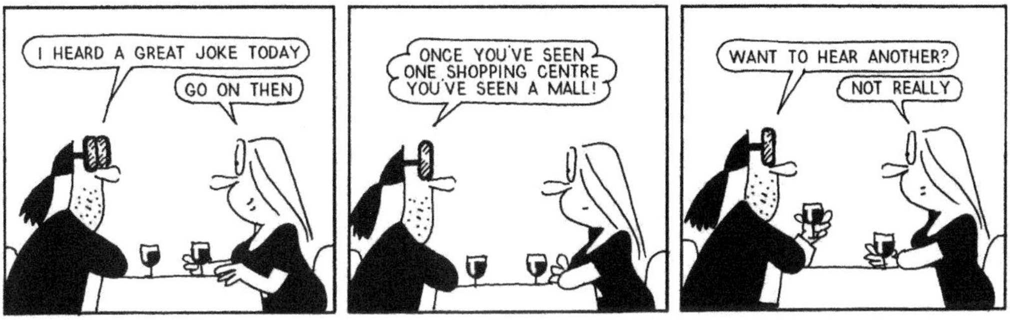
I HEARD A GREAT JOKE TODAY
GO ON THEN
ONCE YOU'VE SEEN ONE SHOPPING CENTRE YOU'VE SEEN A MALL!
WANT TO HEAR ANOTHER?
NOT REALLY

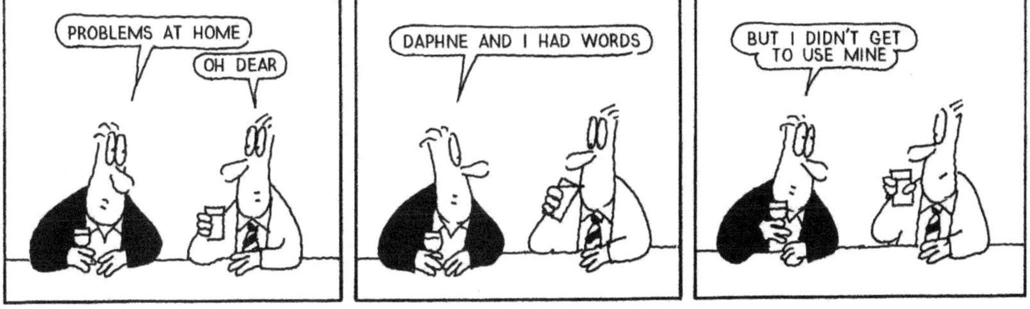
PROBLEMS AT HOME
OH DEAR
DAPHNE AND I HAD WORDS
BUT I DIDN'T GET TO USE MINE

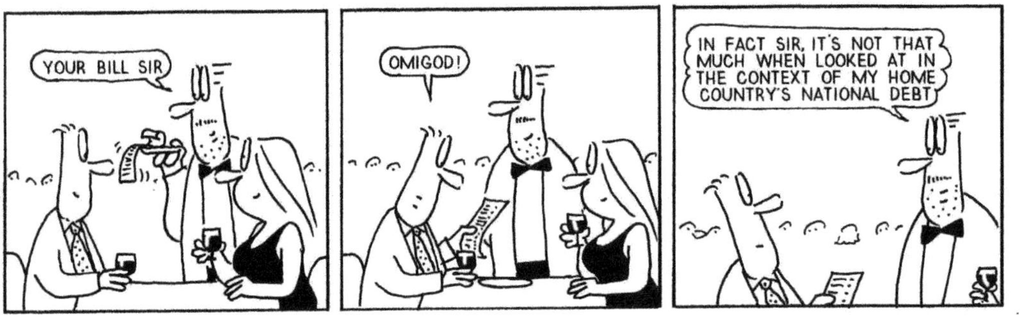
YOUR BILL SIR
OMIGOD!
IN FACT SIR, IT'S NOT THAT MUCH WHEN LOOKED AT IN THE CONTEXT OF MY HOME COUNTRY'S NATIONAL DEBT

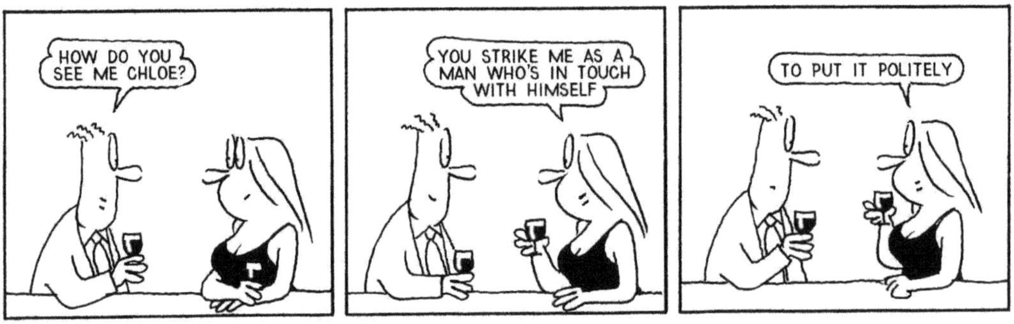
HOW DO YOU SEE ME CHLOE?
YOU STRIKE ME AS A MAN WHO'S IN TOUCH WITH HIMSELF
TO PUT IT POLITELY

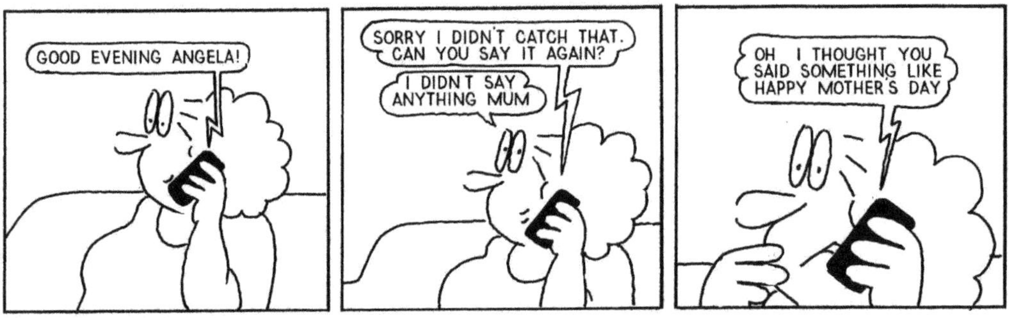
GOOD EVENING ANGELA!
SORRY I DIDN'T CATCH THAT. CAN YOU SAY IT AGAIN?
I DIDN'T SAY ANYTHING MUM
OH I THOUGHT YOU SAID SOMETHING LIKE HAPPY MOTHER'S DAY

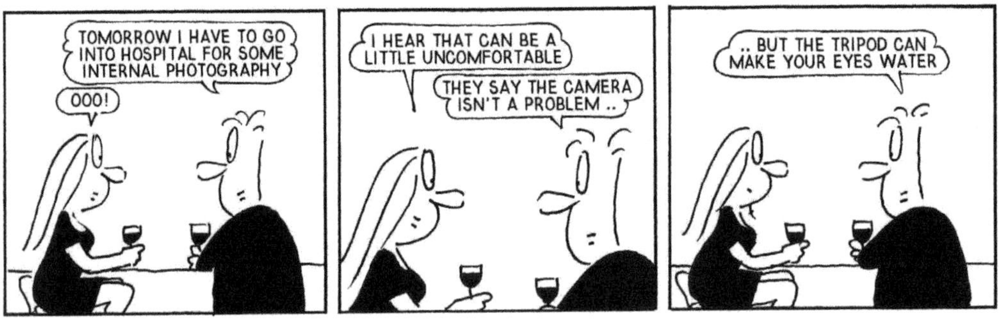
TOMORROW I HAVE TO GO INTO HOSPITAL FOR SOME INTERNAL PHOTOGRAPHY
OOO!
I HEAR THAT CAN BE A LITTLE UNCOMFORTABLE
THEY SAY THE CAMERA ISN'T A PROBLEM ..
.. BUT THE TRIPOD CAN MAKE YOUR EYES WATER

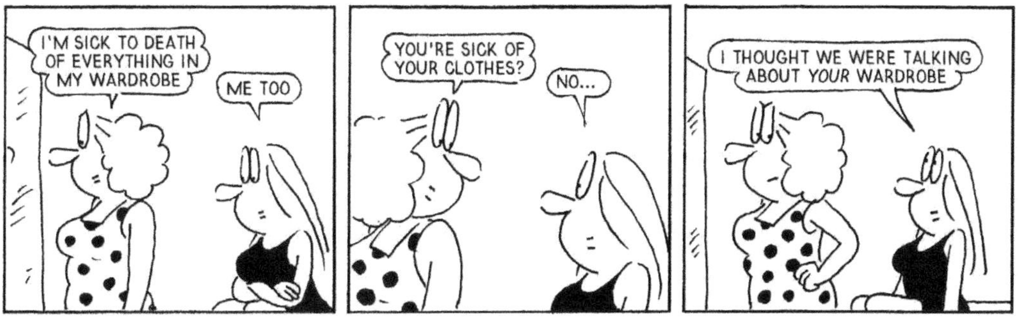
I'M SICK TO DEATH OF EVERYTHING IN MY WARDROBE
ME TOO
YOU'RE SICK OF YOUR CLOTHES?
NO...
I THOUGHT WE WERE TALKING ABOUT *YOUR* WARDROBE

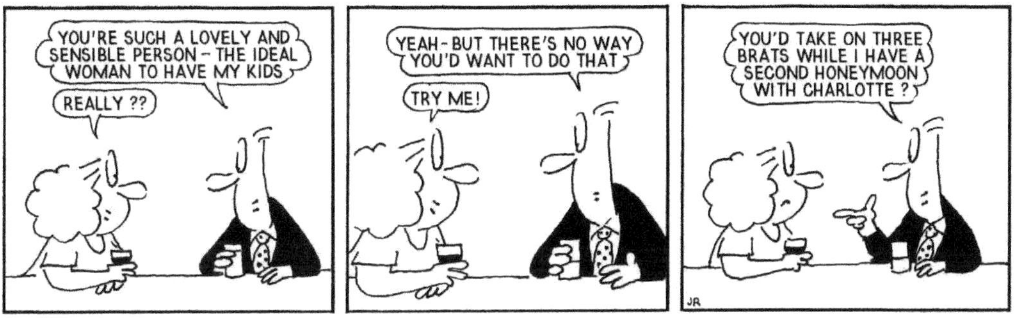
YOU'RE SUCH A LOVELY AND SENSIBLE PERSON – THE IDEAL WOMAN TO HAVE MY KIDS
REALLY ??
YEAH – BUT THERE'S NO WAY YOU'D WANT TO DO THAT
TRY ME!
YOU'D TAKE ON THREE BRATS WHILE I HAVE A SECOND HONEYMOON WITH CHARLOTTE ?
JR

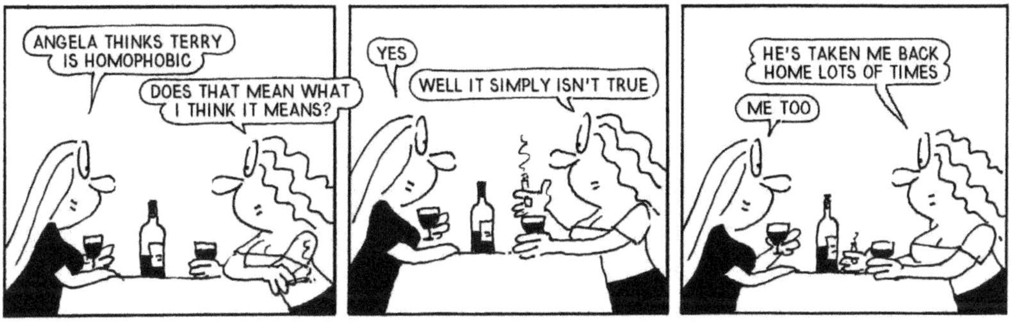
ANGELA THINKS TERRY IS HOMOPHOBIC
DOES THAT MEAN WHAT I THINK IT MEANS?
YES
WELL IT SIMPLY ISN'T TRUE
HE'S TAKEN ME BACK HOME LOTS OF TIMES
ME TOO

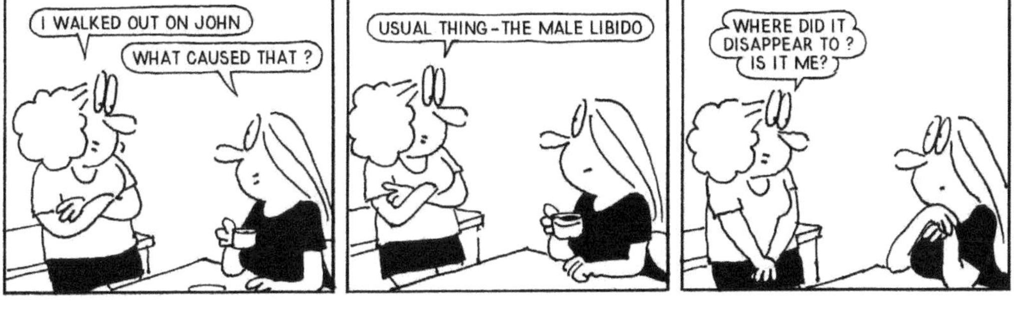
I WALKED OUT ON JOHN
WHAT CAUSED THAT ?
USUAL THING – THE MALE LIBIDO
WHERE DID IT DISAPPEAR TO ? IS IT ME?

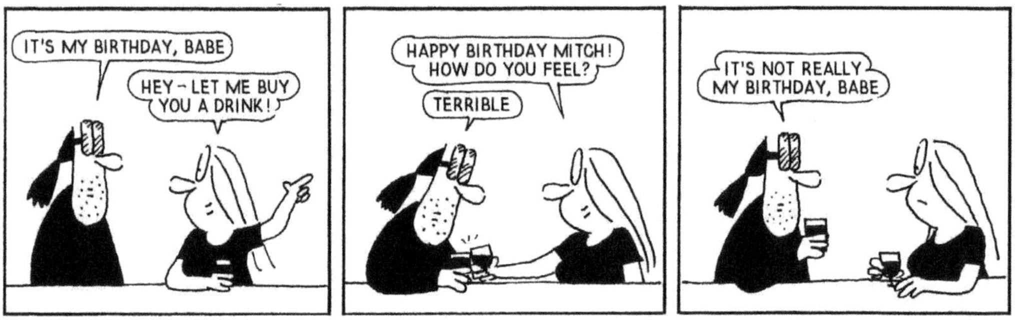
IT'S MY BIRTHDAY, BABE
HEY – LET ME BUY YOU A DRINK!
HAPPY BIRTHDAY MITCH! HOW DO YOU FEEL?
TERRIBLE
IT'S NOT REALLY MY BIRTHDAY, BABE

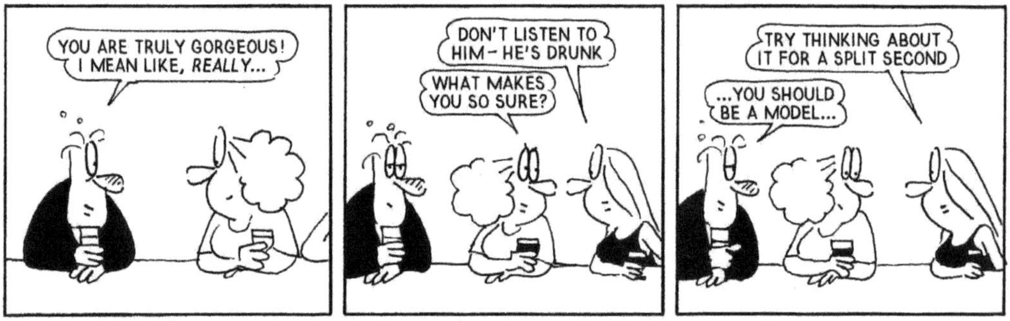
YOU ARE TRULY GORGEOUS! I MEAN LIKE, *REALLY*...
DON'T LISTEN TO HIM – HE'S DRUNK
WHAT MAKES YOU SO SURE?
TRY THINKING ABOUT IT FOR A SPLIT SECOND
...YOU SHOULD BE A MODEL...

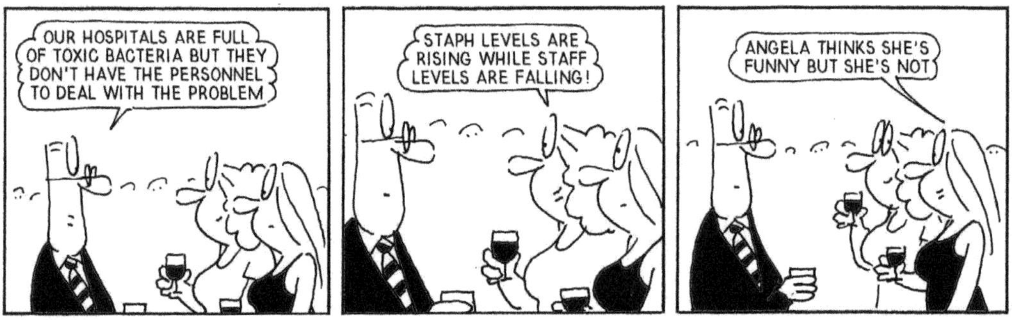
OUR HOSPITALS ARE FULL OF TOXIC BACTERIA BUT THEY DON'T HAVE THE PERSONNEL TO DEAL WITH THE PROBLEM
STAPH LEVELS ARE RISING WHILE STAFF LEVELS ARE FALLING!
ANGELA THINKS SHE'S FUNNY BUT SHE'S NOT

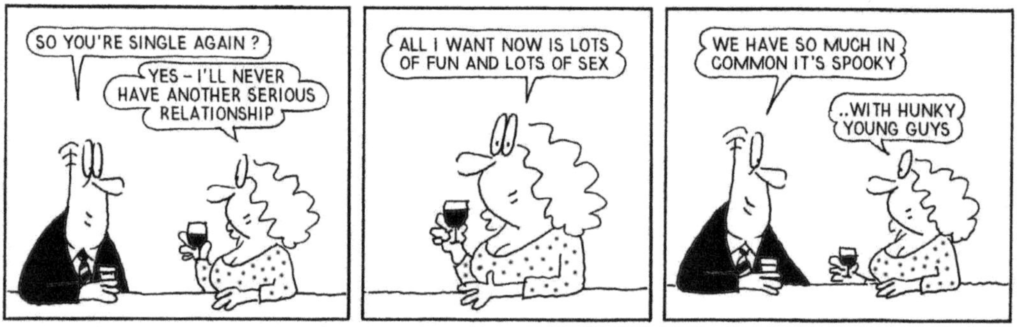
SO YOU'RE SINGLE AGAIN ?
YES – I'LL NEVER HAVE ANOTHER SERIOUS RELATIONSHIP
ALL I WANT NOW IS LOTS OF FUN AND LOTS OF SEX
WE HAVE SO MUCH IN COMMON IT'S SPOOKY
..WITH HUNKY YOUNG GUYS

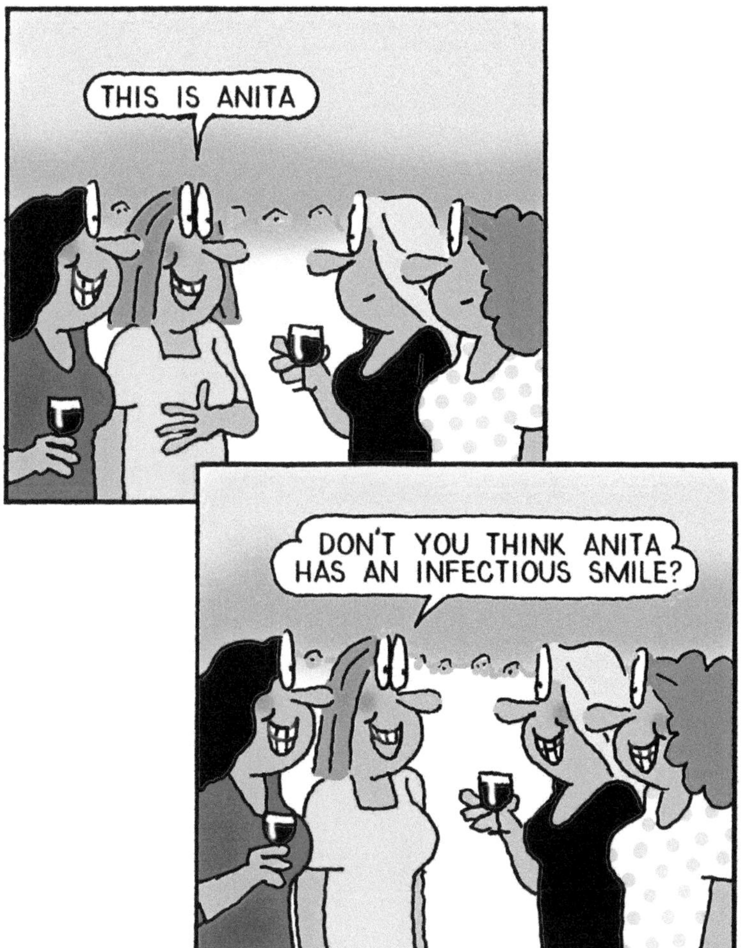
THIS IS ANITA
DON'T YOU THINK ANITA HAS AN INFECTIOUS SMILE?
Gray

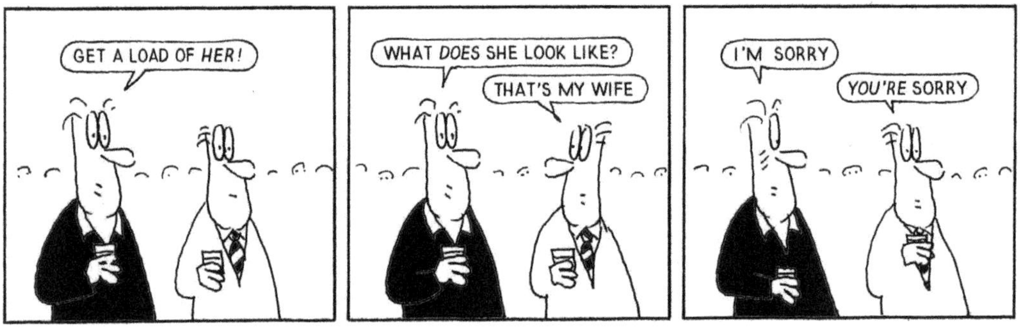
GET A LOAD OF HER!
WHAT DOES SHE LOOK LIKE?
THAT'S MY WIFE
I'M SORRY
YOU'RE SORRY

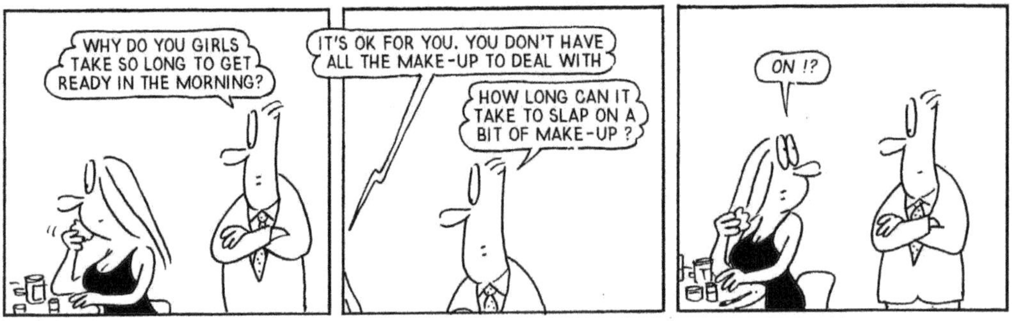
WHY DO YOU GIRLS TAKE SO LONG TO GET READY IN THE MORNING?
IT'S OK FOR YOU. YOU DON'T HAVE ALL THE MAKE-UP TO DEAL WITH
HOW LONG CAN IT TAKE TO SLAP ON A BIT OF MAKE-UP ?
ON !?

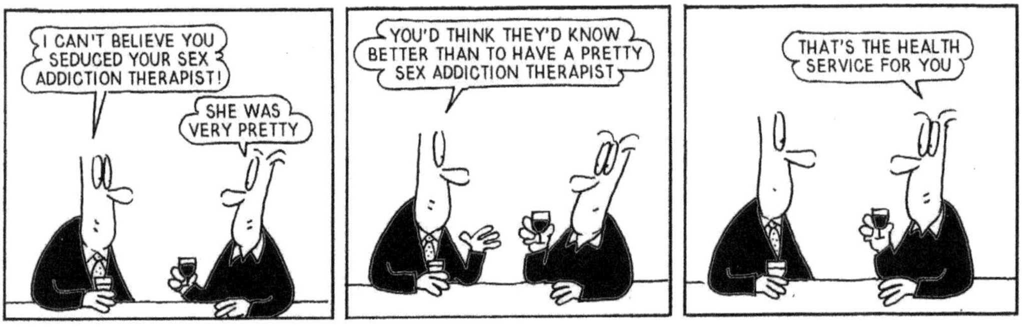
I CAN'T BELIEVE YOU SEDUCED YOUR SEX ADDICTION THERAPIST!
SHE WAS VERY PRETTY
YOU'D THINK THEY'D KNOW BETTER THAN TO HAVE A PRETTY SEX ADDICTION THERAPIST
THAT'S THE HEALTH SERVICE FOR YOU

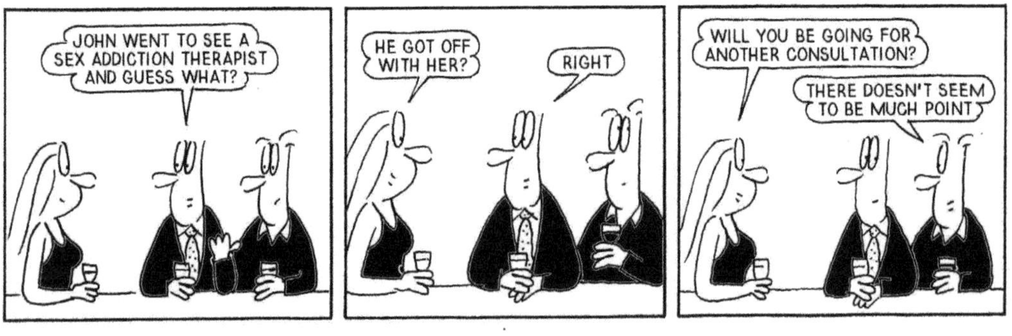
JOHN WENT TO SEE A SEX ADDICTION THERAPIST AND GUESS WHAT?
HE GOT OFF WITH HER?
RIGHT
WILL YOU BE GOING FOR ANOTHER CONSULTATION?
THERE DOESN'T SEEM TO BE MUCH POINT

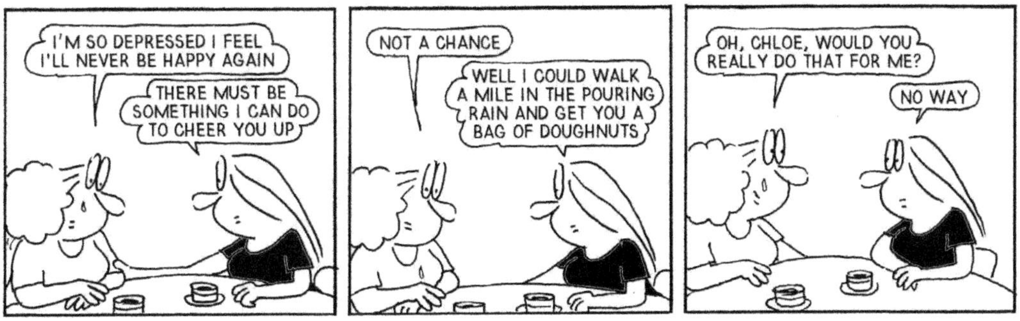
I'M SO DEPRESSED I FEEL I'LL NEVER BE HAPPY AGAIN
THERE MUST BE SOMETHING I CAN DO TO CHEER YOU UP
NOT A CHANCE
WELL I COULD WALK A MILE IN THE POURING RAIN AND GET YOU A BAG OF DOUGHNUTS
OH, CHLOE, WOULD YOU REALLY DO THAT FOR ME?
NO WAY

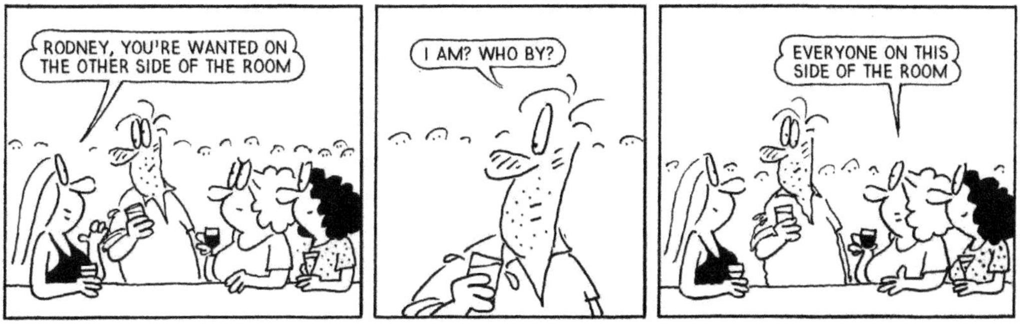
RODNEY, YOU'RE WANTED ON THE OTHER SIDE OF THE ROOM
I AM? WHO BY?
EVERYONE ON THIS SIDE OF THE ROOM

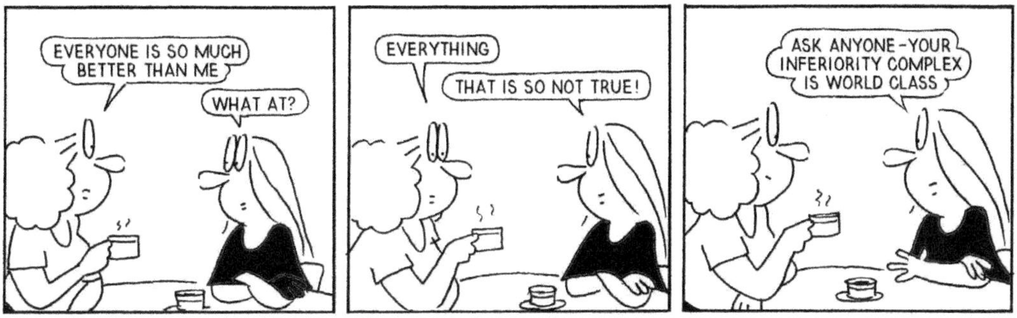
EVERYONE IS SO MUCH BETTER THAN ME
WHAT AT?
EVERYTHING
THAT IS SO NOT TRUE!
ASK ANYONE - YOUR INFERIORITY COMPLEX IS WORLD CLASS

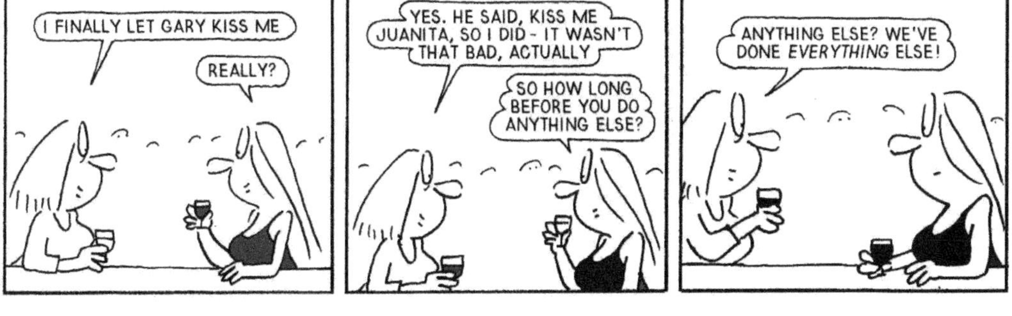
I FINALLY LET GARY KISS ME
REALLY?
YES. HE SAID, KISS ME JUANITA, SO I DID - IT WASN'T THAT BAD, ACTUALLY
SO HOW LONG BEFORE YOU DO ANYTHING ELSE?
ANYTHING ELSE? WE'VE DONE *EVERYTHING* ELSE!

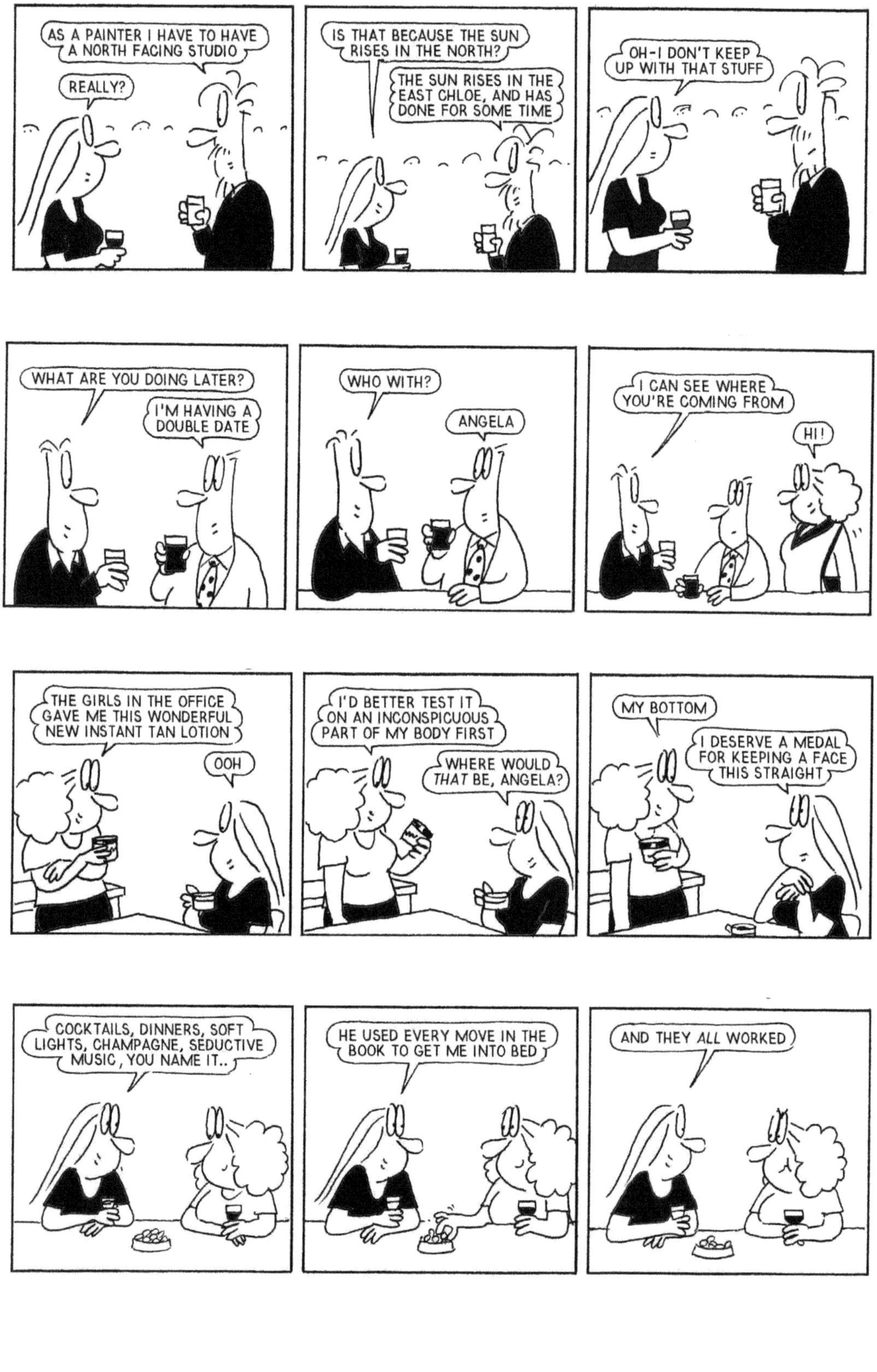
AS A PAINTER I HAVE TO HAVE A NORTH FACING STUDIO
REALLY?
IS THAT BECAUSE THE SUN RISES IN THE NORTH?
THE SUN RISES IN THE EAST CHLOE, AND HAS DONE FOR SOME TIME
OH-I DON'T KEEP UP WITH THAT STUFF
WHAT ARE YOU DOING LATER?
I'M HAVING A DOUBLE DATE
WHO WITH?
ANGELA
I CAN SEE WHERE YOU'RE COMING FROM
HI!
THE GIRLS IN THE OFFICE GAVE ME THIS WONDERFUL NEW INSTANT TAN LOTION
OOH
I'D BETTER TEST IT ON AN INCONSPICUOUS PART OF MY BODY FIRST
WHERE WOULD *THAT* BE, ANGELA?
MY BOTTOM
I DESERVE A MEDAL FOR KEEPING A FACE THIS STRAIGHT
COCKTAILS, DINNERS, SOFT LIGHTS, CHAMPAGNE, SEDUCTIVE MUSIC, YOU NAME IT..
HE USED EVERY MOVE IN THE BOOK TO GET ME INTO BED
AND THEY *ALL* WORKED

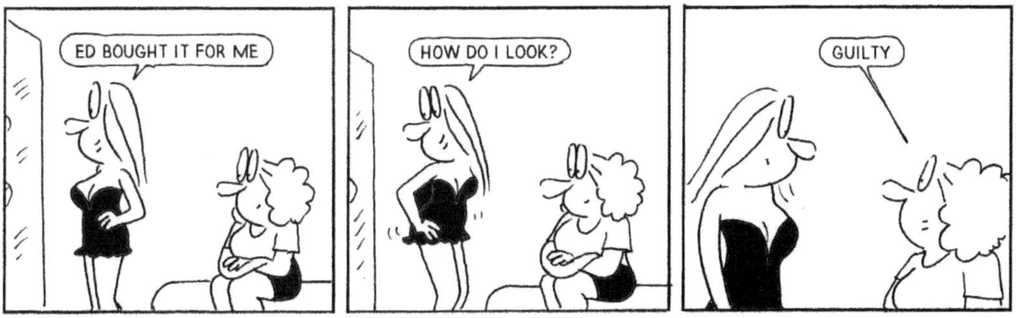
ED BOUGHT IT FOR ME
HOW DO I LOOK?
GUILTY

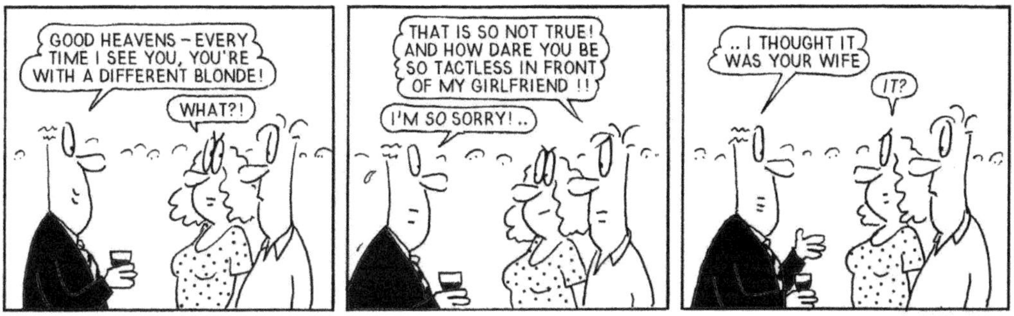
GOOD HEAVENS – EVERY TIME I SEE YOU, YOU'RE WITH A DIFFERENT BLONDE!
WHAT?!
THAT IS SO NOT TRUE! AND HOW DARE YOU BE SO TACTLESS IN FRONT OF MY GIRLFRIEND !!
I'M SO SORRY! ..
.. I THOUGHT IT WAS YOUR WIFE
IT?

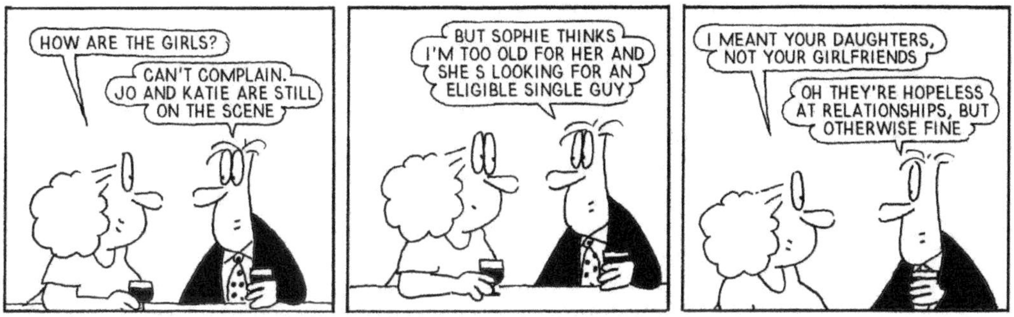
HOW ARE THE GIRLS?
CAN'T COMPLAIN. JO AND KATIE ARE STILL ON THE SCENE
BUT SOPHIE THINKS I'M TOO OLD FOR HER AND SHE S LOOKING FOR AN ELIGIBLE SINGLE GUY
I MEANT YOUR DAUGHTERS, NOT YOUR GIRLFRIENDS
OH THEY'RE HOPELESS AT RELATIONSHIPS, BUT OTHERWISE FINE

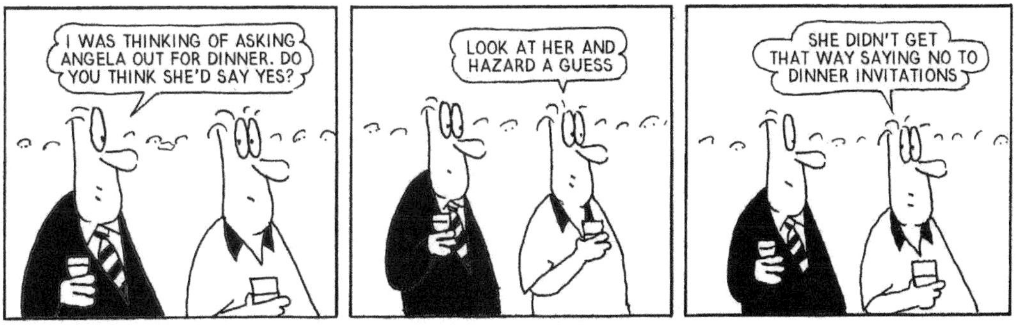
I WAS THINKING OF ASKING ANGELA OUT FOR DINNER. DO YOU THINK SHE'D SAY YES?
LOOK AT HER AND HAZARD A GUESS
SHE DIDN'T GET THAT WAY SAYING NO TO DINNER INVITATIONS

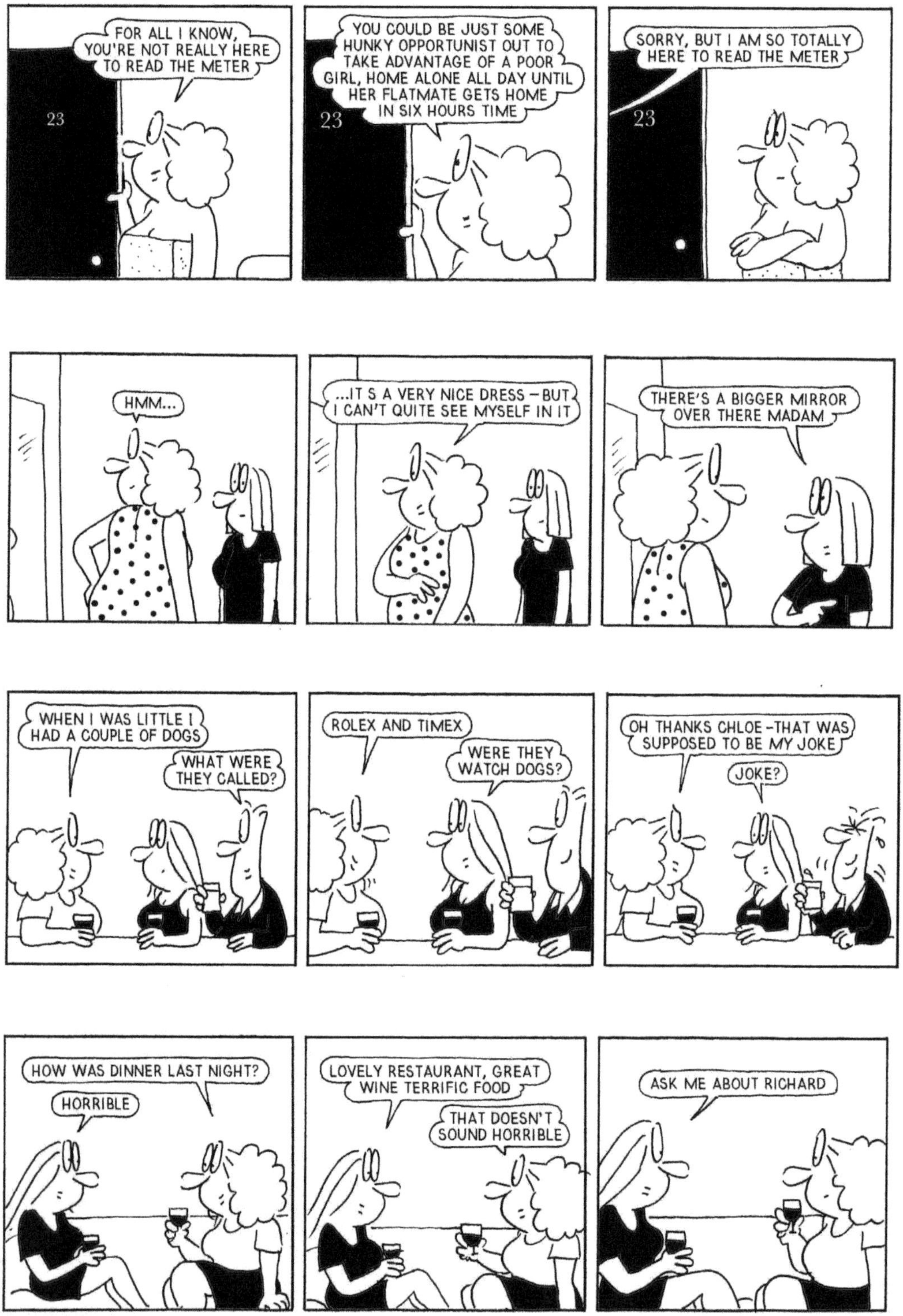

FOR ALL I KNOW, YOU'RE NOT REALLY HERE TO READ THE METER
23
YOU COULD BE JUST SOME HUNKY OPPORTUNIST OUT TO TAKE ADVANTAGE OF A POOR GIRL, HOME ALONE ALL DAY UNTIL HER FLATMATE GETS HOME IN SIX HOURS TIME
23
SORRY, BUT I AM SO TOTALLY HERE TO READ THE METER
23
HMM...
...IT S A VERY NICE DRESS – BUT I CAN'T QUITE SEE MYSELF IN IT
THERE'S A BIGGER MIRROR OVER THERE MADAM
WHEN I WAS LITTLE I HAD A COUPLE OF DOGS
WHAT WERE THEY CALLED?
ROLEX AND TIMEX
WERE THEY WATCH DOGS?
OH THANKS CHLOE –THAT WAS SUPPOSED TO BE MY JOKE
JOKE?
HOW WAS DINNER LAST NIGHT?
HORRIBLE
LOVELY RESTAURANT, GREAT WINE TERRIFIC FOOD
THAT DOESN'T SOUND HORRIBLE
ASK ME ABOUT RICHARD

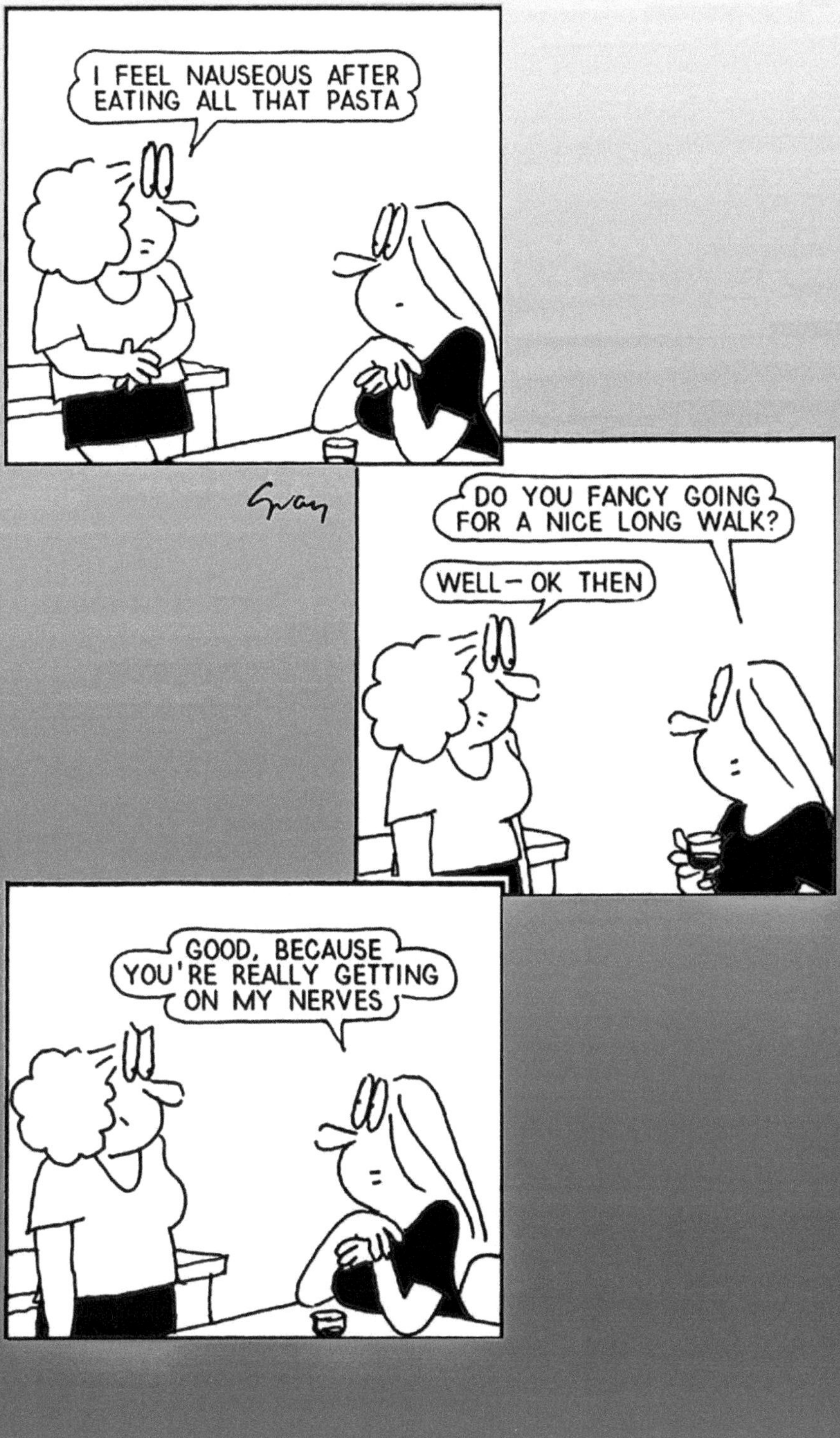
I FEEL NAUSEOUS AFTER EATING ALL THAT PASTA
DO YOU FANCY GOING FOR A NICE LONG WALK?
WELL- OK THEN
GOOD, BECAUSE YOU'RE REALLY GETTING ON MY NERVES

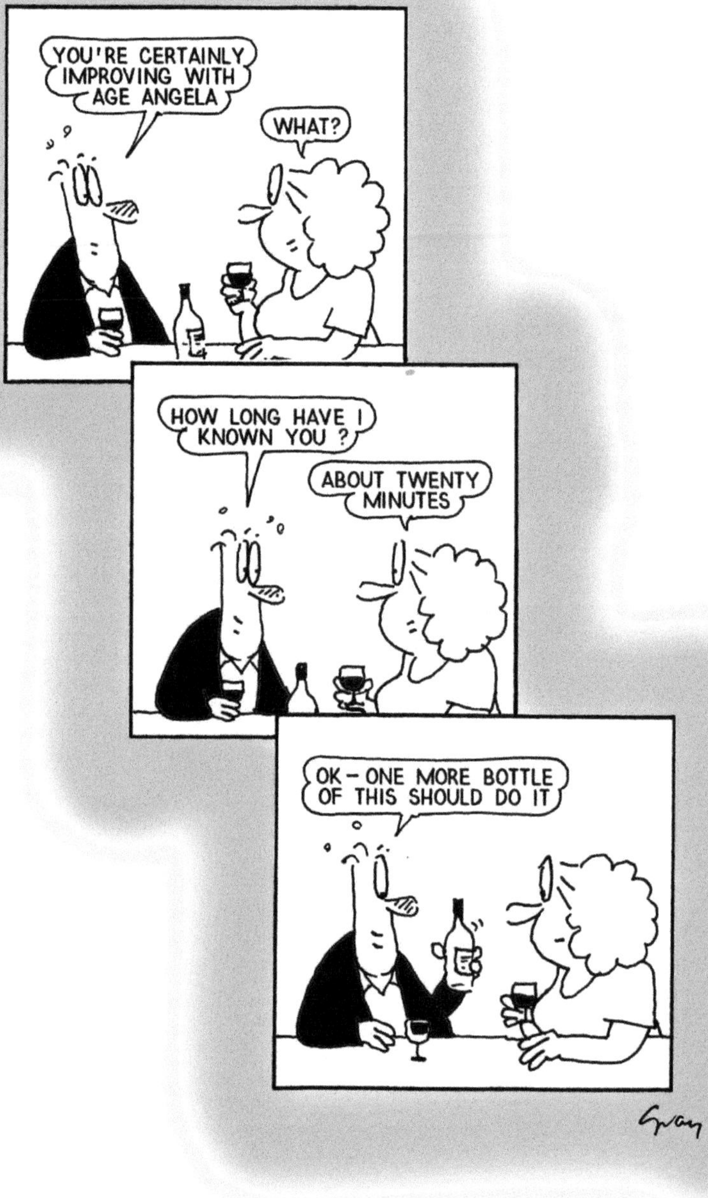
YOU'RE CERTAINLY IMPROVING WITH AGE ANGELA
WHAT?
HOW LONG HAVE I KNOWN YOU ?
ABOUT TWENTY MINUTES
OK – ONE MORE BOTTLE OF THIS SHOULD DO IT
Gray

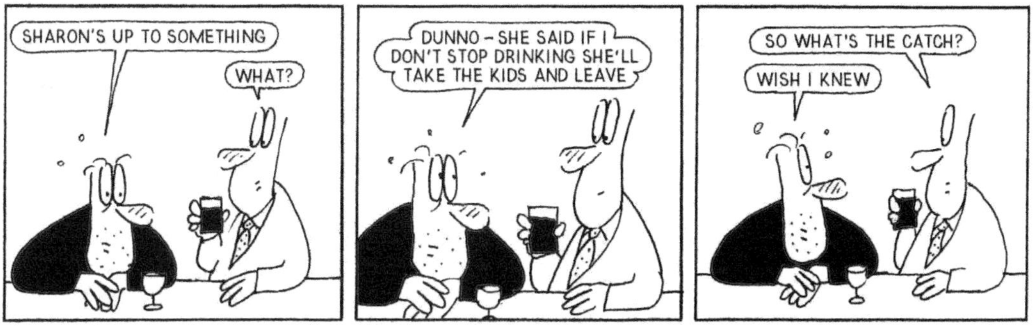
SHARON'S UP TO SOMETHING
WHAT?
DUNNO – SHE SAID IF I DON'T STOP DRINKING SHE'LL TAKE THE KIDS AND LEAVE
SO WHAT'S THE CATCH?
WISH I KNEW

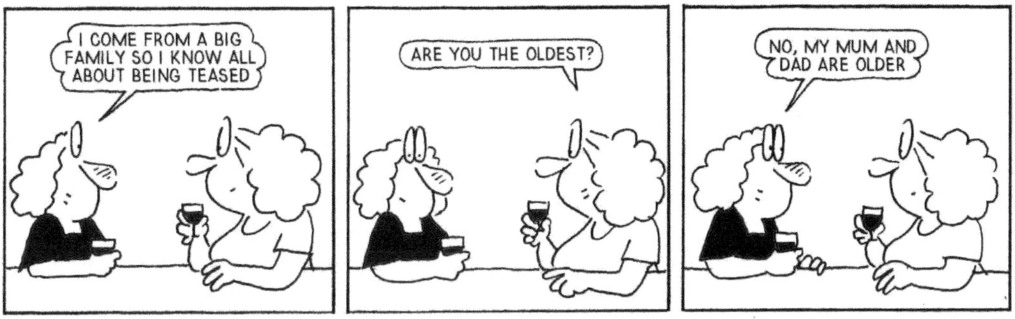
I COME FROM A BIG FAMILY SO I KNOW ALL ABOUT BEING TEASED
ARE YOU THE OLDEST?
NO, MY MUM AND DAD ARE OLDER

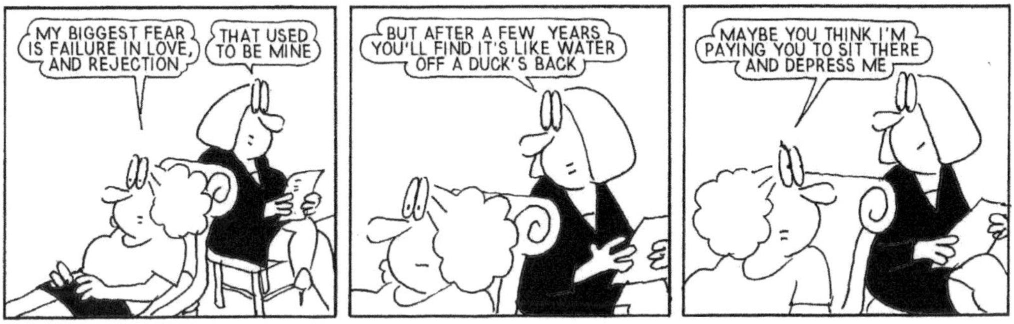
MY BIGGEST FEAR IS FAILURE IN LOVE, AND REJECTION
THAT USED TO BE MINE
BUT AFTER A FEW YEARS YOU'LL FIND IT'S LIKE WATER OFF A DUCK'S BACK
MAYBE YOU THINK I'M PAYING YOU TO SIT THERE AND DEPRESS ME

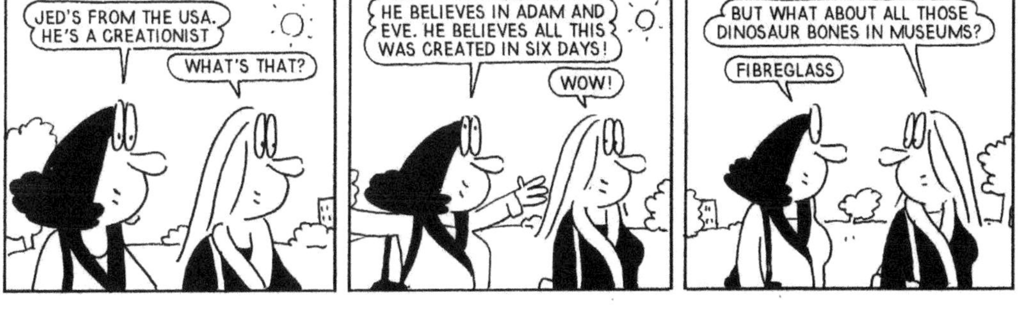
JED'S FROM THE USA. HE'S A CREATIONIST
WHAT'S THAT?
HE BELIEVES IN ADAM AND EVE. HE BELIEVES ALL THIS WAS CREATED IN SIX DAYS!
WOW!
BUT WHAT ABOUT ALL THOSE DINOSAUR BONES IN MUSEUMS?
FIBREGLASS

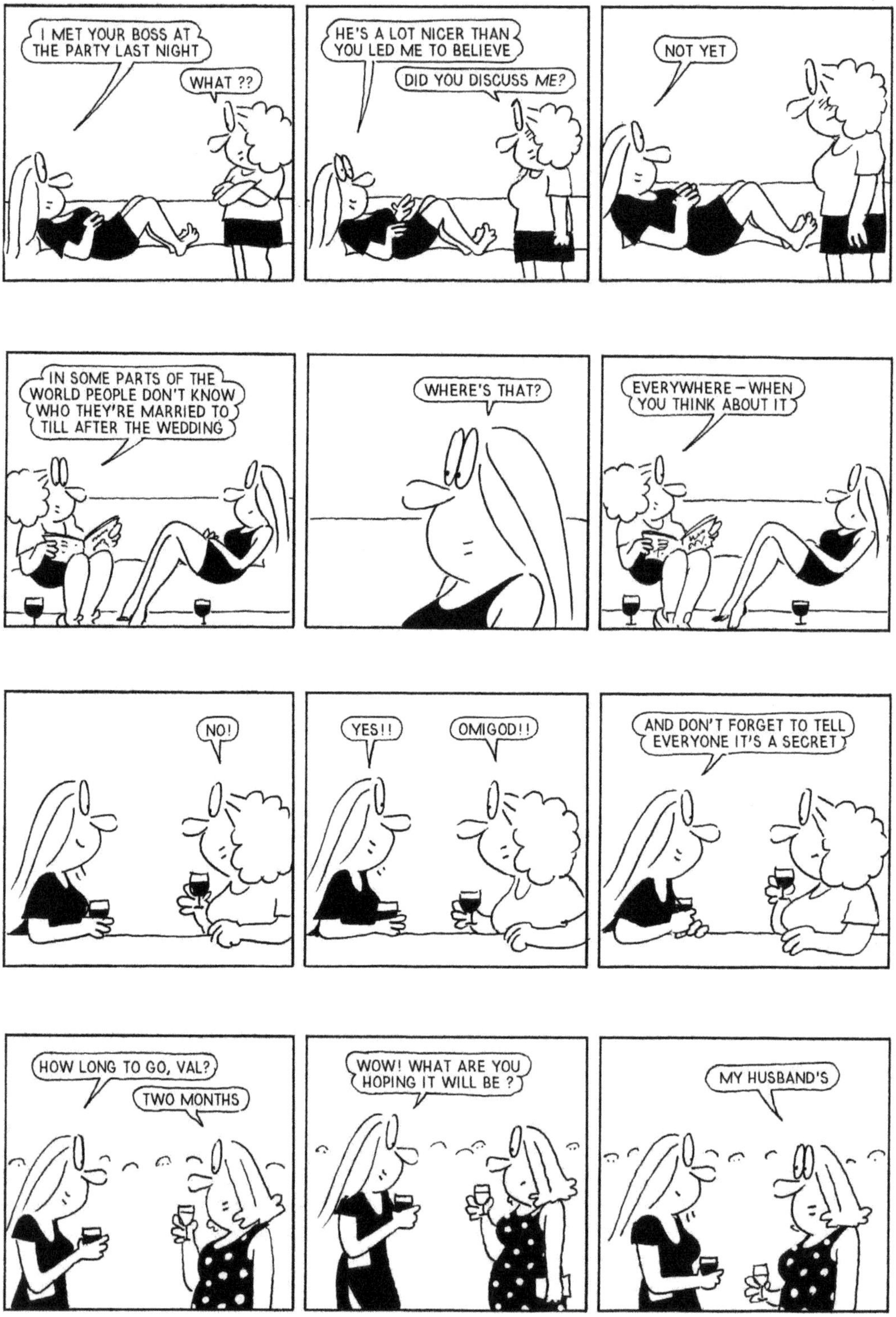
I MET YOUR BOSS AT THE PARTY LAST NIGHT
WHAT ??
HE'S A LOT NICER THAN YOU LED ME TO BELIEVE
DID YOU DISCUSS *ME?*
NOT YET
IN SOME PARTS OF THE WORLD PEOPLE DON'T KNOW WHO THEY'RE MARRIED TO TILL AFTER THE WEDDING
WHERE'S THAT?
EVERYWHERE – WHEN YOU THINK ABOUT IT
NO!
YES!!
OMIGOD!!
AND DON'T FORGET TO TELL EVERYONE IT'S A SECRET
HOW LONG TO GO, VAL?
TWO MONTHS
WOW! WHAT ARE YOU HOPING IT WILL BE ?
MY HUSBAND'S

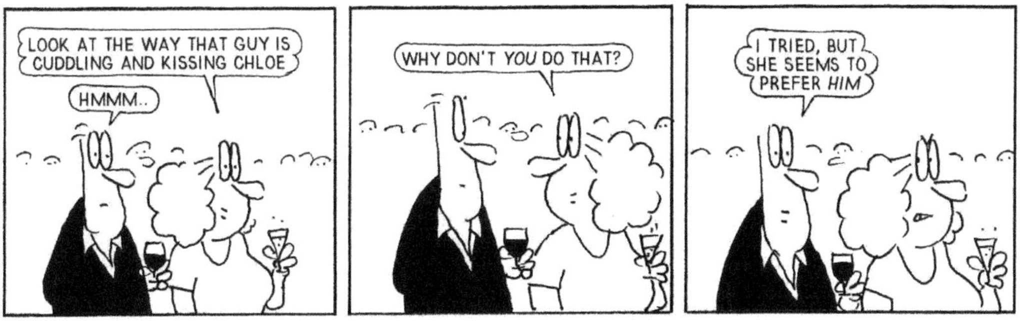
LOOK AT THE WAY THAT GUY IS CUDDLING AND KISSING CHLOE
HMMM..
WHY DON'T *YOU* DO THAT?
I TRIED, BUT SHE SEEMS TO PREFER *HIM*

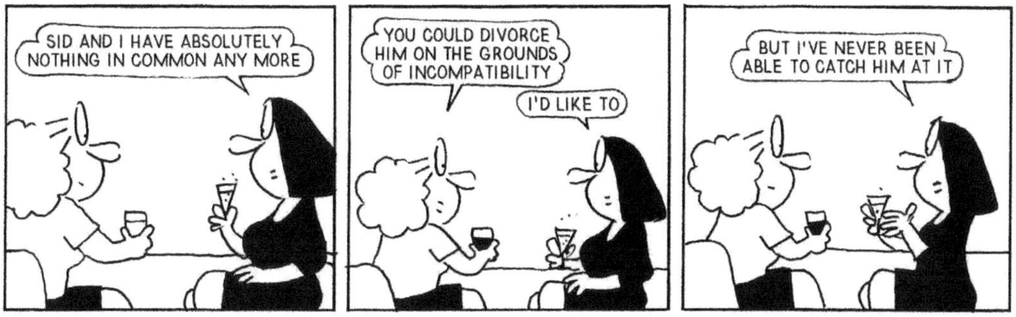
SID AND I HAVE ABSOLUTELY NOTHING IN COMMON ANY MORE
YOU COULD DIVORCE HIM ON THE GROUNDS OF INCOMPATIBILITY
I'D LIKE TO
BUT I'VE NEVER BEEN ABLE TO CATCH HIM AT IT

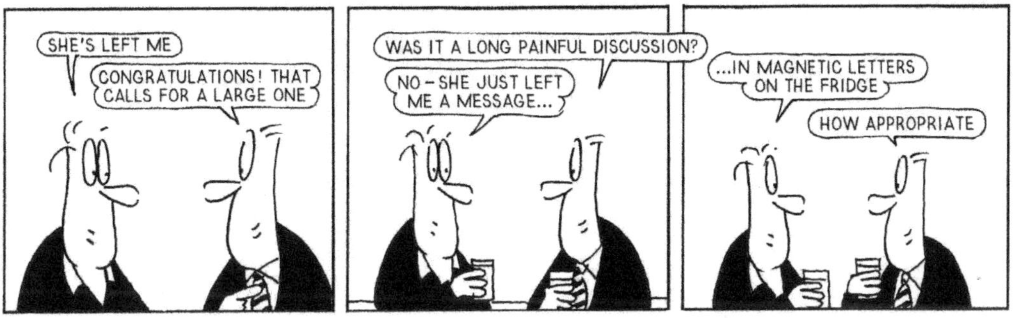
SHE'S LEFT ME
CONGRATULATIONS! THAT CALLS FOR A LARGE ONE
WAS IT A LONG PAINFUL DISCUSSION?
NO – SHE JUST LEFT ME A MESSAGE...
...IN MAGNETIC LETTERS ON THE FRIDGE
HOW APPROPRIATE

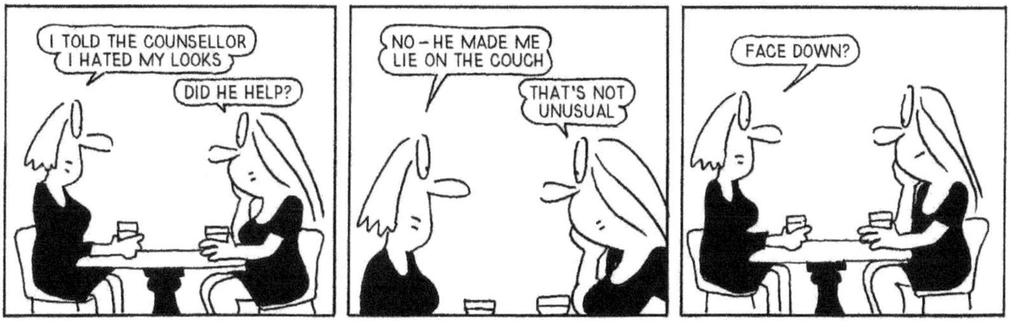
I TOLD THE COUNSELLOR I HATED MY LOOKS
DID HE HELP?
NO – HE MADE ME LIE ON THE COUCH
THAT'S NOT UNUSUAL
FACE DOWN?

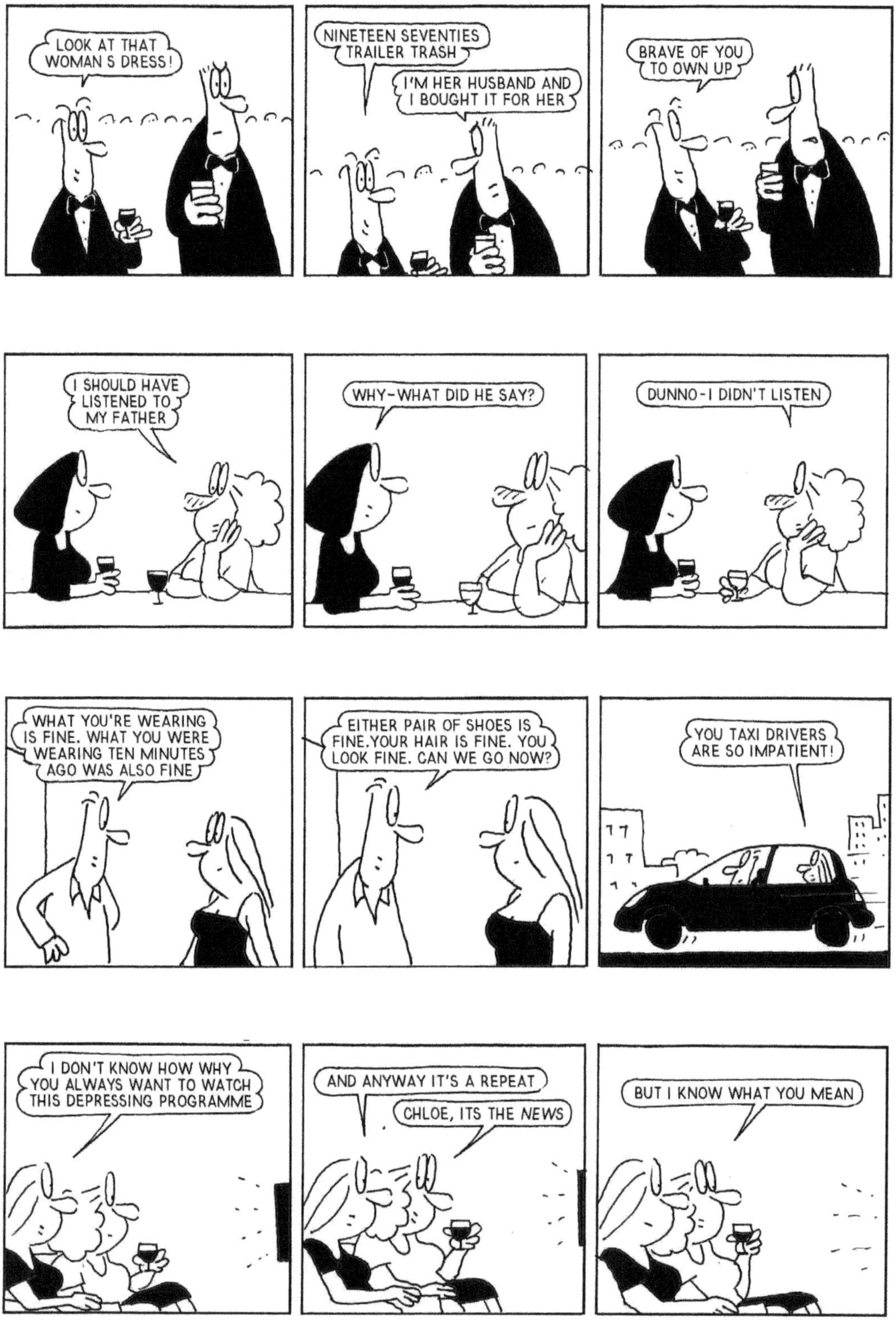
LOOK AT THAT WOMAN S DRESS!
NINETEEN SEVENTIES TRAILER TRASH
I'M HER HUSBAND AND I BOUGHT IT FOR HER
BRAVE OF YOU TO OWN UP
I SHOULD HAVE LISTENED TO MY FATHER
WHY-WHAT DID HE SAY?
DUNNO-I DIDN'T LISTEN
WHAT YOU'RE WEARING IS FINE. WHAT YOU WERE WEARING TEN MINUTES AGO WAS ALSO FINE
EITHER PAIR OF SHOES IS FINE.YOUR HAIR IS FINE. YOU LOOK FINE. CAN WE GO NOW?
YOU TAXI DRIVERS ARE SO IMPATIENT!
I DON'T KNOW HOW WHY YOU ALWAYS WANT TO WATCH THIS DEPRESSING PROGRAMME
AND ANYWAY IT'S A REPEAT
CHLOE, ITS THE *NEWS*
BUT I KNOW WHAT YOU MEAN

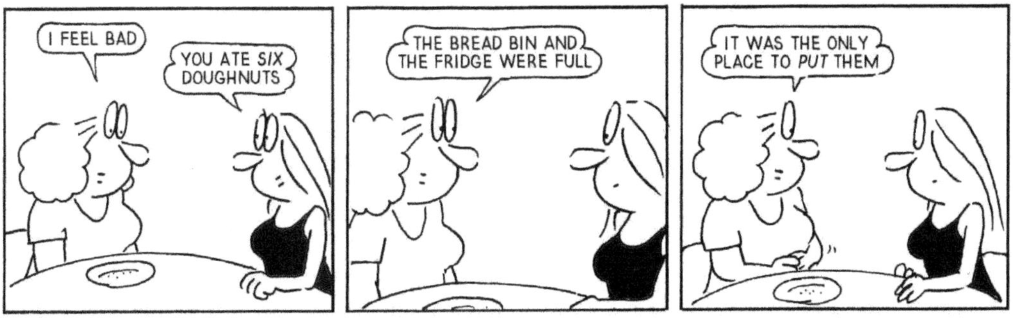
I FEEL BAD
YOU ATE *SIX* DOUGHNUTS
THE BREAD BIN AND THE FRIDGE WERE FULL
IT WAS THE ONLY PLACE TO *PUT* THEM

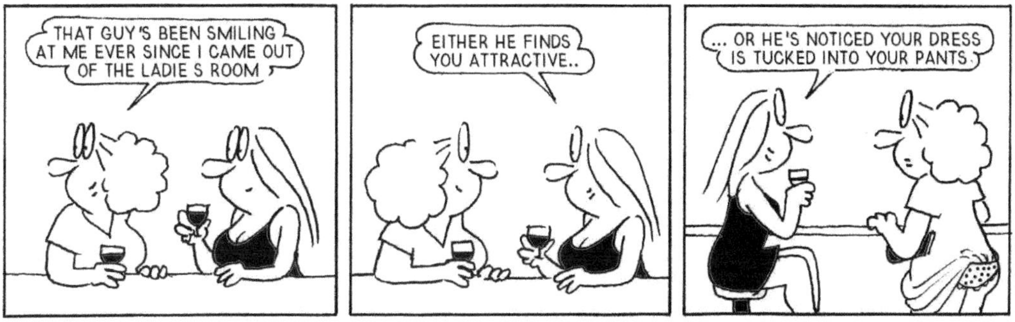
THAT GUY'S BEEN SMILING AT ME EVER SINCE I CAME OUT OF THE LADIE S ROOM
EITHER HE FINDS YOU ATTRACTIVE..
... OR HE'S NOTICED YOUR DRESS IS TUCKED INTO YOUR PANTS.

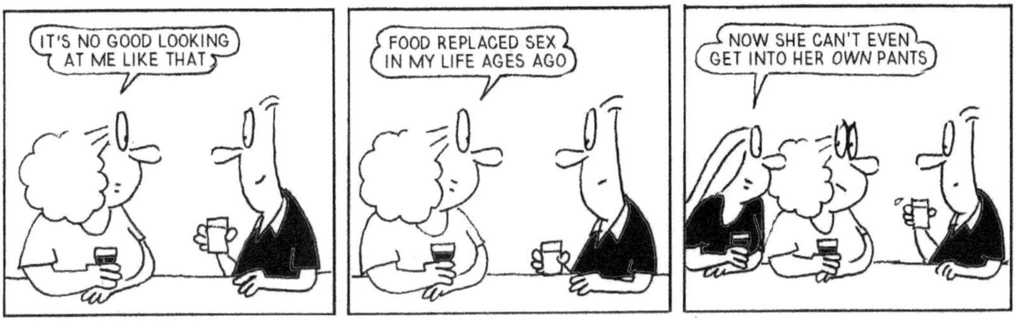
IT'S NO GOOD LOOKING AT ME LIKE THAT
FOOD REPLACED SEX IN MY LIFE AGES AGO
NOW SHE CAN'T EVEN GET INTO HER *OWN* PANTS

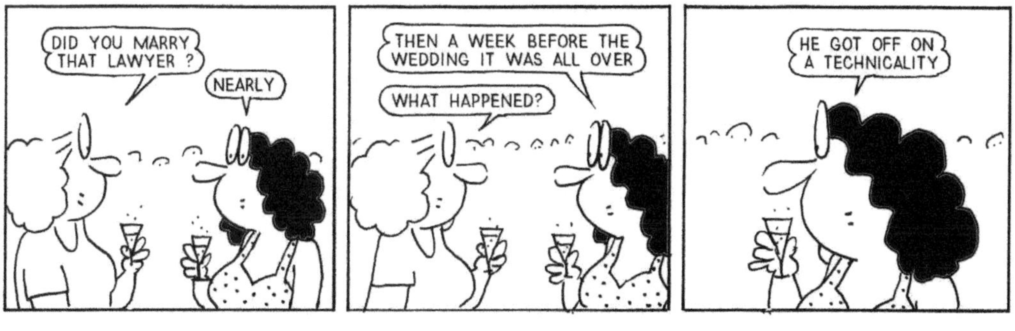
DID YOU MARRY THAT LAWYER ?
NEARLY
THEN A WEEK BEFORE THE WEDDING IT WAS ALL OVER
WHAT HAPPENED?
HE GOT OFF ON A TECHNICALITY

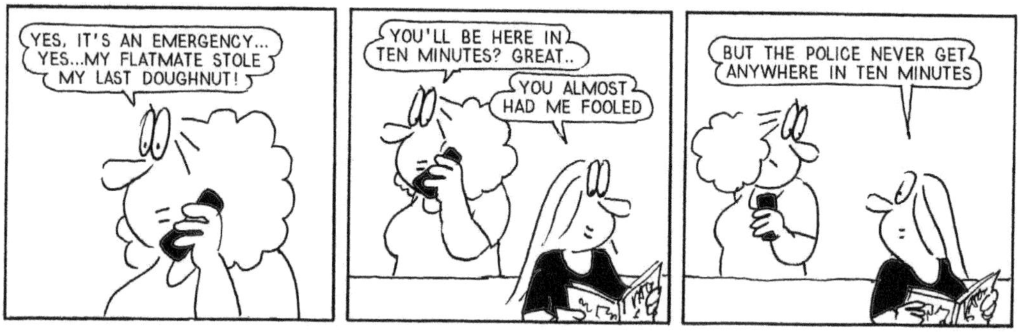
YES, IT'S AN EMERGENCY... YES...MY FLATMATE STOLE MY LAST DOUGHNUT!
YOU'LL BE HERE IN TEN MINUTES? GREAT..
YOU ALMOST HAD ME FOOLED
BUT THE POLICE NEVER GET ANYWHERE IN TEN MINUTES

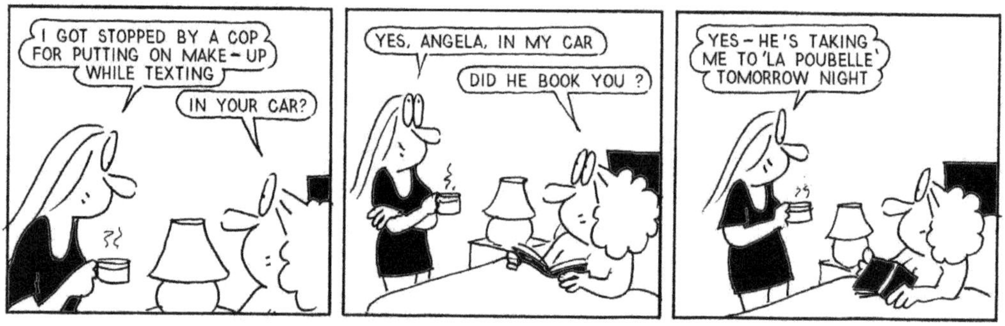
I GOT STOPPED BY A COP FOR PUTTING ON MAKE-UP WHILE TEXTING
IN YOUR CAR?
YES, ANGELA, IN MY CAR
DID HE BOOK YOU ?
YES - HE'S TAKING ME TO 'LA POUBELLE' TOMORROW NIGHT

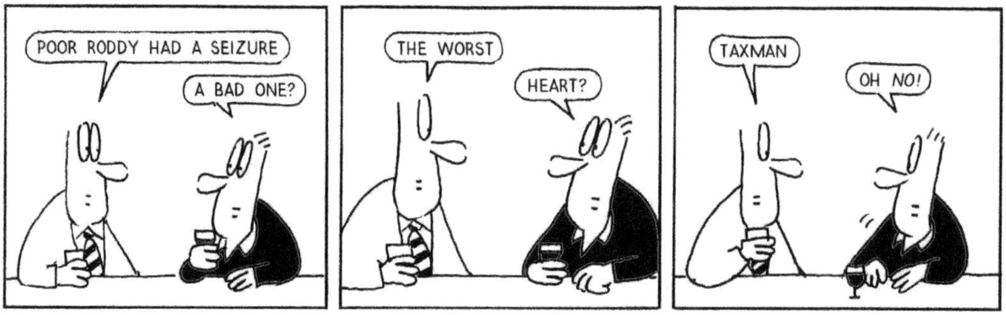
POOR RODDY HAD A SEIZURE
A BAD ONE?
THE WORST
HEART?
TAXMAN
OH NO!

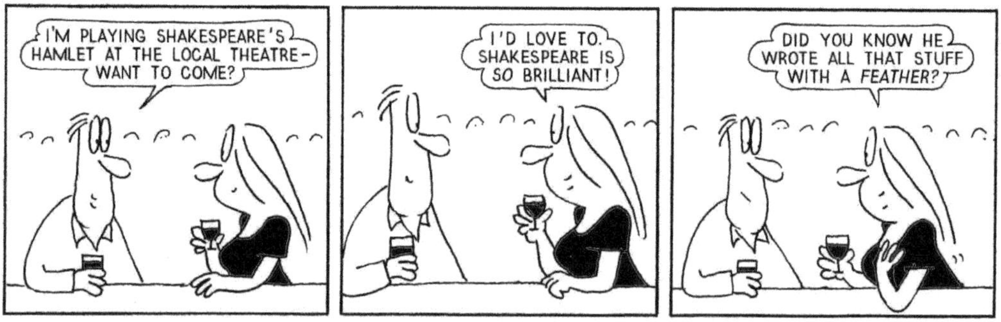
I'M PLAYING SHAKESPEARE'S HAMLET AT THE LOCAL THEATRE- WANT TO COME?
I'D LOVE TO. SHAKESPEARE IS SO BRILLIANT!
DID YOU KNOW HE WROTE ALL THAT STUFF WITH A FEATHER?

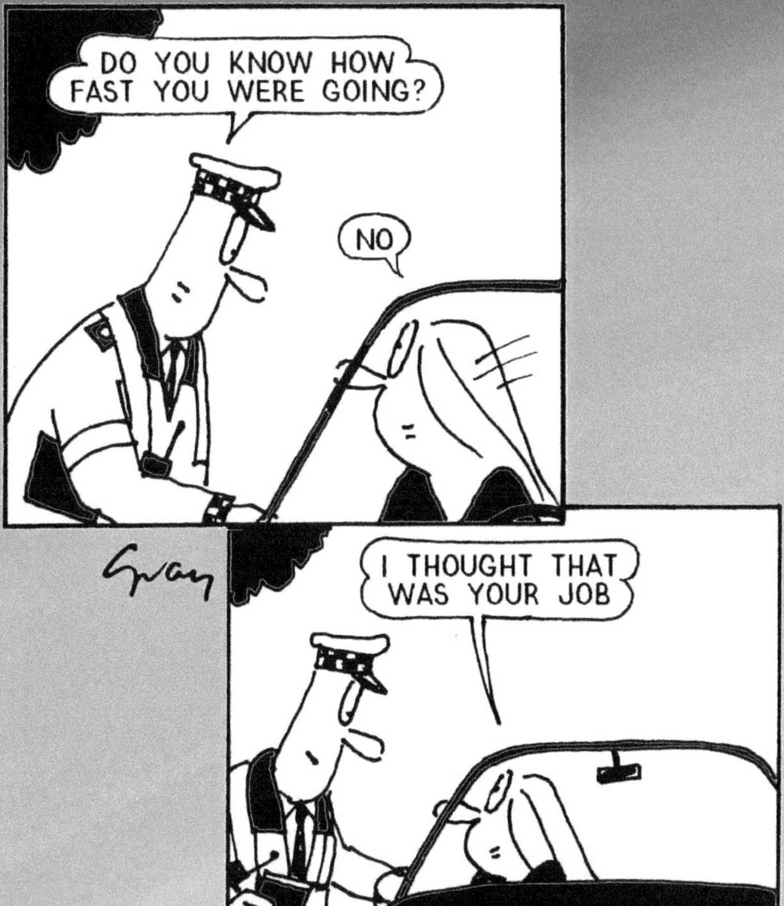
DO YOU KNOW HOW FAST YOU WERE GOING?
NO
I THOUGHT THAT WAS YOUR JOB
Gray

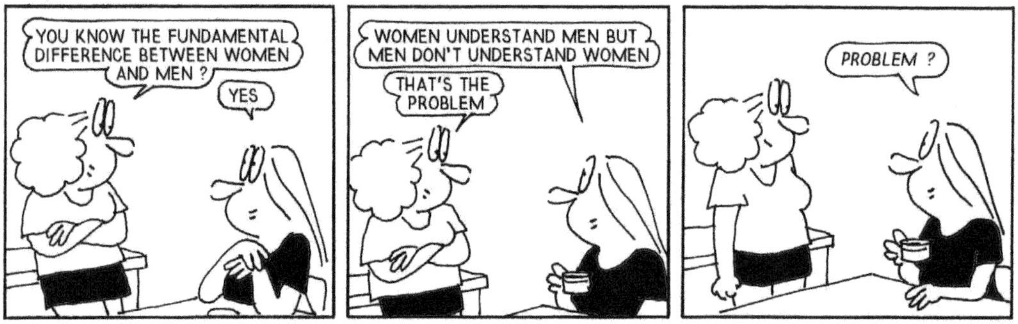
YOU KNOW THE FUNDAMENTAL DIFFERENCE BETWEEN WOMEN AND MEN ?
YES
WOMEN UNDERSTAND MEN BUT MEN DON'T UNDERSTAND WOMEN
THAT'S THE PROBLEM
PROBLEM ?

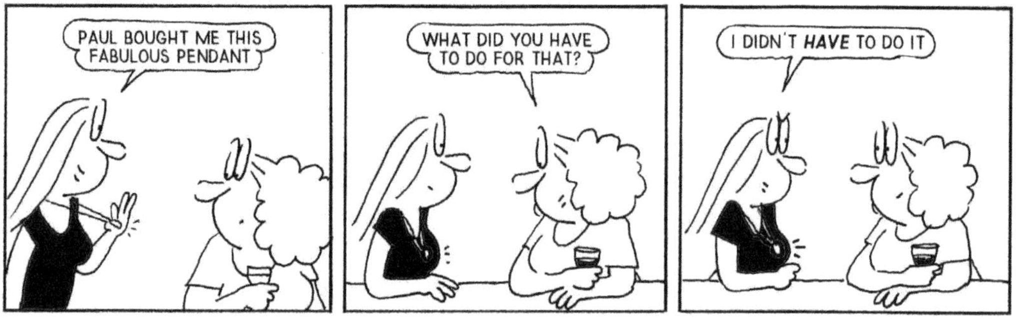
PAUL BOUGHT ME THIS FABULOUS PENDANT
WHAT DID YOU HAVE TO DO FOR THAT?
I DIDN'T **HAVE** TO DO IT

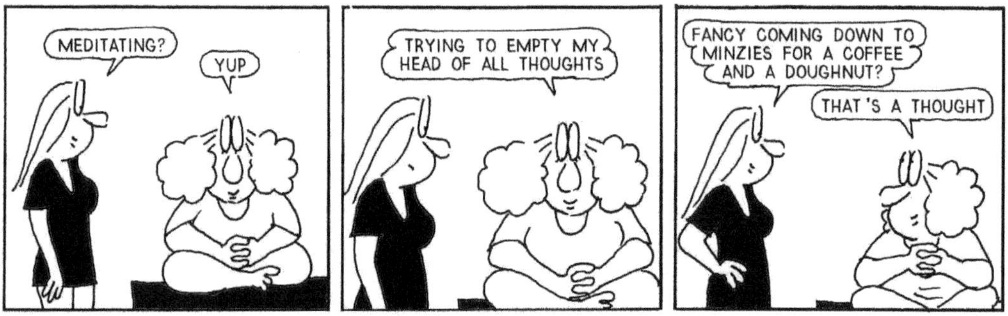
MEDITATING?
YUP
TRYING TO EMPTY MY HEAD OF ALL THOUGHTS
FANCY COMING DOWN TO MINZIES FOR A COFFEE AND A DOUGHNUT?
THAT'S A THOUGHT

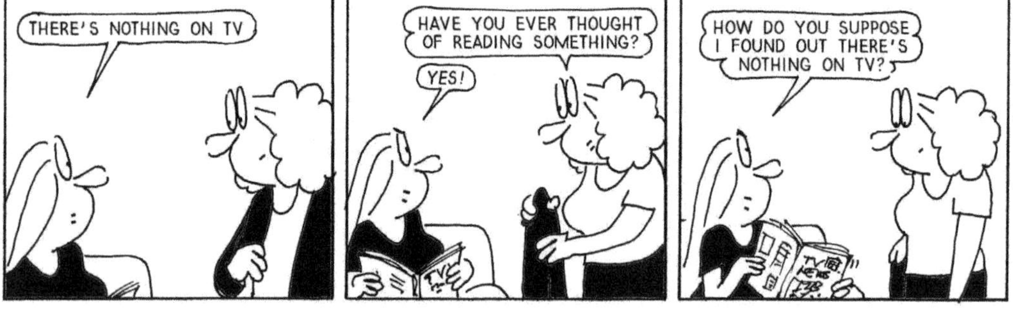
THERE'S NOTHING ON TV
HAVE YOU EVER THOUGHT OF READING SOMETHING?
YES!
HOW DO YOU SUPPOSE I FOUND OUT THERE'S NOTHING ON TV?

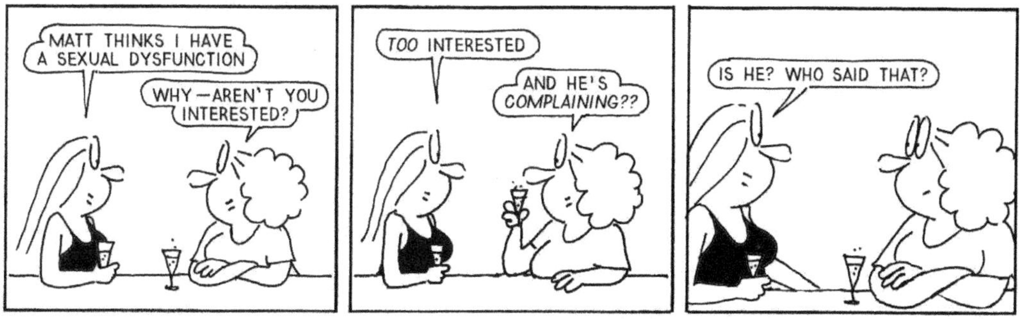
MATT THINKS I HAVE A SEXUAL DYSFUNCTION
WHY—AREN'T YOU INTERESTED?
TOO INTERESTED
AND HE'S *COMPLAINING??*
IS HE? WHO SAID THAT?

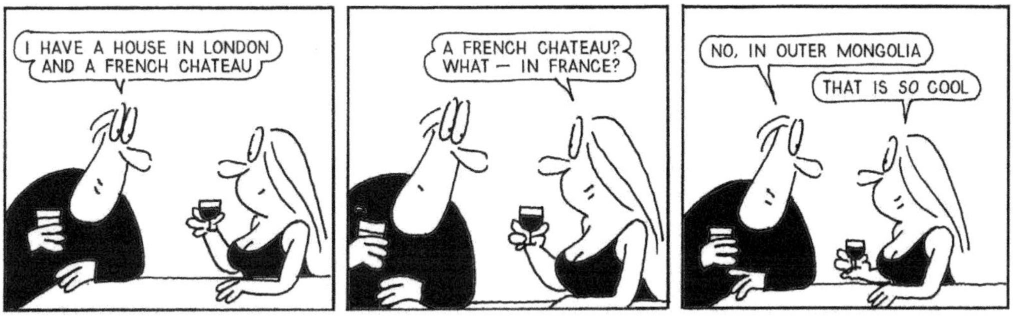
I HAVE A HOUSE IN LONDON AND A FRENCH CHATEAU
A FRENCH CHATEAU? WHAT — IN FRANCE?
NO, IN OUTER MONGOLIA
THAT IS *SO* COOL

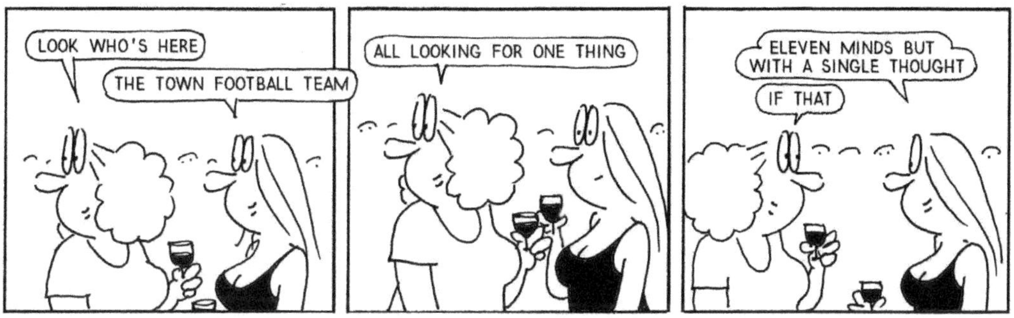
LOOK WHO'S HERE
THE TOWN FOOTBALL TEAM
ALL LOOKING FOR ONE THING
ELEVEN MINDS BUT WITH A SINGLE THOUGHT
IF THAT

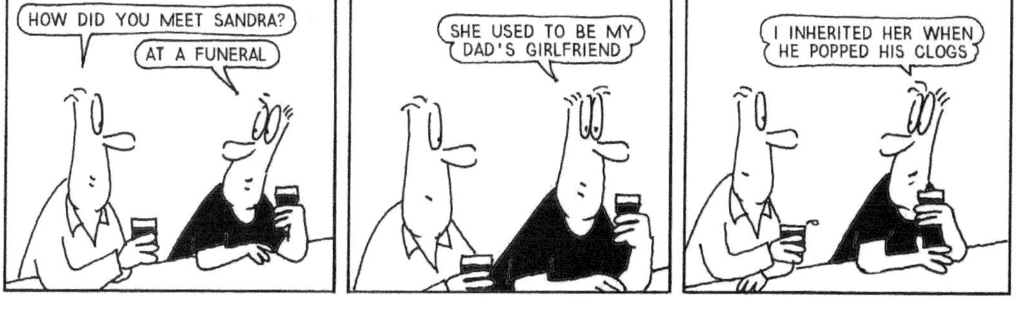
HOW DID YOU MEET SANDRA?
AT A FUNERAL
SHE USED TO BE MY DAD'S GIRLFRIEND
I INHERITED HER WHEN HE POPPED HIS CLOGS

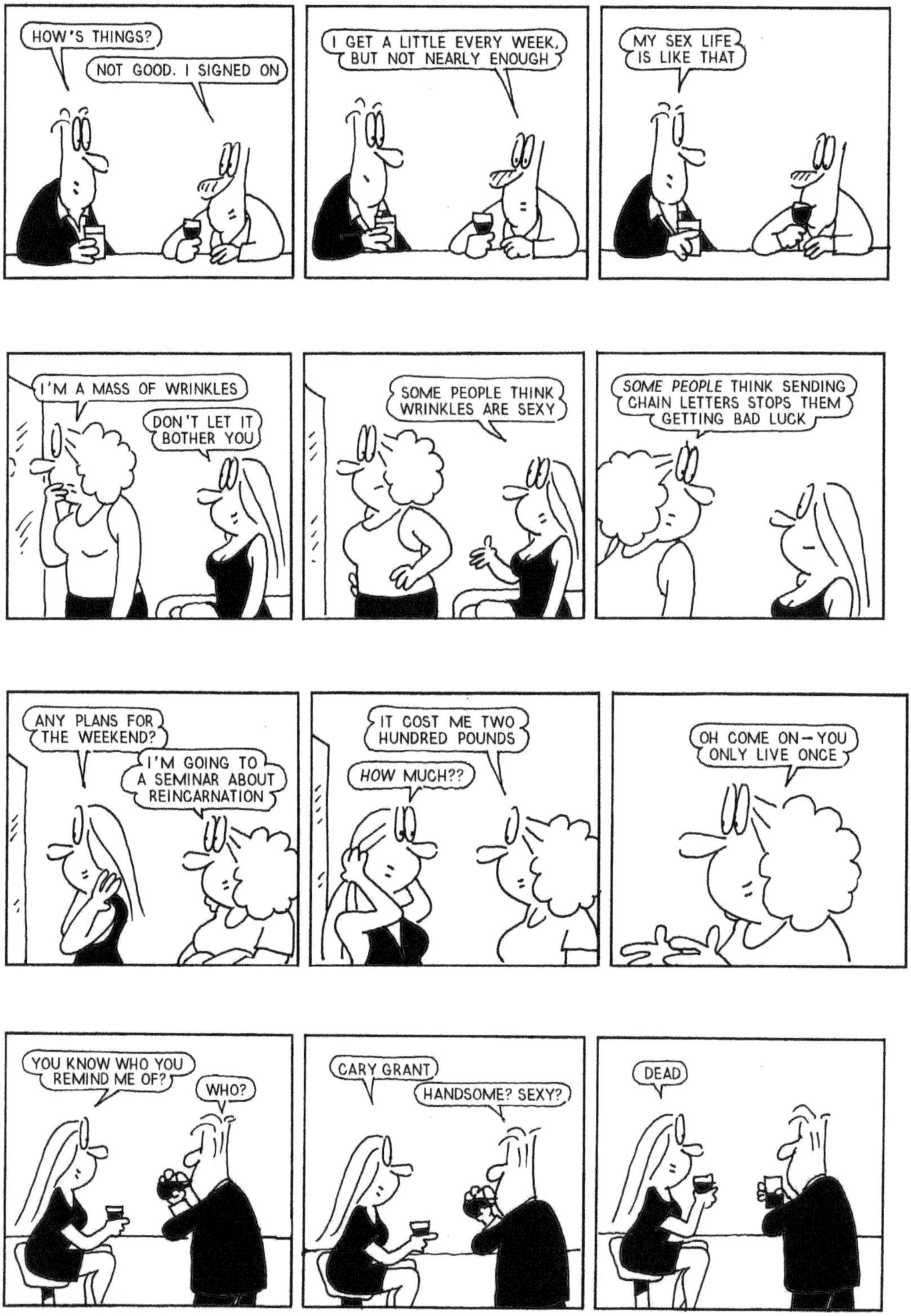
HOW'S THINGS?
NOT GOOD. I SIGNED ON
I GET A LITTLE EVERY WEEK, BUT NOT NEARLY ENOUGH
MY SEX LIFE IS LIKE THAT
I'M A MASS OF WRINKLES
DON'T LET IT BOTHER YOU
SOME PEOPLE THINK WRINKLES ARE SEXY
SOME PEOPLE THINK SENDING CHAIN LETTERS STOPS THEM GETTING BAD LUCK
ANY PLANS FOR THE WEEKEND?
I'M GOING TO A SEMINAR ABOUT REINCARNATION
IT COST ME TWO HUNDRED POUNDS
HOW MUCH??
OH COME ON – YOU ONLY LIVE ONCE
YOU KNOW WHO YOU REMIND ME OF?
WHO?
CARY GRANT
HANDSOME? SEXY?
DEAD

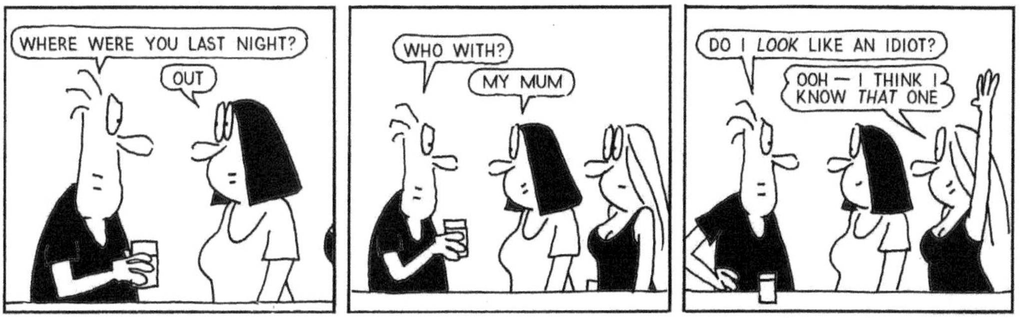
WHERE WERE YOU LAST NIGHT?
OUT
WHO WITH?
MY MUM
DO I *LOOK* LIKE AN IDIOT?
OOH — I THINK I KNOW *THAT* ONE

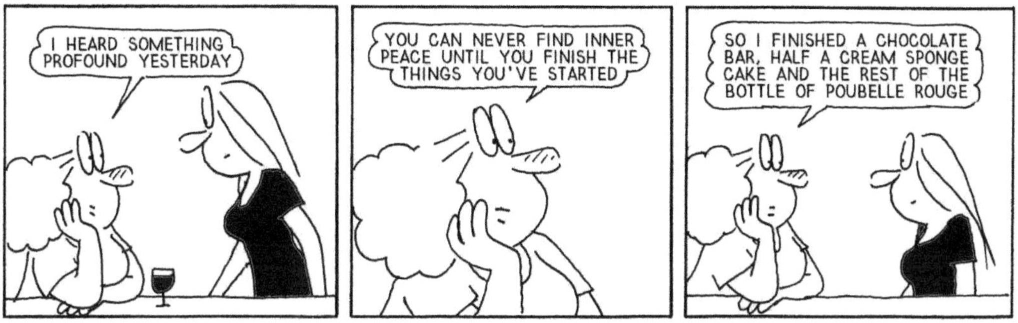
I HEARD SOMETHING PROFOUND YESTERDAY
YOU CAN NEVER FIND INNER PEACE UNTIL YOU FINISH THE THINGS YOU'VE STARTED
SO I FINISHED A CHOCOLATE BAR, HALF A CREAM SPONGE CAKE AND THE REST OF THE BOTTLE OF POUBELLE ROUGE

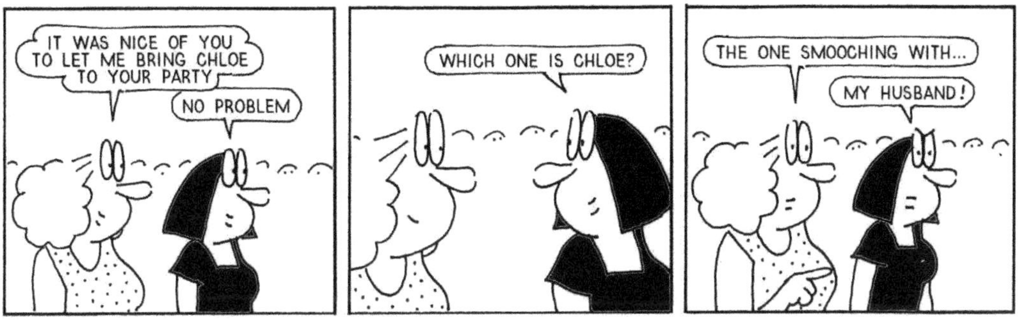
IT WAS NICE OF YOU TO LET ME BRING CHLOE TO YOUR PARTY
NO PROBLEM
WHICH ONE IS CHLOE?
THE ONE SMOOCHING WITH...
MY HUSBAND!

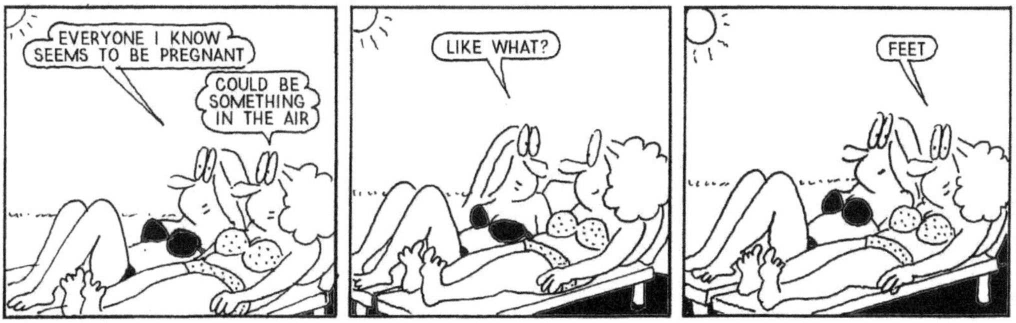
EVERYONE I KNOW SEEMS TO BE PREGNANT
COULD BE SOMETHING IN THE AIR
LIKE WHAT?
FEET

YOU DON'T LOOK TOO HAPPY
I GOT ROBBED
HAVE YOU INFORMED THE POLICE ?
THE POLICE TEND NOT TO INVOLVE THEMSELVES IN DIVORCE

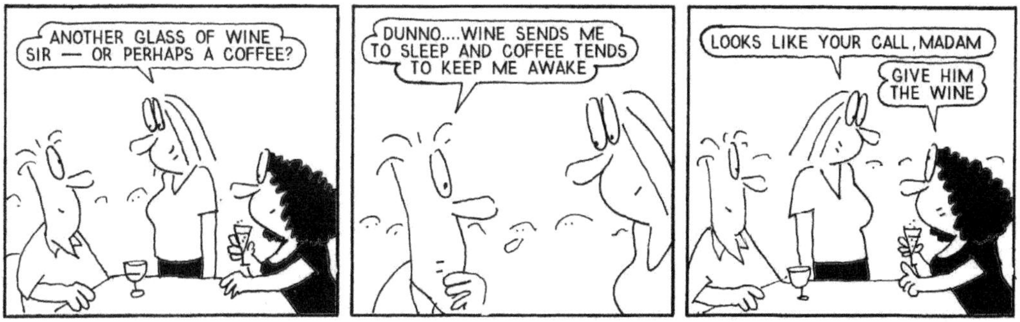
ANOTHER GLASS OF WINE SIR — OR PERHAPS A COFFEE?
DUNNO....WINE SENDS ME TO SLEEP AND COFFEE TENDS TO KEEP ME AWAKE
LOOKS LIKE YOUR CALL, MADAM
GIVE HIM THE WINE

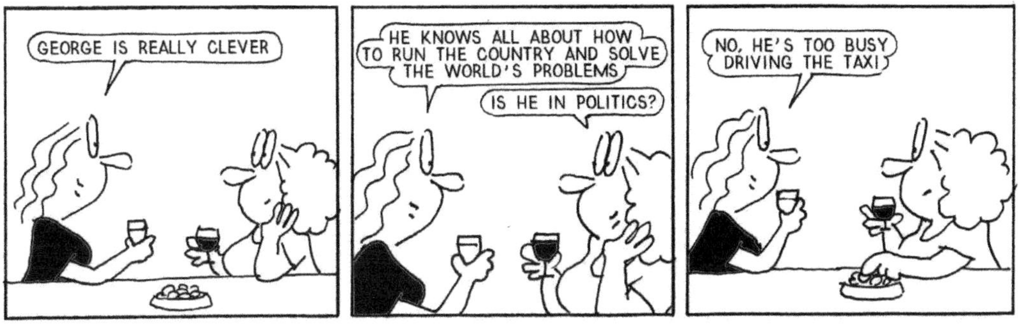
GEORGE IS REALLY CLEVER
HE KNOWS ALL ABOUT HOW TO RUN THE COUNTRY AND SOLVE THE WORLD'S PROBLEMS
IS HE IN POLITICS?
NO, HE'S TOO BUSY DRIVING THE TAXI

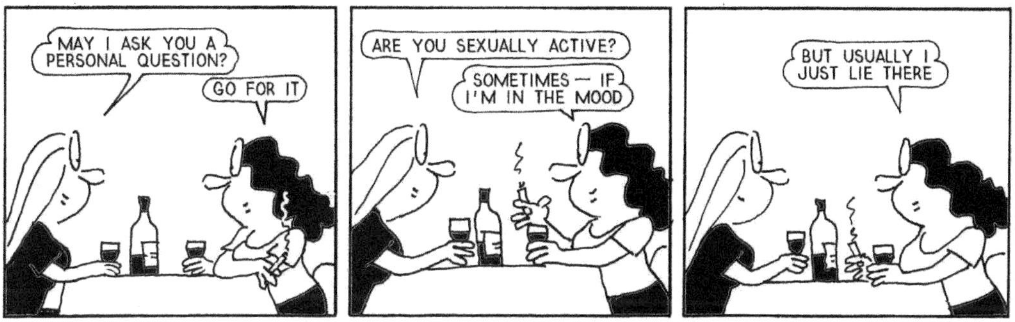
MAY I ASK YOU A PERSONAL QUESTION?
GO FOR IT
ARE YOU SEXUALLY ACTIVE?
SOMETIMES — IF I'M IN THE MOOD
BUT USUALLY I JUST LIE THERE

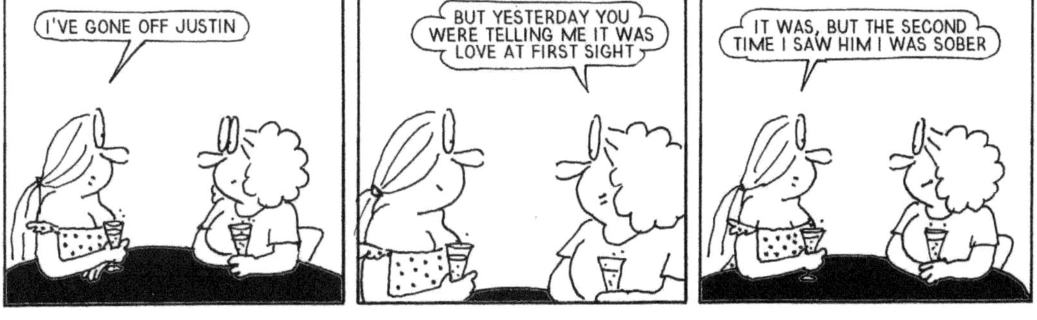
I'VE GONE OFF JUSTIN
BUT YESTERDAY YOU WERE TELLING ME IT WAS LOVE AT FIRST SIGHT
IT WAS, BUT THE SECOND TIME I SAW HIM I WAS SOBER

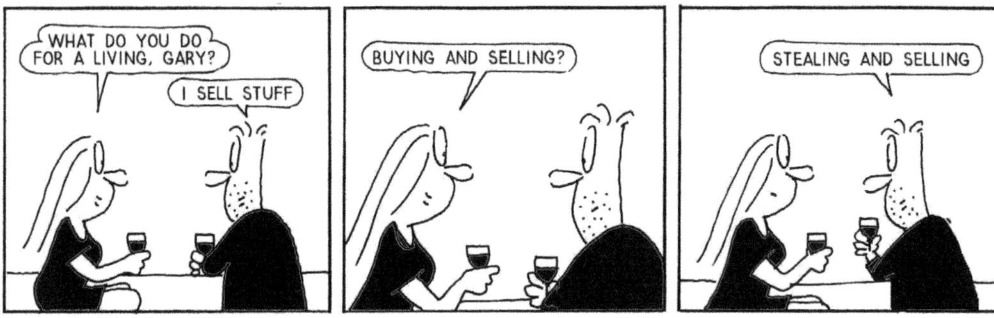
WHAT DO YOU DO FOR A LIVING, GARY?
I SELL STUFF
BUYING AND SELLING?
STEALING AND SELLING

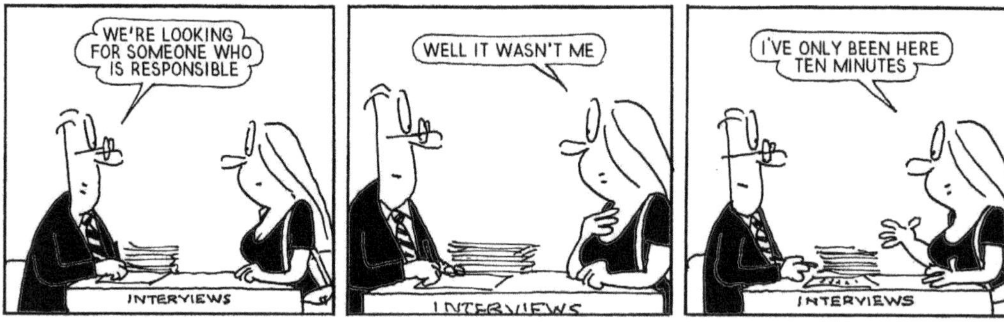
WE'RE LOOKING FOR SOMEONE WHO IS RESPONSIBLE
INTERVIEWS
WELL IT WASN'T ME
I'VE ONLY BEEN HERE TEN MINUTES
INTERVIEWS

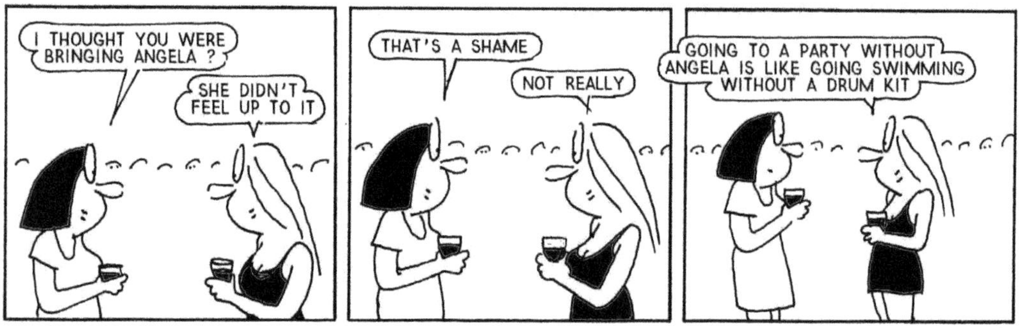
I THOUGHT YOU WERE BRINGING ANGELA ?
SHE DIDN'T FEEL UP TO IT
THAT'S A SHAME
NOT REALLY
GOING TO A PARTY WITHOUT ANGELA IS LIKE GOING SWIMMING WITHOUT A DRUM KIT

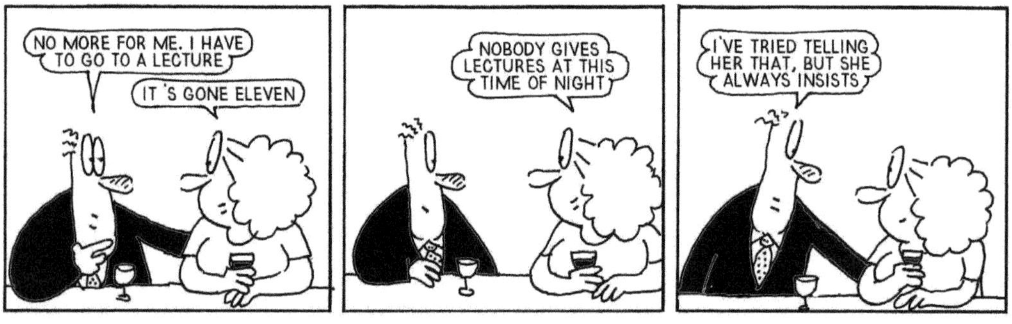
NO MORE FOR ME. I HAVE TO GO TO A LECTURE
IT'S GONE ELEVEN
NOBODY GIVES LECTURES AT THIS TIME OF NIGHT
I'VE TRIED TELLING HER THAT, BUT SHE ALWAYS INSISTS

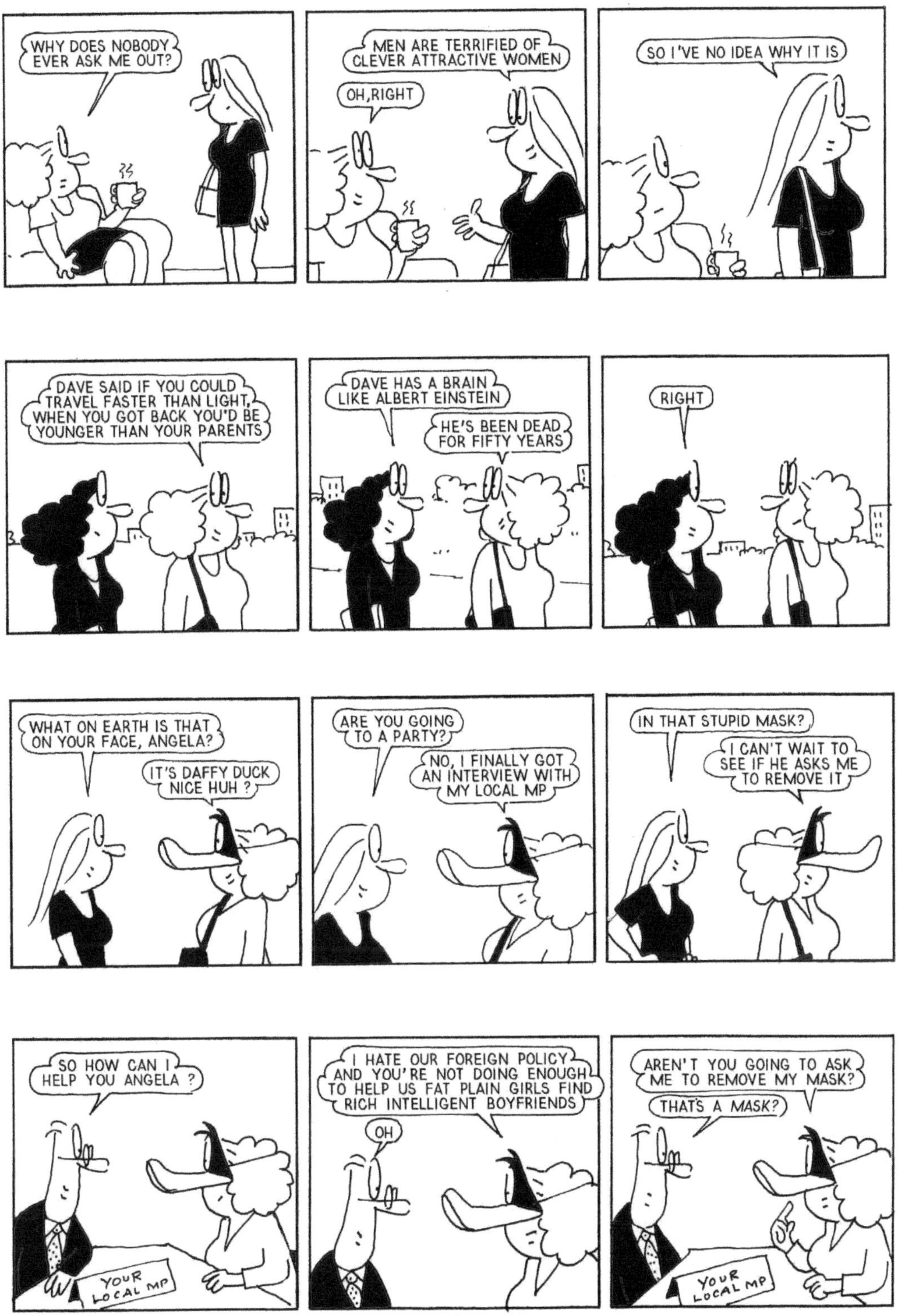
WHY DOES NOBODY EVER ASK ME OUT?
MEN ARE TERRIFIED OF CLEVER ATTRACTIVE WOMEN
OH,RIGHT
SO I'VE NO IDEA WHY IT IS
DAVE SAID IF YOU COULD TRAVEL FASTER THAN LIGHT, WHEN YOU GOT BACK YOU'D BE YOUNGER THAN YOUR PARENTS
DAVE HAS A BRAIN LIKE ALBERT EINSTEIN
HE'S BEEN DEAD FOR FIFTY YEARS
RIGHT
WHAT ON EARTH IS THAT ON YOUR FACE, ANGELA?
IT'S DAFFY DUCK NICE HUH ?
ARE YOU GOING TO A PARTY?
NO, I FINALLY GOT AN INTERVIEW WITH MY LOCAL MP
IN THAT STUPID MASK?
I CAN'T WAIT TO SEE IF HE ASKS ME TO REMOVE IT
SO HOW CAN I HELP YOU ANGELA ?
YOUR LOCAL MP
I HATE OUR FOREIGN POLICY AND YOU'RE NOT DOING ENOUGH TO HELP US FAT PLAIN GIRLS FIND RICH INTELLIGENT BOYFRIENDS
OH
AREN'T YOU GOING TO ASK ME TO REMOVE MY MASK?
THAT'S A *MASK*?
YOUR LOCAL MP

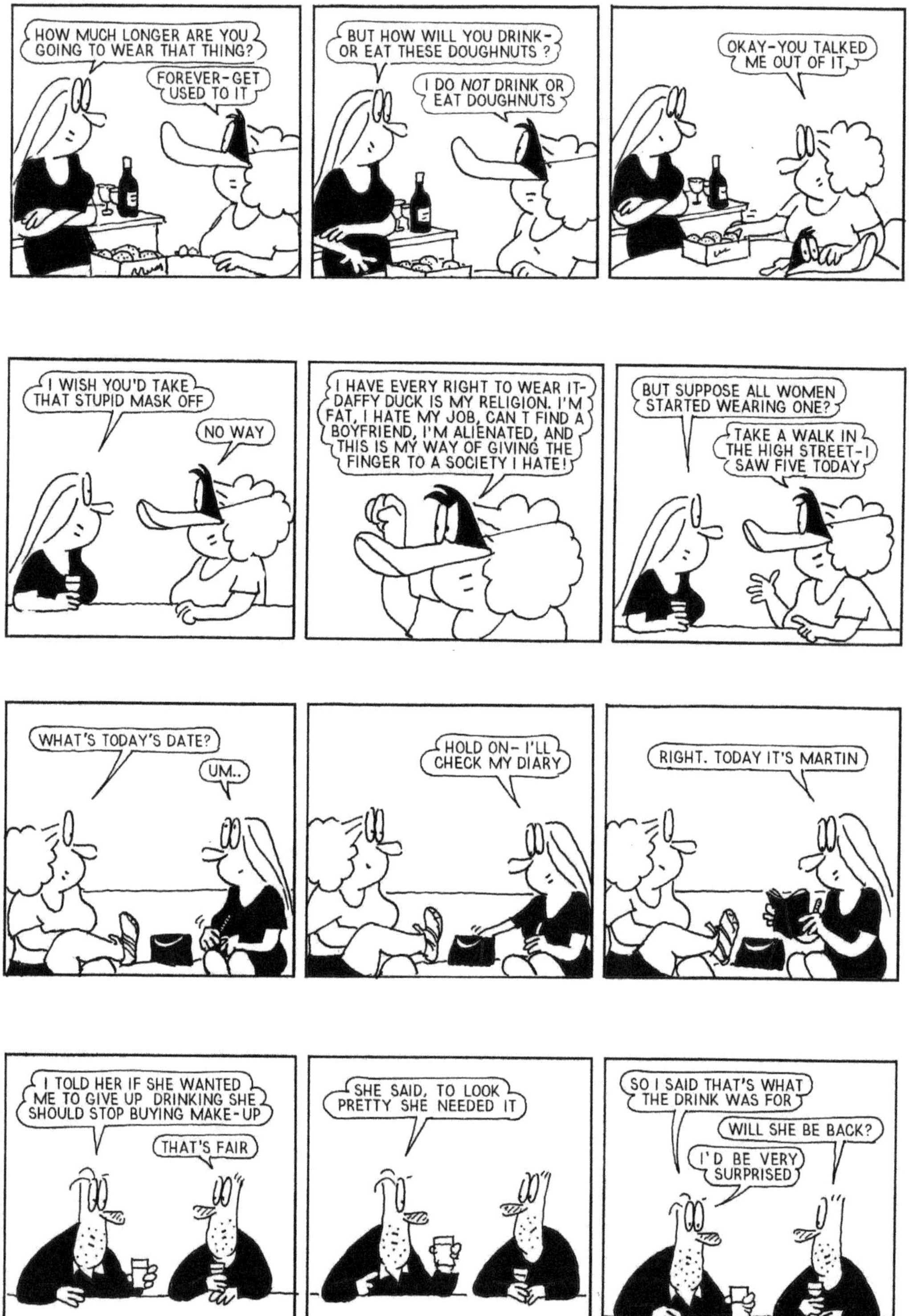
HOW MUCH LONGER ARE YOU GOING TO WEAR THAT THING?
FOREVER-GET USED TO IT
BUT HOW WILL YOU DRINK- OR EAT THESE DOUGHNUTS ?
I DO *NOT* DRINK OR EAT DOUGHNUTS
OKAY-YOU TALKED ME OUT OF IT
I WISH YOU'D TAKE THAT STUPID MASK OFF
NO WAY
I HAVE EVERY RIGHT TO WEAR IT- DAFFY DUCK IS MY RELIGION. I'M FAT, I HATE MY JOB, CAN T FIND A BOYFRIEND, I'M ALIENATED, AND THIS IS MY WAY OF GIVING THE FINGER TO A SOCIETY I HATE!
BUT SUPPOSE ALL WOMEN STARTED WEARING ONE?
TAKE A WALK IN THE HIGH STREET-I SAW FIVE TODAY
WHAT'S TODAY'S DATE?
UM..
HOLD ON- I'LL CHECK MY DIARY
RIGHT. TODAY IT'S MARTIN
I TOLD HER IF SHE WANTED ME TO GIVE UP DRINKING SHE SHOULD STOP BUYING MAKE-UP
THAT'S FAIR
SHE SAID, TO LOOK PRETTY SHE NEEDED IT
SO I SAID THAT'S WHAT THE DRINK WAS FOR
WILL SHE BE BACK?
I'D BE VERY SURPRISED

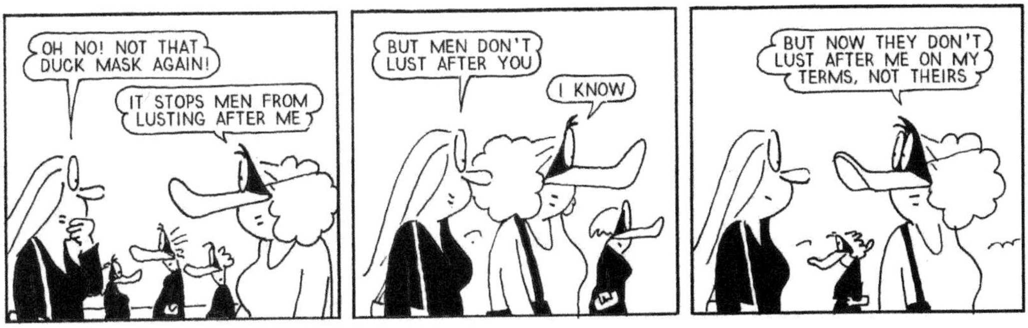
OH NO! NOT THAT DUCK MASK AGAIN!
IT STOPS MEN FROM LUSTING AFTER ME
BUT MEN DON'T LUST AFTER YOU
I KNOW
BUT NOW THEY DON'T LUST AFTER ME ON MY TERMS, NOT THEIRS

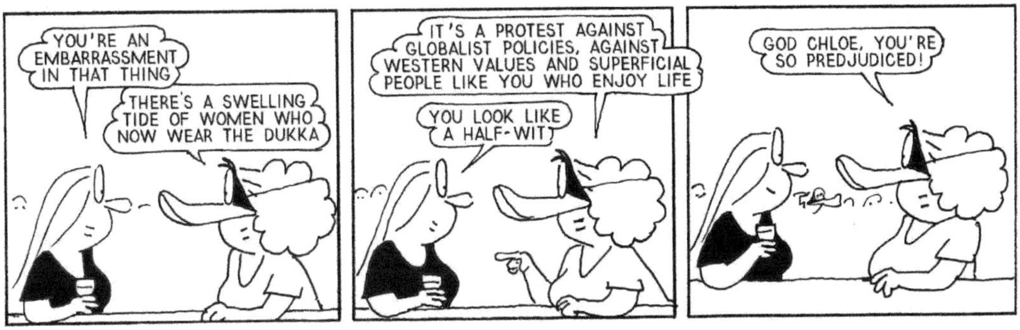
YOU'RE AN EMBARRASSMENT IN THAT THING
THERE'S A SWELLING TIDE OF WOMEN WHO NOW WEAR THE DUKKA
IT'S A PROTEST AGAINST GLOBALIST POLICIES, AGAINST WESTERN VALUES AND SUPERFICIAL PEOPLE LIKE YOU WHO ENJOY LIFE
YOU LOOK LIKE A HALF-WIT
GOD CHLOE, YOU'RE SO PREDJUDICED!

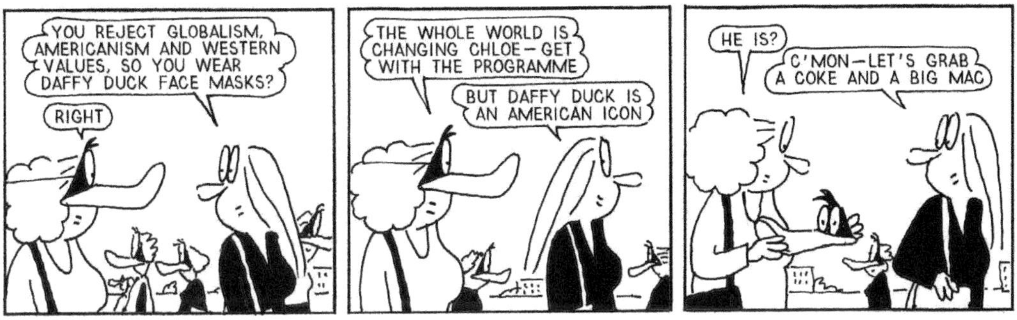
YOU REJECT GLOBALISM, AMERICANISM AND WESTERN VALUES, SO YOU WEAR DAFFY DUCK FACE MASKS?
RIGHT
THE WHOLE WORLD IS CHANGING CHLOE—GET WITH THE PROGRAMME
BUT DAFFY DUCK IS AN AMERICAN ICON
HE IS?
C'MON—LET'S GRAB A COKE AND A BIG MAC

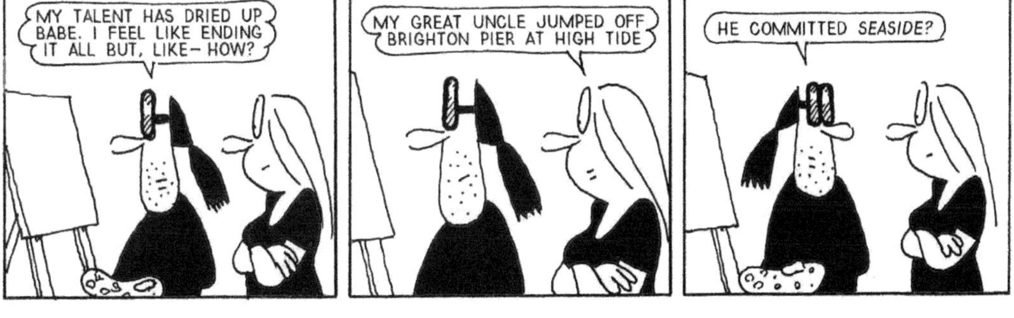
MY TALENT HAS DRIED UP BABE. I FEEL LIKE ENDING IT ALL BUT, LIKE—HOW?
MY GREAT UNCLE JUMPED OFF BRIGHTON PIER AT HIGH TIDE
HE COMMITTED *SEASIDE?*

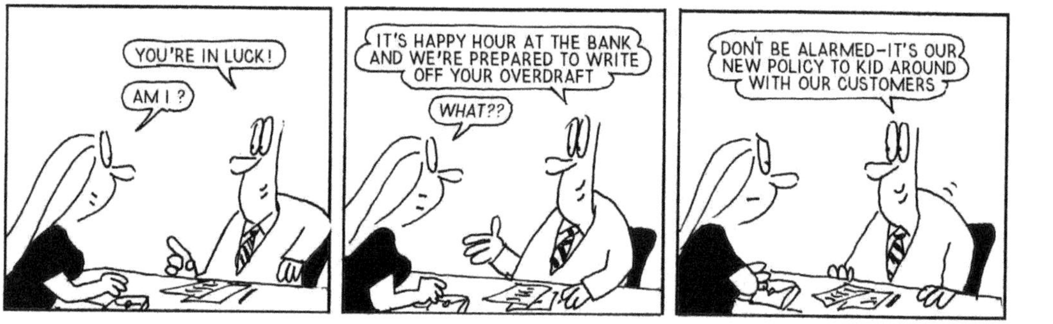
YOU'RE IN LUCK!
AM I ?
IT'S HAPPY HOUR AT THE BANK AND WE'RE PREPARED TO WRITE OFF YOUR OVERDRAFT
WHAT??
DON'T BE ALARMED–IT'S OUR NEW POLICY TO KID AROUND WITH OUR CUSTOMERS

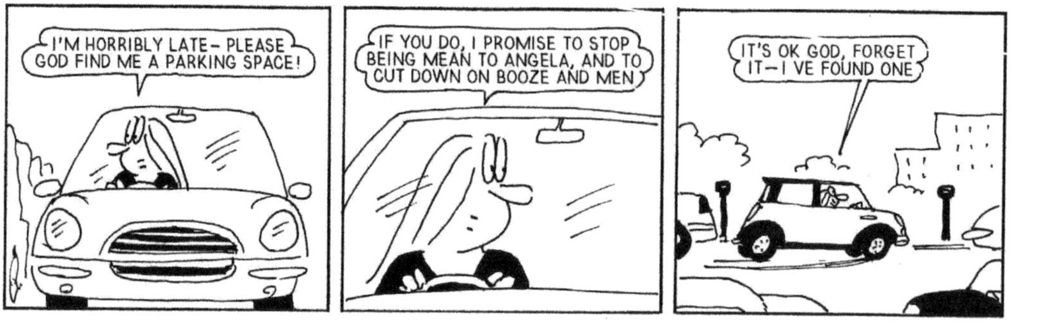
I'M HORRIBLY LATE– PLEASE GOD FIND ME A PARKING SPACE!
IF YOU DO, I PROMISE TO STOP BEING MEAN TO ANGELA, AND TO CUT DOWN ON BOOZE AND MEN
IT'S OK GOD, FORGET IT–I VE FOUND ONE

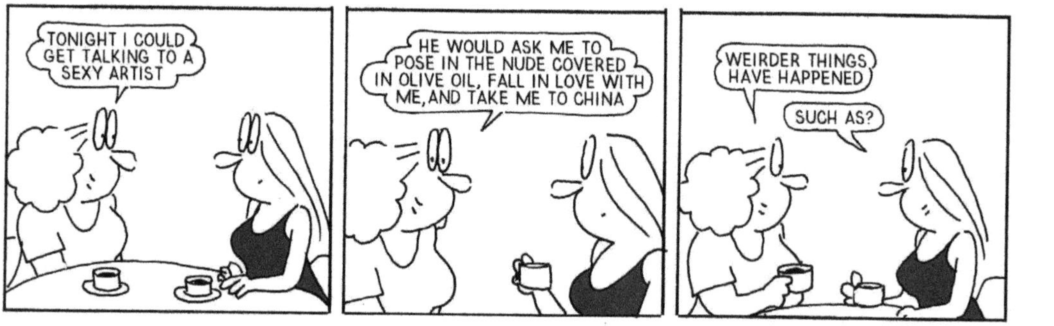
TONIGHT I COULD GET TALKING TO A SEXY ARTIST
HE WOULD ASK ME TO POSE IN THE NUDE COVERED IN OLIVE OIL, FALL IN LOVE WITH ME, AND TAKE ME TO CHINA
WEIRDER THINGS HAVE HAPPENED
SUCH AS?

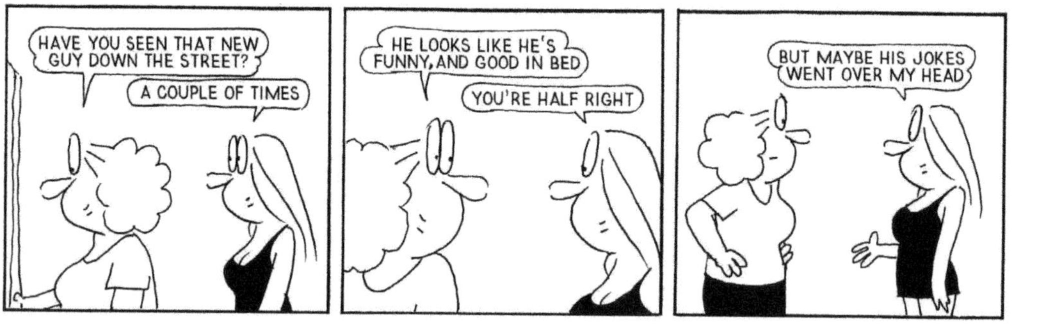
HAVE YOU SEEN THAT NEW GUY DOWN THE STREET?
A COUPLE OF TIMES
HE LOOKS LIKE HE'S FUNNY, AND GOOD IN BED
YOU'RE HALF RIGHT
BUT MAYBE HIS JOKES WENT OVER MY HEAD

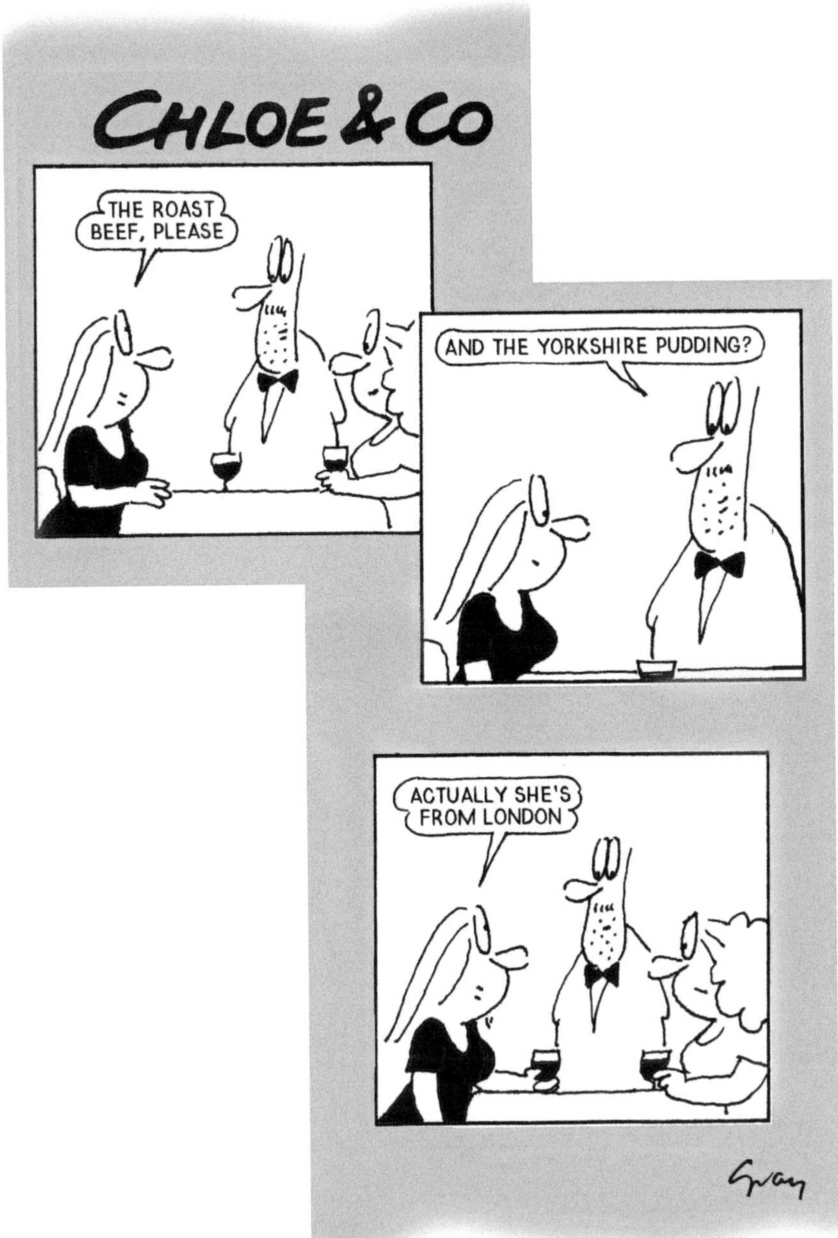
CHLOE & CO
THE ROAST BEEF, PLEASE
AND THE YORKSHIRE PUDDING?
ACTUALLY SHE'S FROM LONDON
Gray

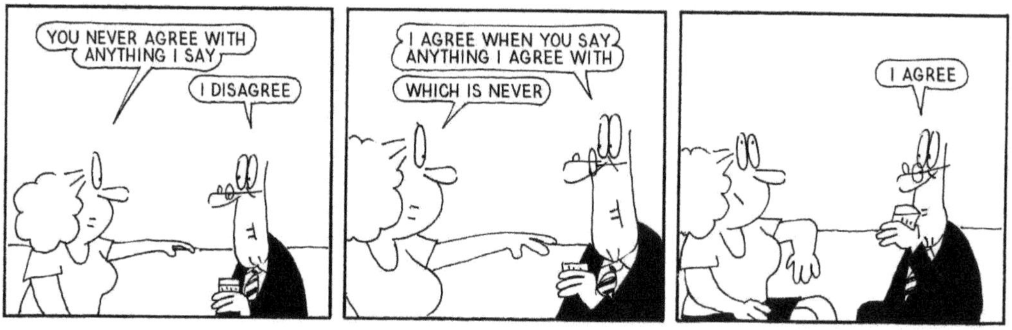
YOU NEVER AGREE WITH ANYTHING I SAY
I DISAGREE
I AGREE WHEN YOU SAY ANYTHING I AGREE WITH
WHICH IS NEVER
I AGREE

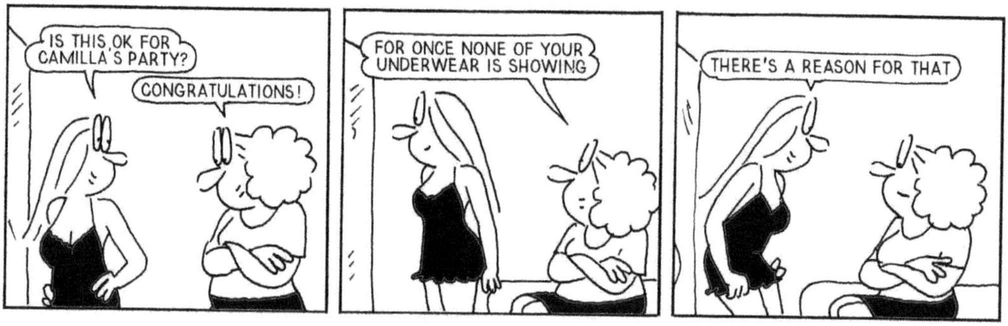
IS THIS OK FOR CAMILLA'S PARTY?
CONGRATULATIONS!
FOR ONCE NONE OF YOUR UNDERWEAR IS SHOWING
THERE'S A REASON FOR THAT

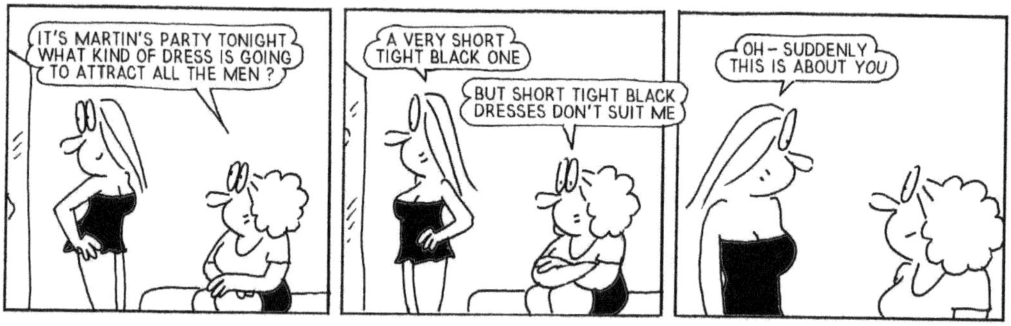
IT'S MARTIN'S PARTY TONIGHT WHAT KIND OF DRESS IS GOING TO ATTRACT ALL THE MEN ?
A VERY SHORT TIGHT BLACK ONE
BUT SHORT TIGHT BLACK DRESSES DON'T SUIT ME
OH – SUDDENLY THIS IS ABOUT *YOU*

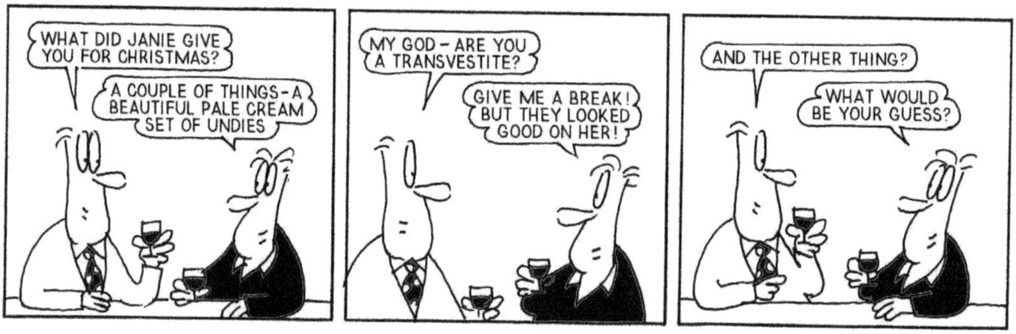
WHAT DID JANIE GIVE YOU FOR CHRISTMAS?
A COUPLE OF THINGS – A BEAUTIFUL PALE CREAM SET OF UNDIES
MY GOD – ARE YOU A TRANSVESTITE?
GIVE ME A BREAK! BUT THEY LOOKED GOOD ON HER!
AND THE OTHER THING?
WHAT WOULD BE YOUR GUESS?

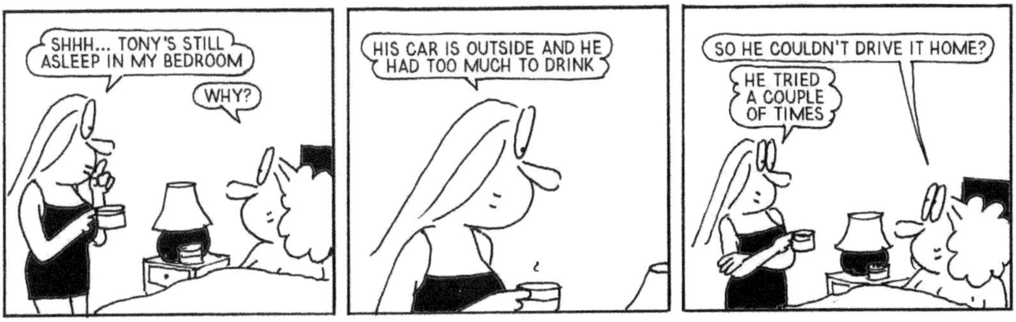
SHHH... TONY'S STILL ASLEEP IN MY BEDROOM
WHY?
HIS CAR IS OUTSIDE AND HE HAD TOO MUCH TO DRINK
SO HE COULDN'T DRIVE IT HOME?
HE TRIED A COUPLE OF TIMES

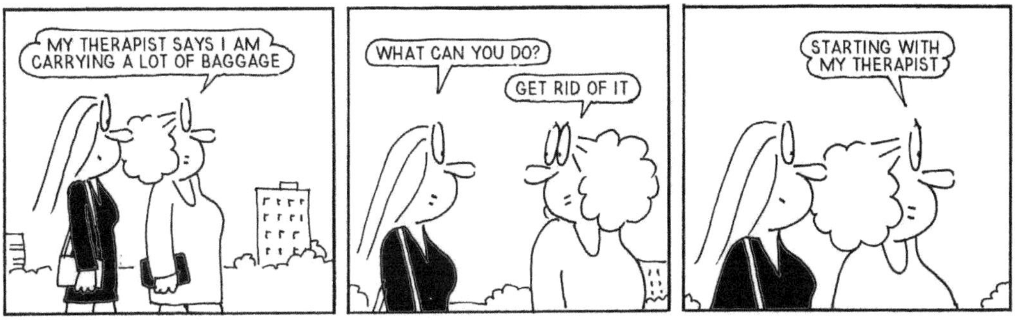
MY THERAPIST SAYS I AM CARRYING A LOT OF BAGGAGE
WHAT CAN YOU DO?
GET RID OF IT
STARTING WITH MY THERAPIST

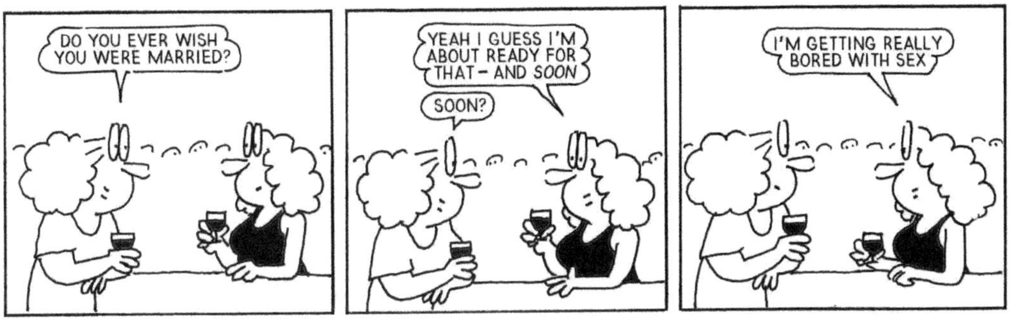
DO YOU EVER WISH YOU WERE MARRIED?
YEAH I GUESS I'M ABOUT READY FOR THAT – AND *SOON*
SOON?
I'M GETTING REALLY BORED WITH SEX

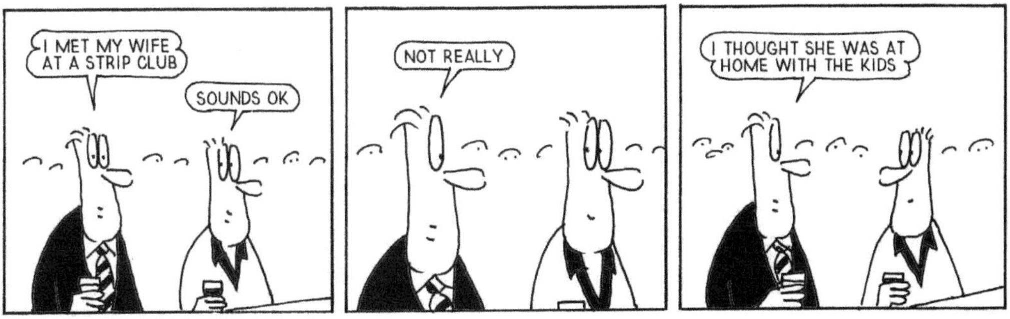
I MET MY WIFE AT A STRIP CLUB
SOUNDS OK
NOT REALLY
I THOUGHT SHE WAS AT HOME WITH THE KIDS

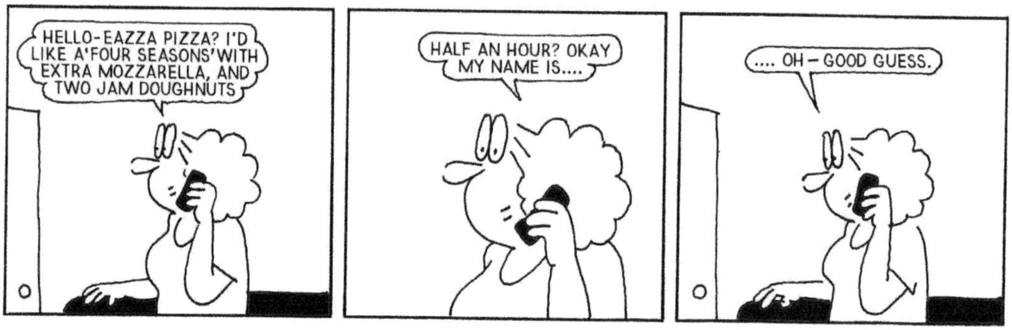
HELLO-EAZZA PIZZA? I'D LIKE A'FOUR SEASONS'WITH EXTRA MOZZARELLA, AND TWO JAM DOUGHNUTS
HALF AN HOUR? OKAY MY NAME IS....
.... OH – GOOD GUESS.

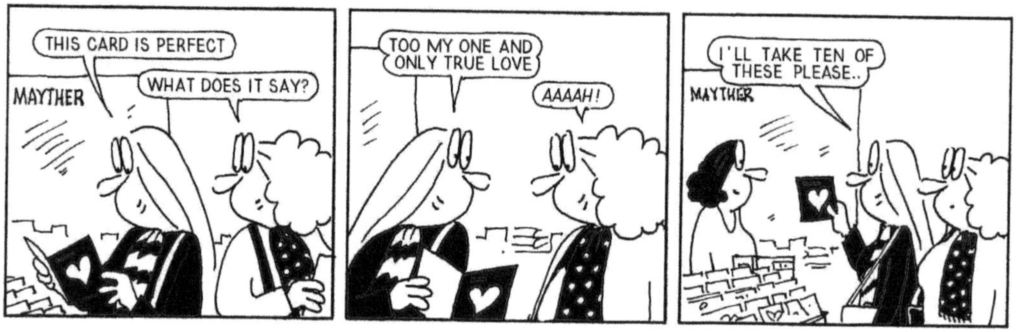
THIS CARD IS PERFECT
MAYTHER
WHAT DOES IT SAY?
TOO MY ONE AND ONLY TRUE LOVE
AAAAH!
I'LL TAKE TEN OF THESE PLEASE..
MAYTHER

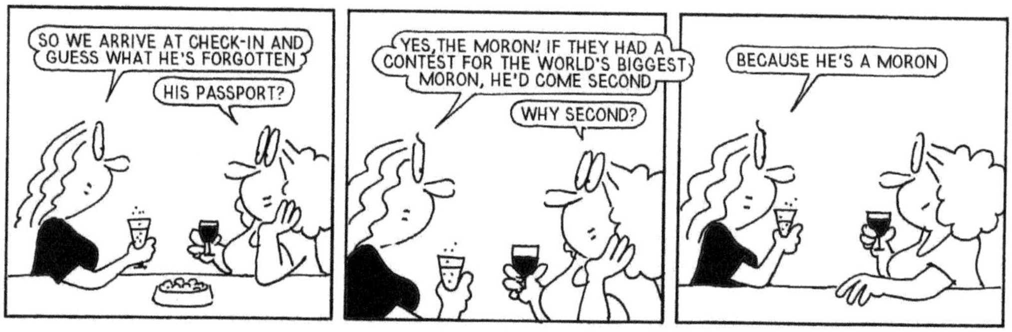
SO WE ARRIVE AT CHECK-IN AND GUESS WHAT HE'S FORGOTTEN
HIS PASSPORT?
YES, THE MORON! IF THEY HAD A CONTEST FOR THE WORLD'S BIGGEST MORON, HE'D COME SECOND
WHY SECOND?
BECAUSE HE'S A MORON

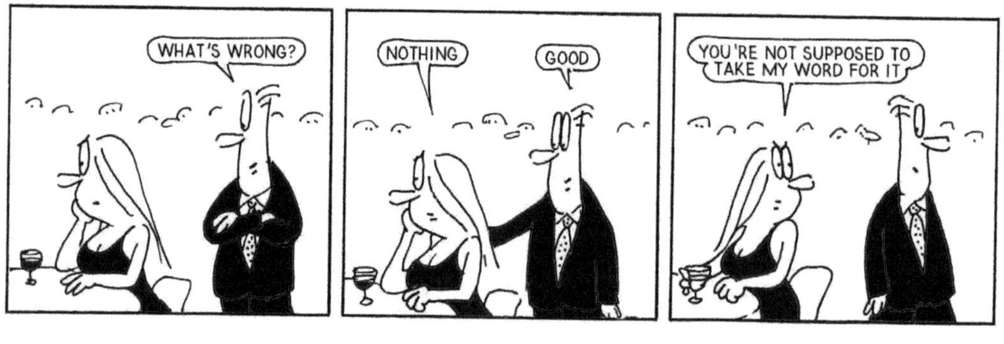
WHAT'S WRONG?
NOTHING
GOOD
YOU'RE NOT SUPPOSED TO TAKE MY WORD FOR IT

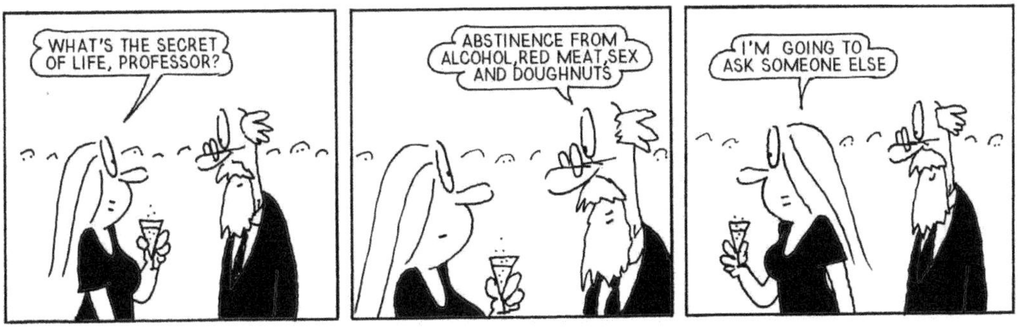
WHAT'S THE SECRET OF LIFE, PROFESSOR?
ABSTINENCE FROM ALCOHOL, RED MEAT, SEX AND DOUGHNUTS
I'M GOING TO ASK SOMEONE ELSE

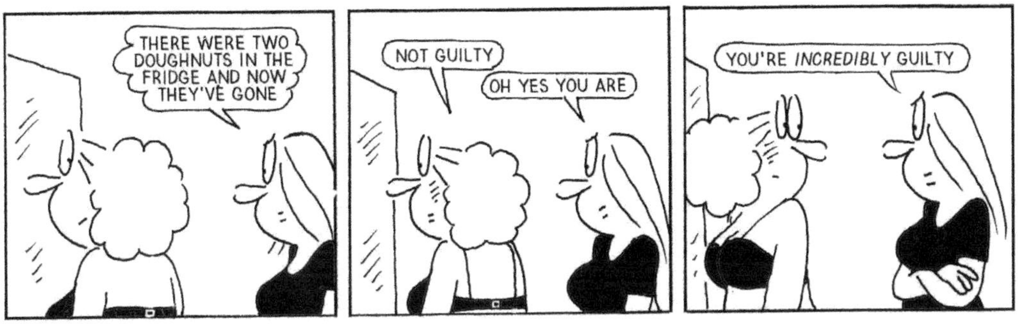
THERE WERE TWO DOUGHNUTS IN THE FRIDGE AND NOW THEY'VE GONE
NOT GUILTY
OH YES YOU ARE
YOU'RE *INCREDIBLY* GUILTY

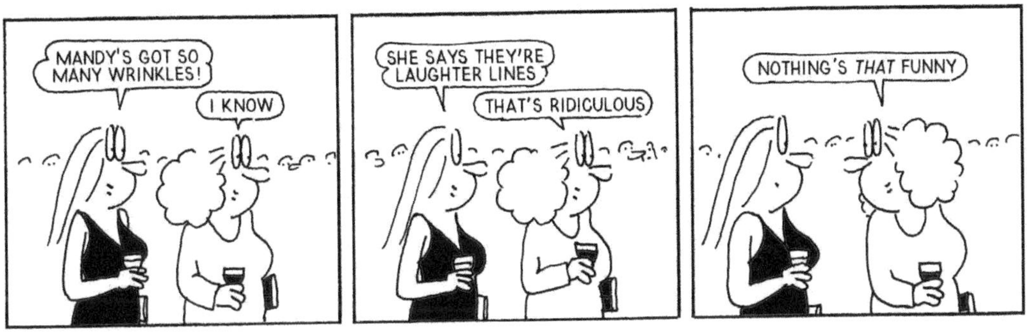
MANDY'S GOT SO MANY WRINKLES!
I KNOW
SHE SAYS THEY'RE LAUGHTER LINES
THAT'S RIDICULOUS
NOTHING'S *THAT* FUNNY

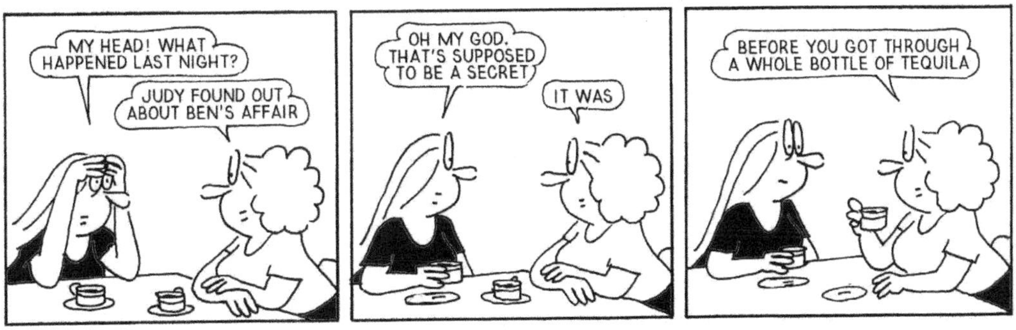
MY HEAD! WHAT HAPPENED LAST NIGHT?
JUDY FOUND OUT ABOUT BEN'S AFFAIR
OH MY GOD. THAT'S SUPPOSED TO BE A SECRET
IT WAS
BEFORE YOU GOT THROUGH A WHOLE BOTTLE OF TEQUILA

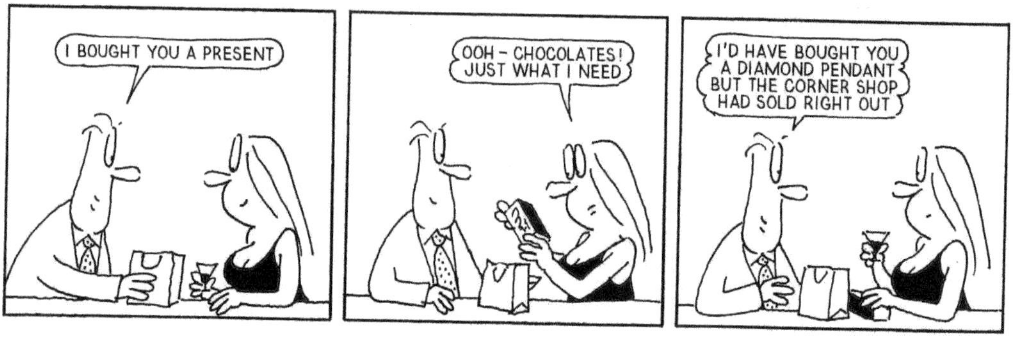
I BOUGHT YOU A PRESENT
OOH – CHOCOLATES! JUST WHAT I NEED
I'D HAVE BOUGHT YOU A DIAMOND PENDANT BUT THE CORNER SHOP HAD SOLD RIGHT OUT

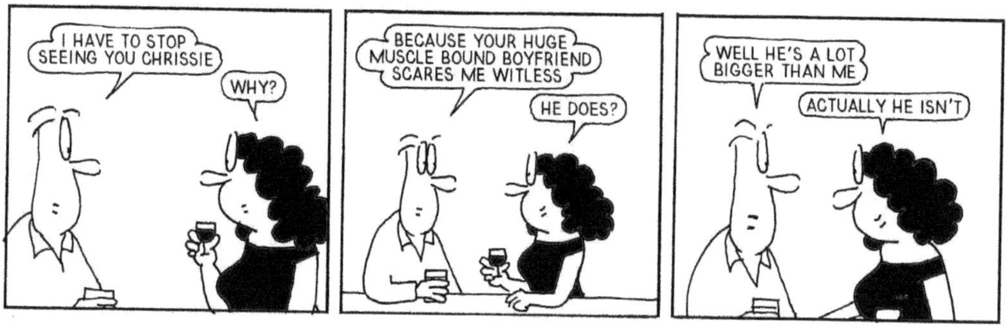
I HAVE TO STOP SEEING YOU CHRISSIE
WHY?
BECAUSE YOUR HUGE MUSCLE BOUND BOYFRIEND SCARES ME WITLESS
HE DOES?
WELL HE'S A LOT BIGGER THAN ME
ACTUALLY HE ISN'T

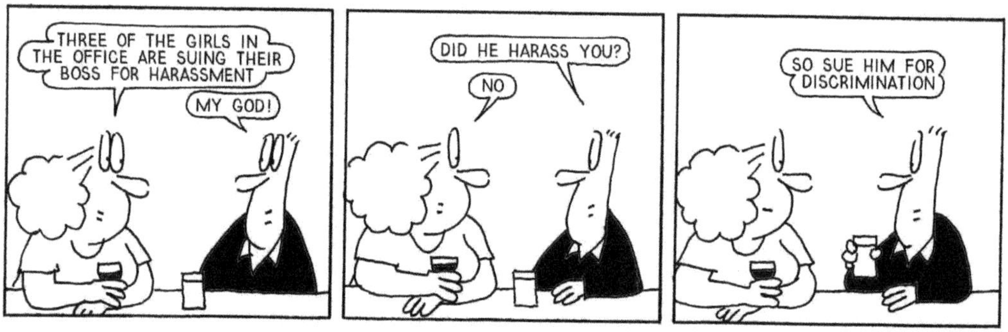
THREE OF THE GIRLS IN THE OFFICE ARE SUING THEIR BOSS FOR HARASSMENT
MY GOD!
DID HE HARASS YOU?
NO
SO SUE HIM FOR DISCRIMINATION

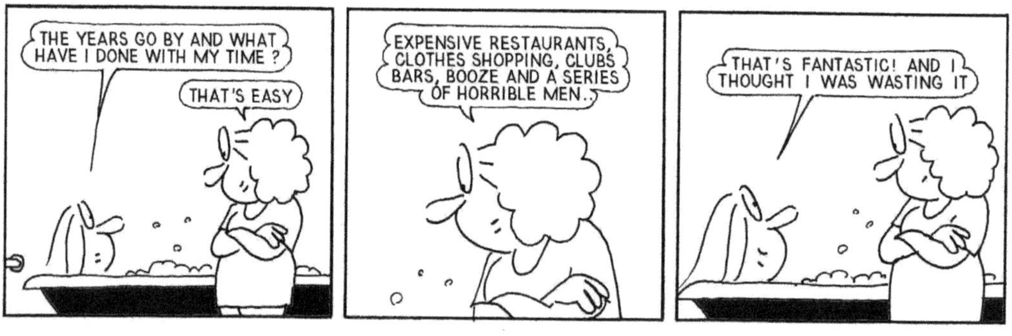
THE YEARS GO BY AND WHAT HAVE I DONE WITH MY TIME ?
THAT'S EASY
EXPENSIVE RESTAURANTS, CLOTHES SHOPPING, CLUBS BARS, BOOZE AND A SERIES OF HORRIBLE MEN..
THAT'S FANTASTIC! AND I THOUGHT I WAS WASTING IT

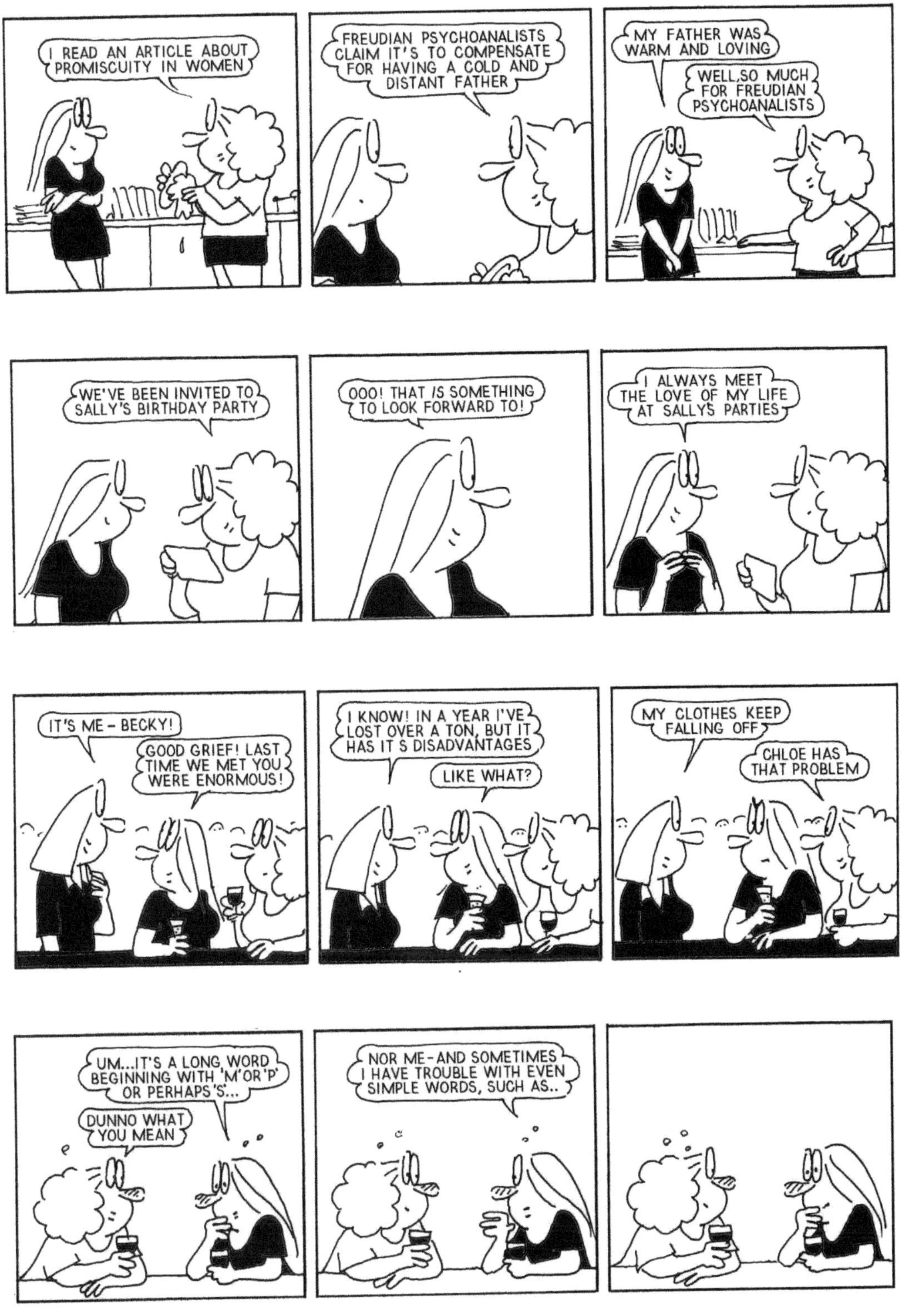
I READ AN ARTICLE ABOUT PROMISCUITY IN WOMEN
FREUDIAN PSYCHOANALISTS CLAIM IT'S TO COMPENSATE FOR HAVING A COLD AND DISTANT FATHER
MY FATHER WAS WARM AND LOVING
WELL,SO MUCH FOR FREUDIAN PSYCHOANALISTS
WE'VE BEEN INVITED TO SALLY'S BIRTHDAY PARTY
OOO! THAT *IS* SOMETHING TO LOOK FORWARD TO!
I ALWAYS MEET THE LOVE OF MY LIFE AT SALLYS PARTIES
IT'S ME - BECKY!
GOOD GRIEF! LAST TIME WE MET YOU WERE ENORMOUS!
I KNOW! IN A YEAR I'VE LOST OVER A TON, BUT IT HAS IT S DISADVANTAGES
LIKE WHAT?
MY CLOTHES KEEP FALLING OFF
CHLOE HAS THAT PROBLEM
UM...IT'S A LONG WORD BEGINNING WITH 'M'OR'P' OR PERHAPS'S'...
DUNNO WHAT YOU MEAN
NOR ME-AND SOMETIMES I HAVE TROUBLE WITH EVEN SIMPLE WORDS, SUCH AS..

YOU'RE A WRITER?
RIGHT
SO YOU MUST FIND IT EASY TO THINK UP STORIES
FAIRLY
GOOD 'COS YOUR WIFE JUST WALKED IN
Gray

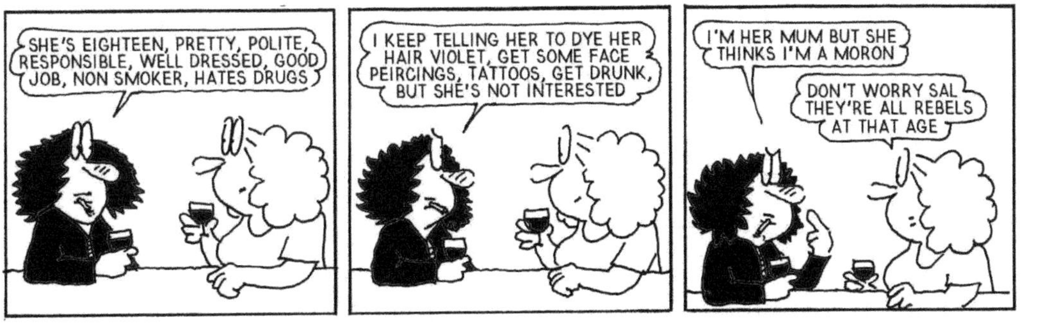
SHE'S EIGHTEEN, PRETTY, POLITE, RESPONSIBLE, WELL DRESSED, GOOD JOB, NON SMOKER, HATES DRUGS
I KEEP TELLING HER TO DYE HER HAIR VIOLET, GET SOME FACE PEIRCINGS, TATTOOS, GET DRUNK, BUT SHE'S NOT INTERESTED
I'M HER MUM BUT SHE THINKS I'M A MORON
DON'T WORRY SAL THEY'RE ALL REBELS AT THAT AGE

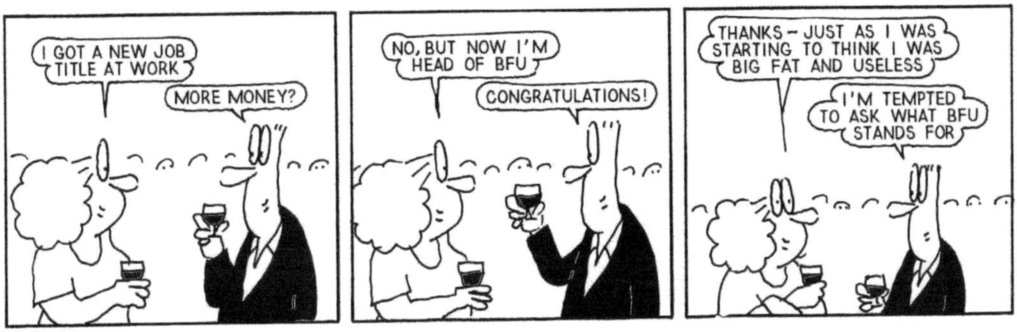
I GOT A NEW JOB TITLE AT WORK
MORE MONEY?
NO, BUT NOW I'M HEAD OF BFU
CONGRATULATIONS!
THANKS – JUST AS I WAS STARTING TO THINK I WAS BIG FAT AND USELESS
I'M TEMPTED TO ASK WHAT BFU STANDS FOR

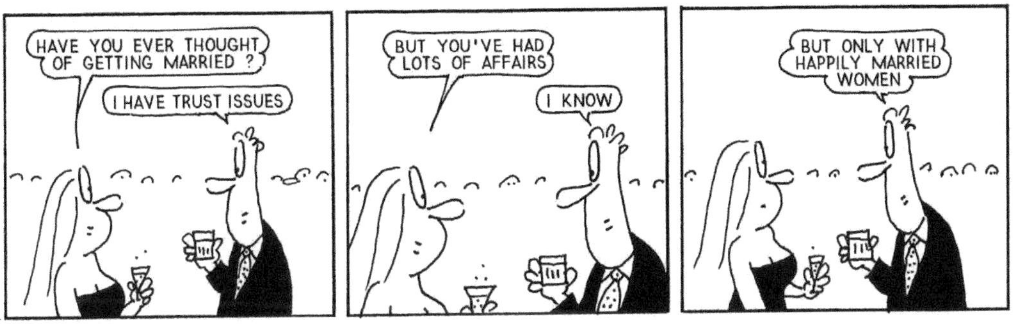
HAVE YOU EVER THOUGHT OF GETTING MARRIED ?
I HAVE TRUST ISSUES
BUT YOU'VE HAD LOTS OF AFFAIRS
I KNOW
BUT ONLY WITH HAPPILY MARRIED WOMEN

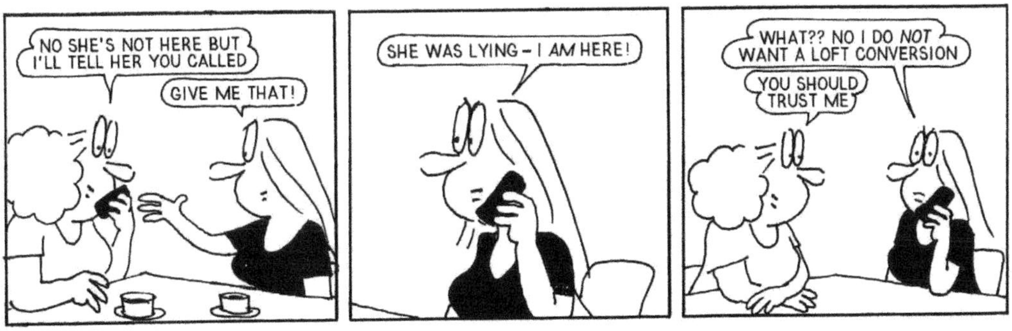
NO SHE'S NOT HERE BUT I'LL TELL HER YOU CALLED
GIVE ME THAT!
SHE WAS LYING – I *AM* HERE!
WHAT?? NO I DO *NOT* WANT A LOFT CONVERSION
YOU SHOULD TRUST ME

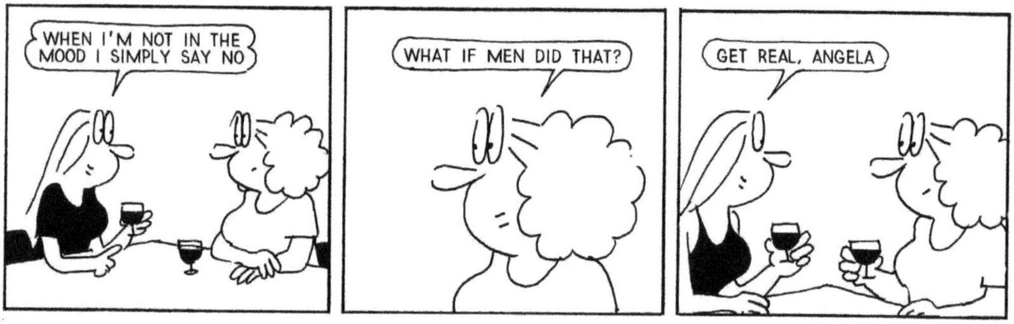
WHEN I'M NOT IN THE MOOD I SIMPLY SAY NO
WHAT IF MEN DID THAT?
GET REAL, ANGELA

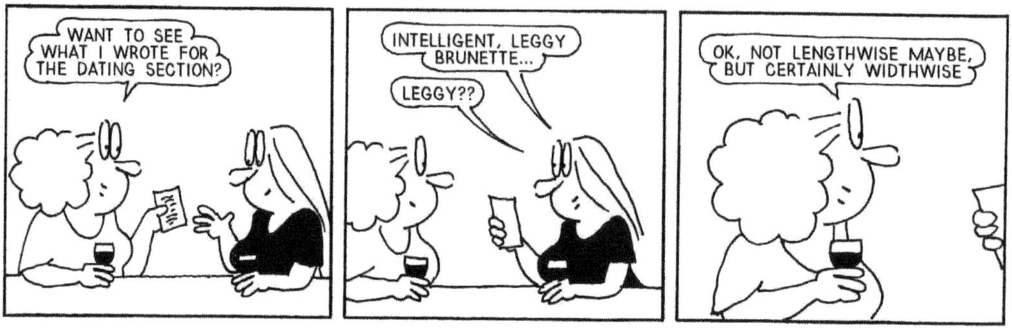
WANT TO SEE WHAT I WROTE FOR THE DATING SECTION?
INTELLIGENT, LEGGY BRUNETTE...
LEGGY??
OK, NOT LENGTHWISE MAYBE, BUT CERTAINLY WIDTHWISE

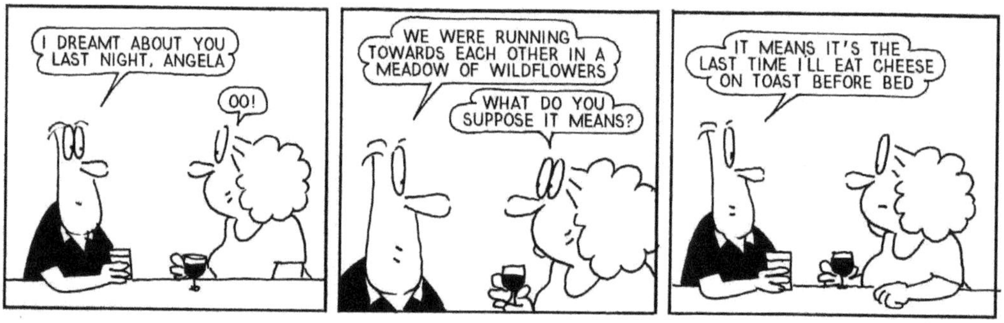
I DREAMT ABOUT YOU LAST NIGHT, ANGELA
OO!
WE WERE RUNNING TOWARDS EACH OTHER IN A MEADOW OF WILDFLOWERS
WHAT DO YOU SUPPOSE IT MEANS?
IT MEANS IT'S THE LAST TIME I'LL EAT CHEESE ON TOAST BEFORE BED

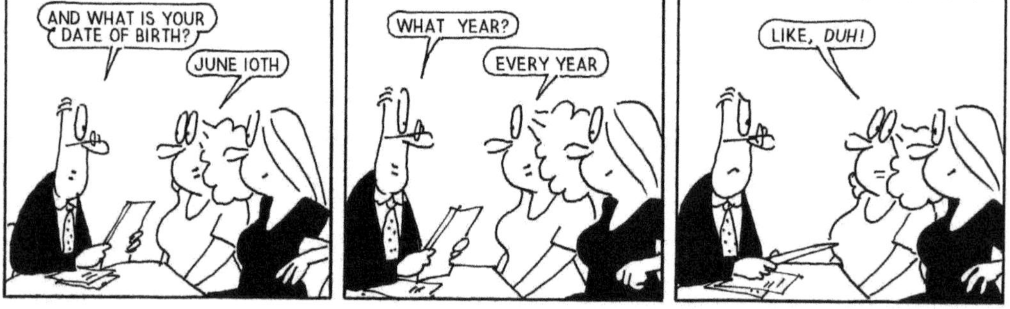
AND WHAT IS YOUR DATE OF BIRTH?
JUNE 10TH
WHAT YEAR?
EVERY YEAR
LIKE, *DUH!*

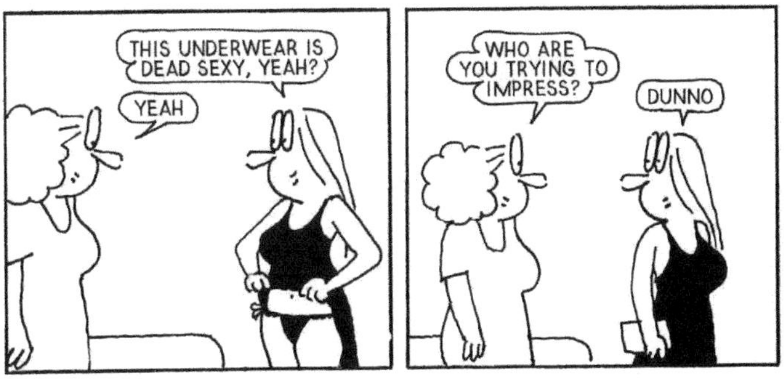
THIS UNDERWEAR IS DEAD SEXY, YEAH?
YEAH
WHO ARE YOU TRYING TO IMPRESS?
DUNNO
ASK ME IN THE MORNING

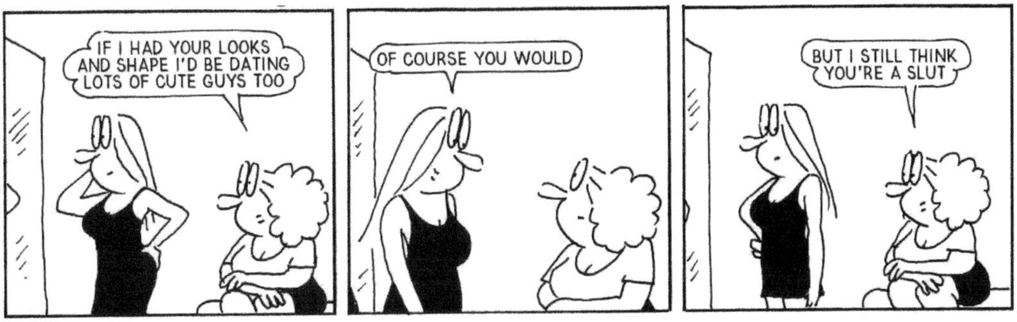
IF I HAD YOUR LOOKS AND SHAPE I'D BE DATING LOTS OF CUTE GUYS TOO
OF COURSE YOU WOULD
BUT I STILL THINK YOU'RE A SLUT

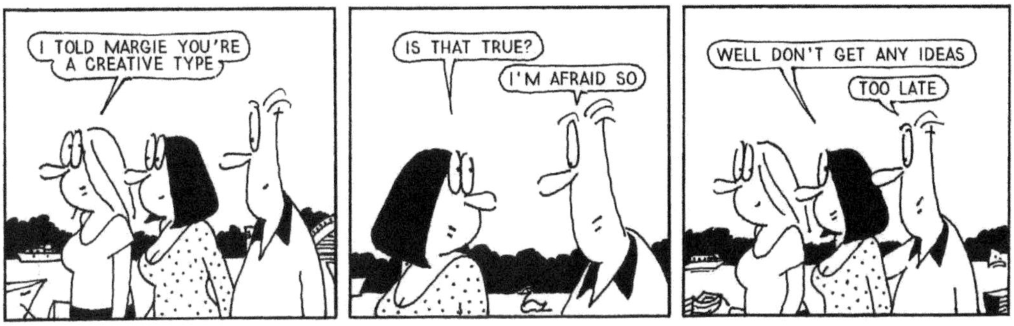
I TOLD MARGIE YOU'RE A CREATIVE TYPE
IS THAT TRUE?
I'M AFRAID SO
WELL DON'T GET ANY IDEAS
TOO LATE

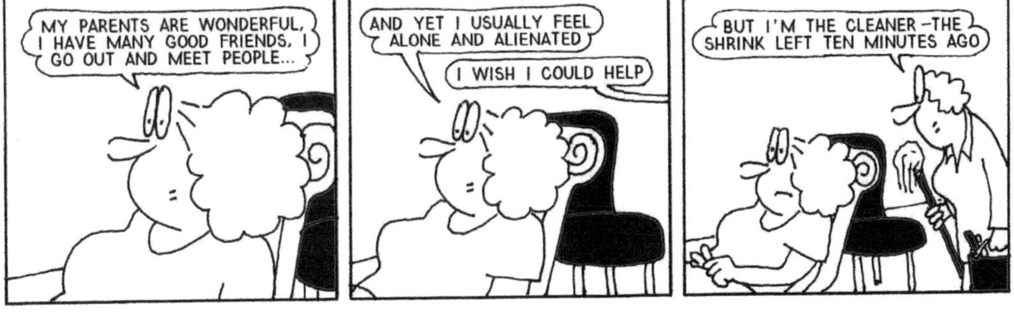
MY PARENTS ARE WONDERFUL, I HAVE MANY GOOD FRIENDS, I GO OUT AND MEET PEOPLE...
AND YET I USUALLY FEEL ALONE AND ALIENATED
I WISH I COULD HELP
BUT I'M THE CLEANER – THE SHRINK LEFT TEN MINUTES AGO

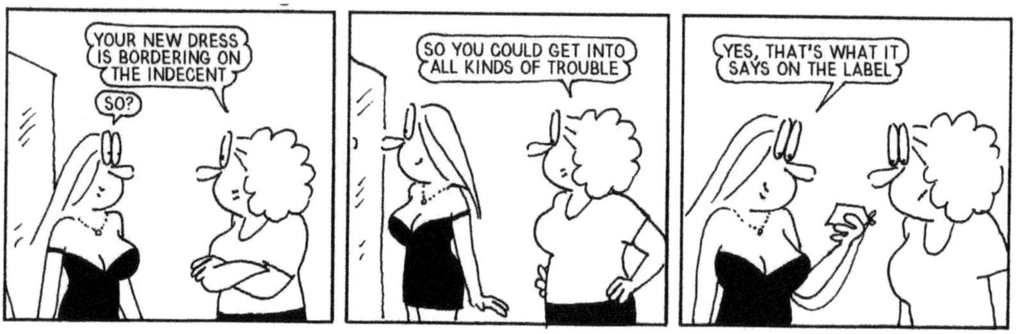
YOUR NEW DRESS IS BORDERING ON THE INDECENT
SO?
SO YOU COULD GET INTO ALL KINDS OF TROUBLE
YES, THAT'S WHAT IT SAYS ON THE LABEL

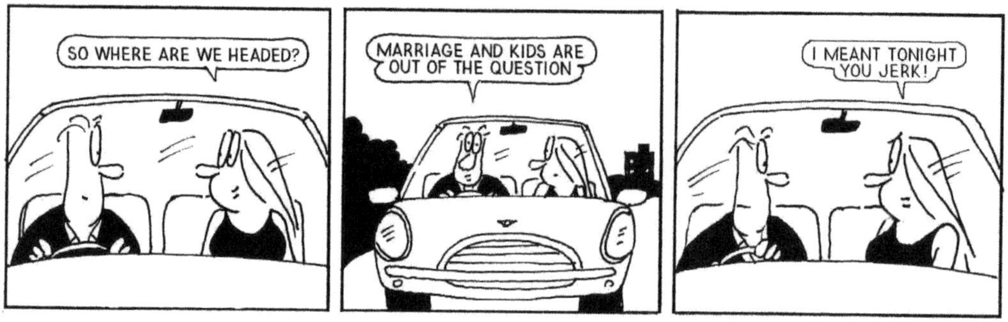
SO WHERE ARE WE HEADED?
MARRIAGE AND KIDS ARE OUT OF THE QUESTION
I MEANT TONIGHT YOU JERK!

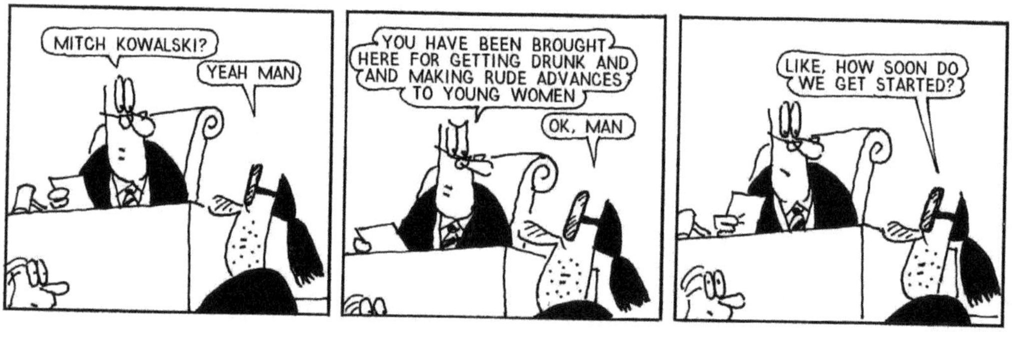
MITCH KOWALSKI?
YEAH MAN
YOU HAVE BEEN BROUGHT HERE FOR GETTING DRUNK AND AND MAKING RUDE ADVANCES TO YOUNG WOMEN
OK, MAN
LIKE, HOW SOON DO WE GET STARTED?

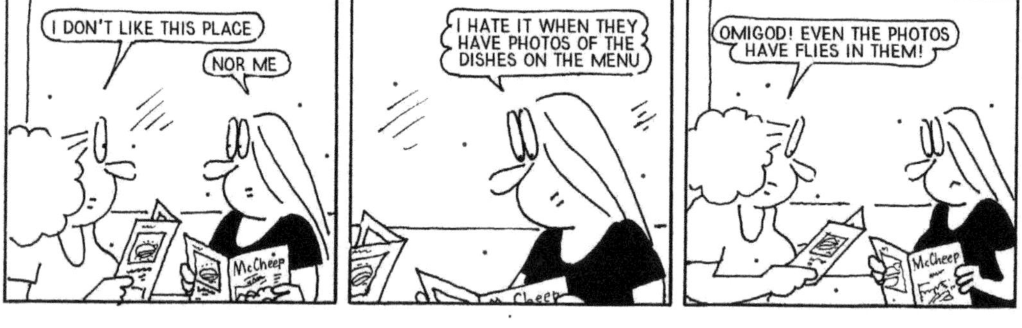
I DON'T LIKE THIS PLACE
NOR ME
I HATE IT WHEN THEY HAVE PHOTOS OF THE DISHES ON THE MENU
OMIGOD! EVEN THE PHOTOS HAVE FLIES IN THEM!

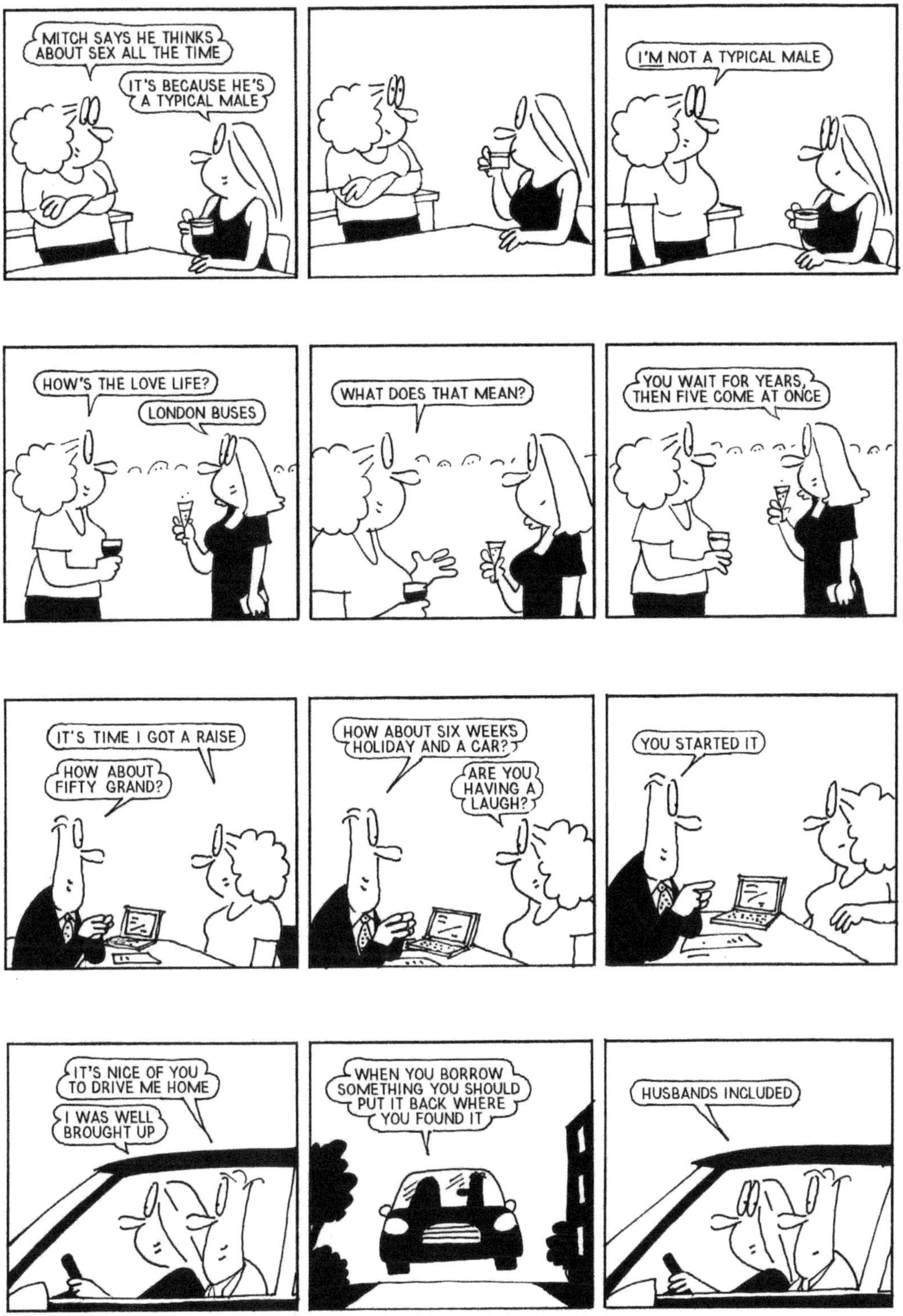
MITCH SAYS HE THINKS ABOUT SEX ALL THE TIME
IT'S BECAUSE HE'S A TYPICAL MALE
I'M NOT A TYPICAL MALE
HOW'S THE LOVE LIFE?
LONDON BUSES
WHAT DOES THAT MEAN?
YOU WAIT FOR YEARS, THEN FIVE COME AT ONCE
IT'S TIME I GOT A RAISE
HOW ABOUT FIFTY GRAND?
HOW ABOUT SIX WEEKS HOLIDAY AND A CAR?
ARE YOU HAVING A LAUGH?
YOU STARTED IT
IT'S NICE OF YOU TO DRIVE ME HOME
I WAS WELL BROUGHT UP
WHEN YOU BORROW SOMETHING YOU SHOULD PUT IT BACK WHERE YOU FOUND IT
HUSBANDS INCLUDED

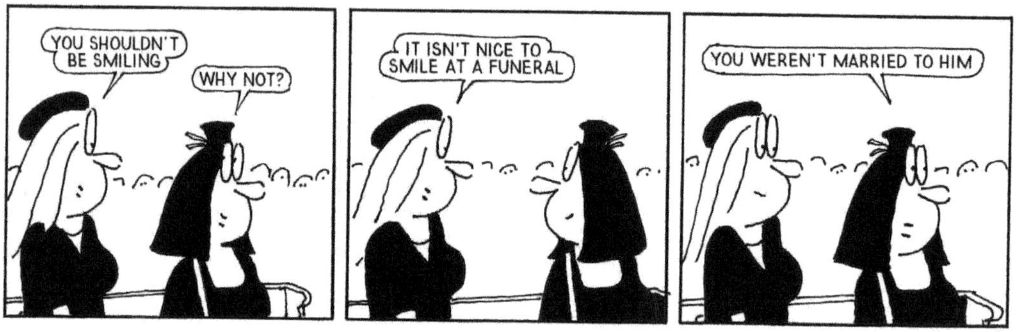
YOU SHOULDN'T BE SMILING
WHY NOT?
IT ISN'T NICE TO SMILE AT A FUNERAL
YOU WEREN'T MARRIED TO HIM

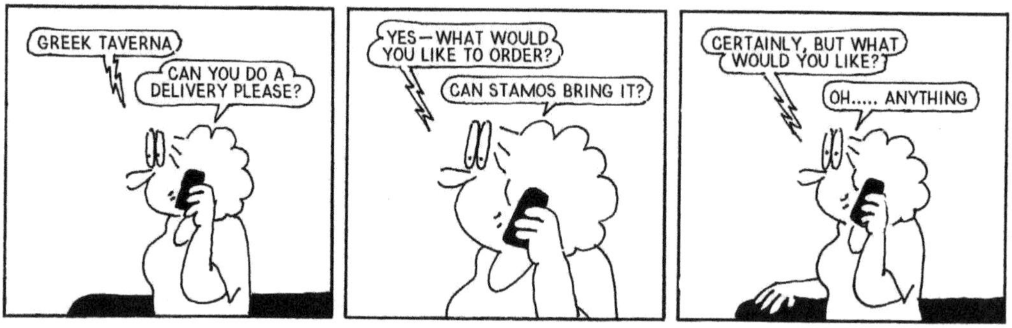
GREEK TAVERNA
CAN YOU DO A DELIVERY PLEASE?
YES—WHAT WOULD YOU LIKE TO ORDER?
CAN STAMOS BRING IT?
CERTAINLY, BUT WHAT WOULD YOU LIKE?
OH..... ANYTHING

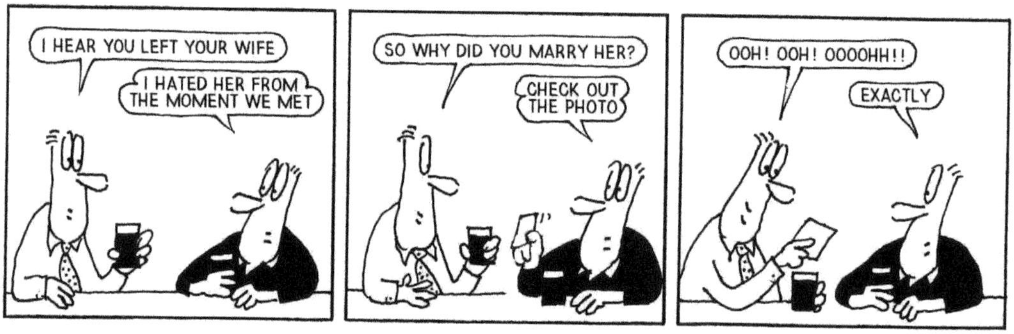
I HEAR YOU LEFT YOUR WIFE
I HATED HER FROM THE MOMENT WE MET
SO WHY DID YOU MARRY HER?
CHECK OUT THE PHOTO
OOH! OOH! OOOOHH!!
EXACTLY

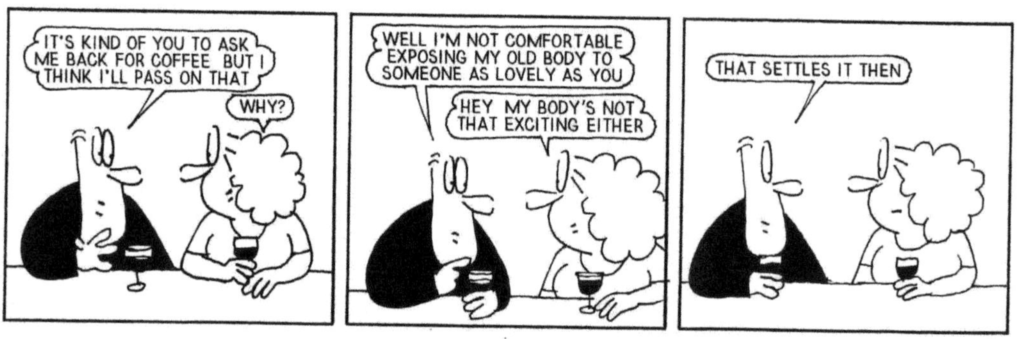
IT'S KIND OF YOU TO ASK ME BACK FOR COFFEE BUT I THINK I'LL PASS ON THAT
WHY?
WELL I'M NOT COMFORTABLE EXPOSING MY OLD BODY TO SOMEONE AS LOVELY AS YOU
HEY MY BODY'S NOT THAT EXCITING EITHER
THAT SETTLES IT THEN

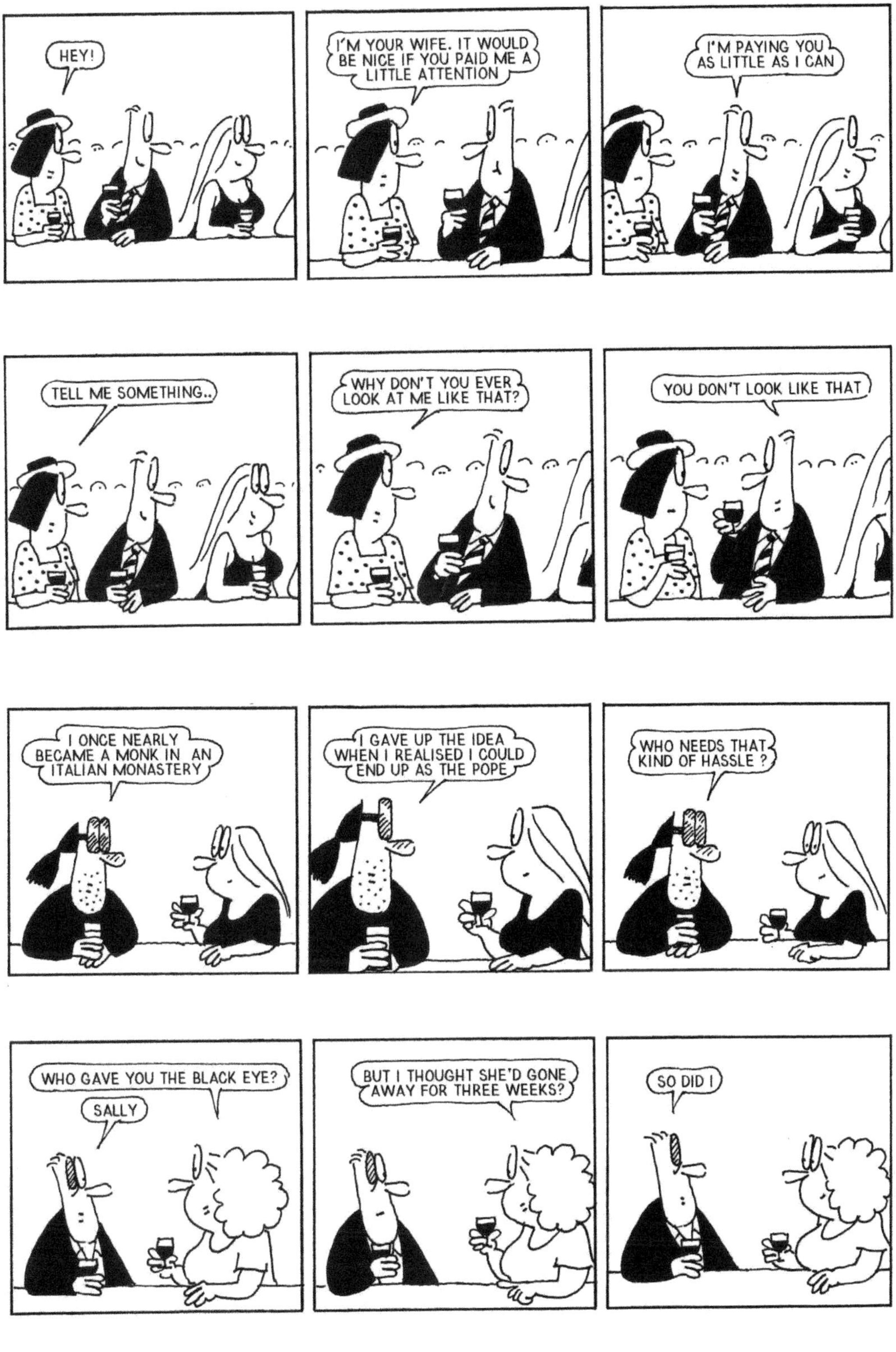
HEY!
I'M YOUR WIFE. IT WOULD BE NICE IF YOU PAID ME A LITTLE ATTENTION
I'M PAYING YOU AS LITTLE AS I CAN
TELL ME SOMETHING..
WHY DON'T YOU EVER LOOK AT ME LIKE THAT?
YOU DON'T LOOK LIKE THAT
I ONCE NEARLY BECAME A MONK IN AN ITALIAN MONASTERY
I GAVE UP THE IDEA WHEN I REALISED I COULD END UP AS THE POPE
WHO NEEDS THAT KIND OF HASSLE ?
WHO GAVE YOU THE BLACK EYE?
SALLY
BUT I THOUGHT SHE'D GONE AWAY FOR THREE WEEKS?
SO DID I

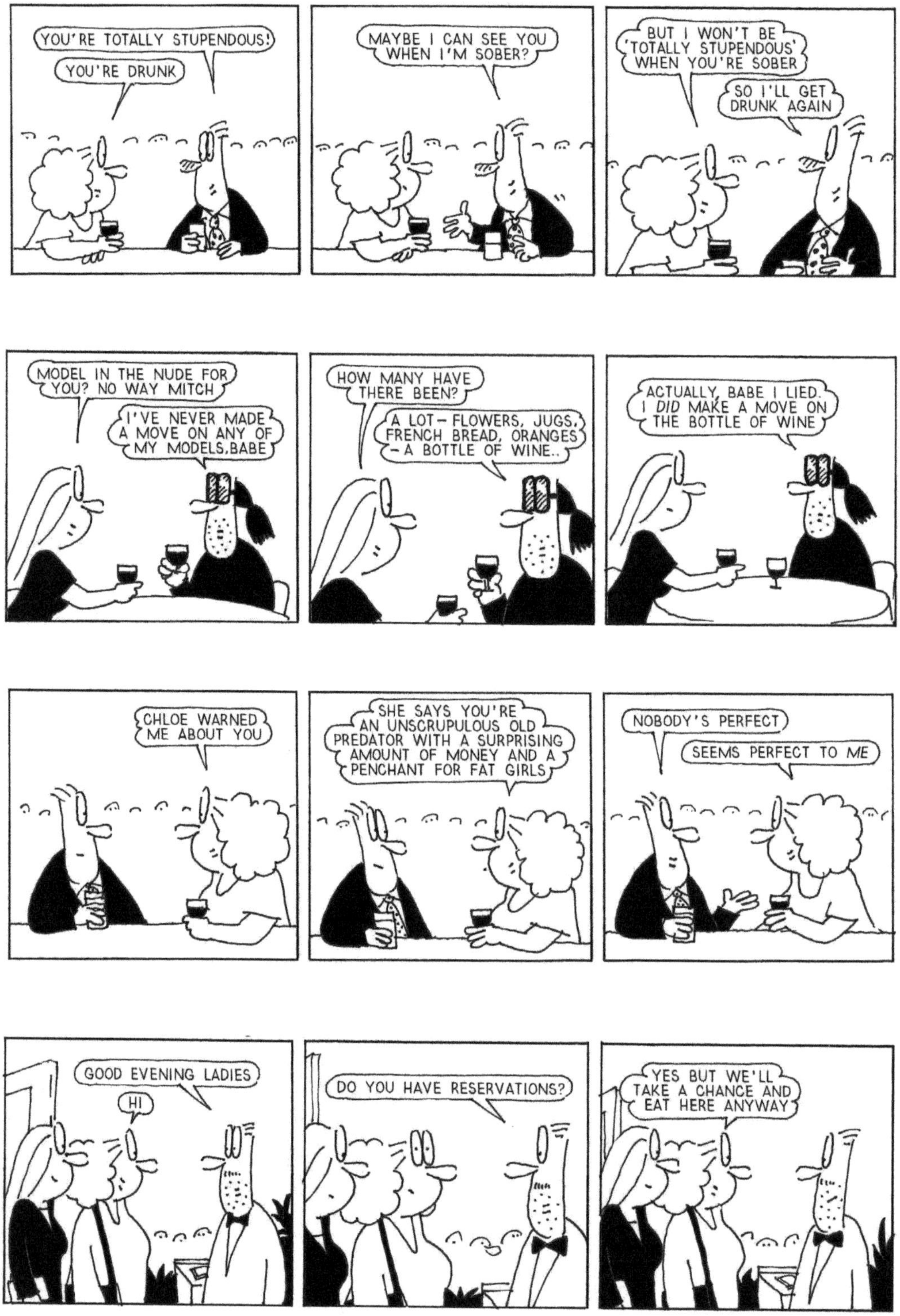
YOU'RE TOTALLY STUPENDOUS!
YOU'RE DRUNK
MAYBE I CAN SEE YOU WHEN I'M SOBER?
BUT I WON'T BE 'TOTALLY STUPENDOUS' WHEN YOU'RE SOBER
SO I'LL GET DRUNK AGAIN
MODEL IN THE NUDE FOR YOU? NO WAY MITCH
I'VE NEVER MADE A MOVE ON ANY OF MY MODELS, BABE
HOW MANY HAVE THERE BEEN?
A LOT – FLOWERS, JUGS, FRENCH BREAD, ORANGES – A BOTTLE OF WINE..
ACTUALLY, BABE I LIED. I *DID* MAKE A MOVE ON THE BOTTLE OF WINE
CHLOE WARNED ME ABOUT YOU
SHE SAYS YOU'RE AN UNSCRUPULOUS OLD PREDATOR WITH A SURPRISING AMOUNT OF MONEY AND A PENCHANT FOR FAT GIRLS
NOBODY'S PERFECT
SEEMS PERFECT TO *ME*
GOOD EVENING LADIES
HI
DO YOU HAVE RESERVATIONS?
YES BUT WE'LL TAKE A CHANCE AND EAT HERE ANYWAY

MOST WOMEN WHO HAVE CONVERSATIONS WITH THEIR CAT ARE DELUSIONAL
WHERE DID YOU HEAR THAT?
MY DOG READ IT IN THE SUNDAY TIMES

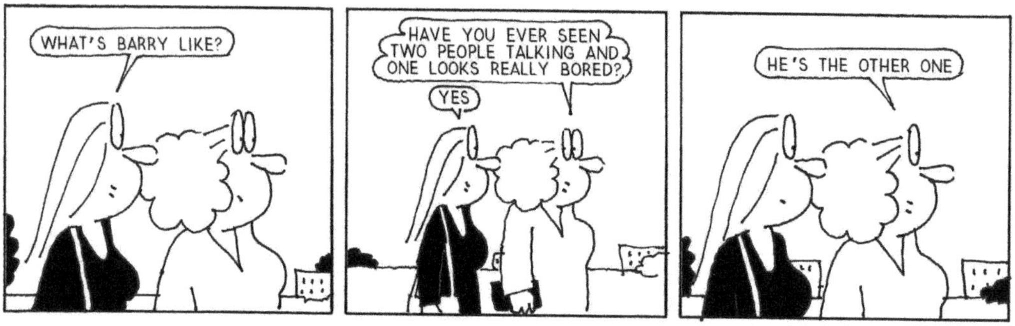
WHAT'S BARRY LIKE?
HAVE YOU EVER SEEN TWO PEOPLE TALKING AND ONE LOOKS REALLY BORED?
YES
HE'S THE OTHER ONE

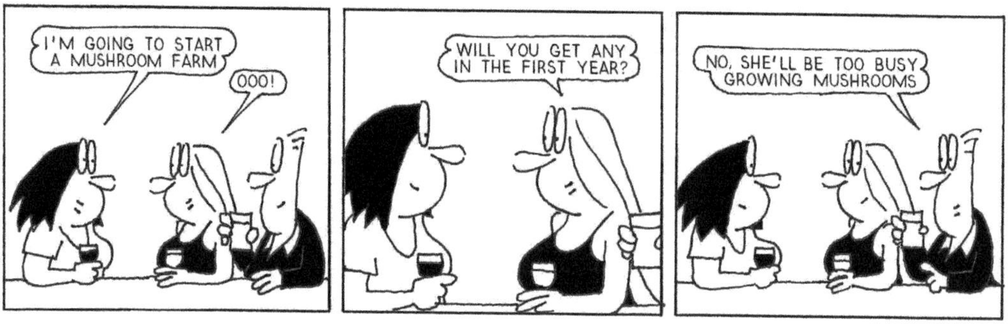
I'M GOING TO START A MUSHROOM FARM
OOO!
WILL YOU GET ANY IN THE FIRST YEAR?
NO, SHE'LL BE TOO BUSY GROWING MUSHROOMS

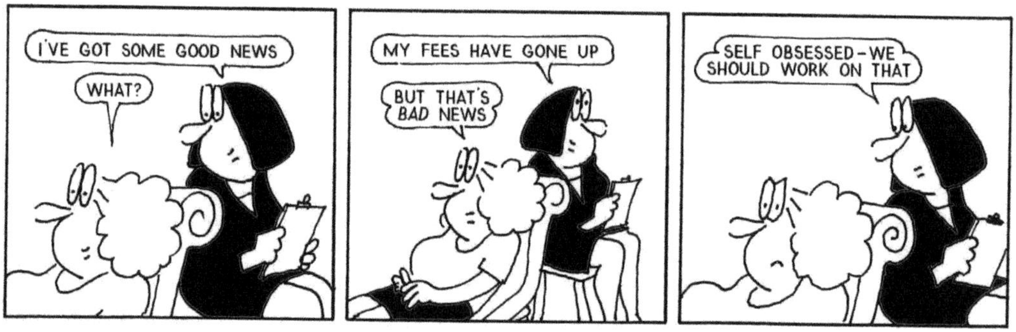
I'VE GOT SOME GOOD NEWS
WHAT?
MY FEES HAVE GONE UP
BUT THAT'S *BAD* NEWS
SELF OBSESSED-WE SHOULD WORK ON THAT

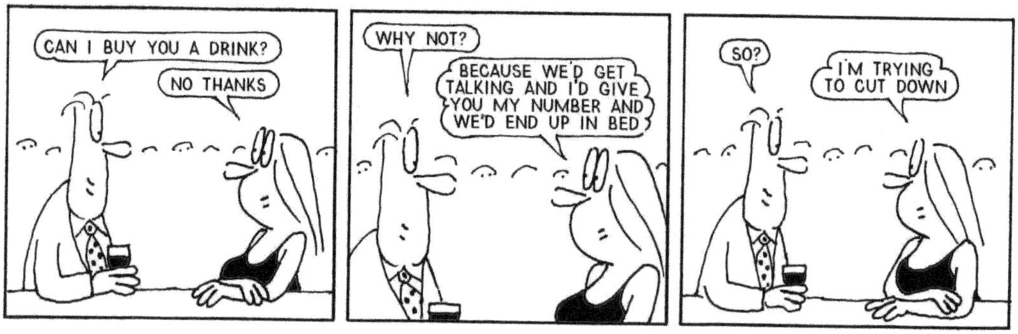
CAN I BUY YOU A DRINK?
NO THANKS
WHY NOT?
BECAUSE WE'D GET TALKING AND I'D GIVE YOU MY NUMBER AND WE'D END UP IN BED
SO?
I'M TRYING TO CUT DOWN

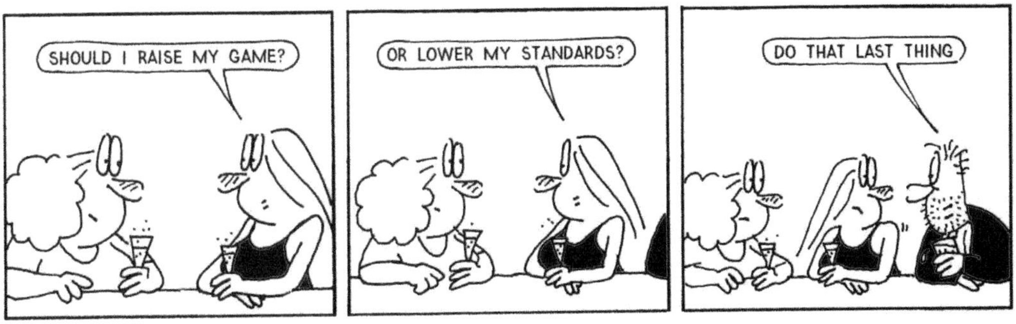
SHOULD I RAISE MY GAME?
OR LOWER MY STANDARDS?
DO THAT LAST THING

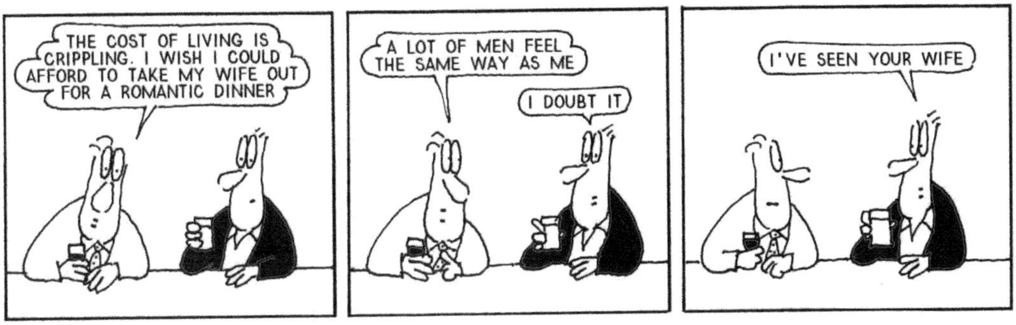
THE COST OF LIVING IS CRIPPLING. I WISH I COULD AFFORD TO TAKE MY WIFE OUT FOR A ROMANTIC DINNER
A LOT OF MEN FEEL THE SAME WAY AS ME
I DOUBT IT
I'VE SEEN YOUR WIFE

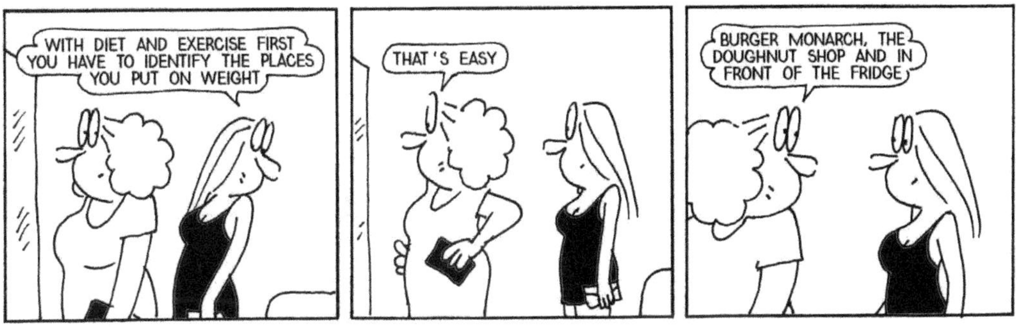
WITH DIET AND EXERCISE FIRST YOU HAVE TO IDENTIFY THE PLACES YOU PUT ON WEIGHT
THAT'S EASY
BURGER MONARCH, THE DOUGHNUT SHOP AND IN FRONT OF THE FRIDGE

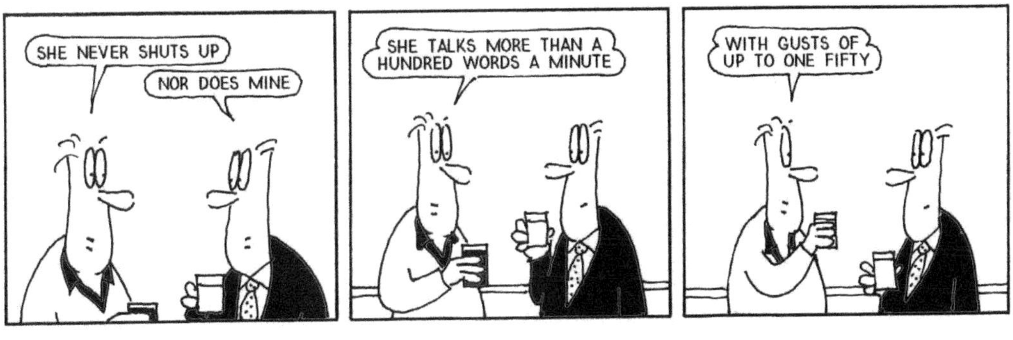
SHE NEVER SHUTS UP
NOR DOES MINE
SHE TALKS MORE THAN A HUNDRED WORDS A MINUTE
WITH GUSTS OF UP TO ONE FIFTY

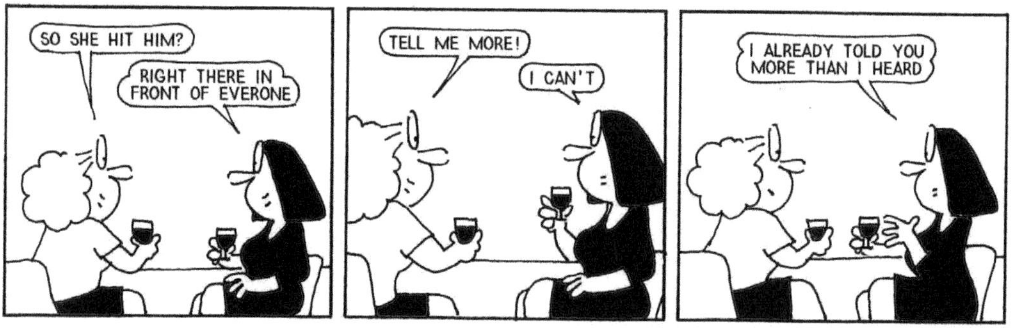
SO SHE HIT HIM?
RIGHT THERE IN FRONT OF EVERONE
TELL ME MORE!
I CAN'T
I ALREADY TOLD YOU MORE THAN I HEARD

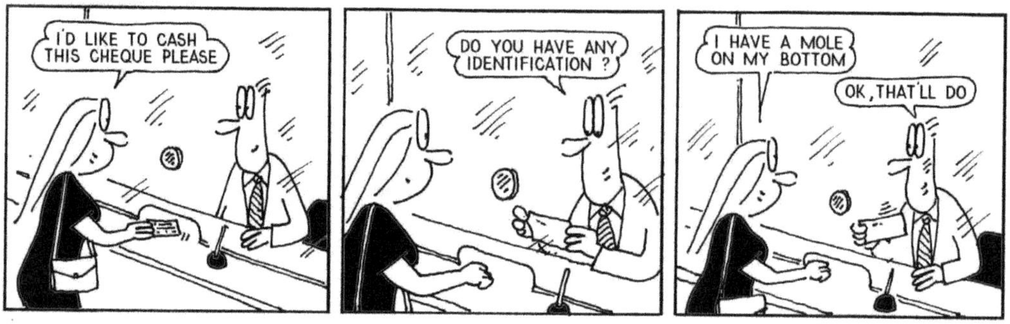
I'D LIKE TO CASH THIS CHEQUE PLEASE
DO YOU HAVE ANY IDENTIFICATION ?
I HAVE A MOLE ON MY BOTTOM
OK, THAT'LL DO

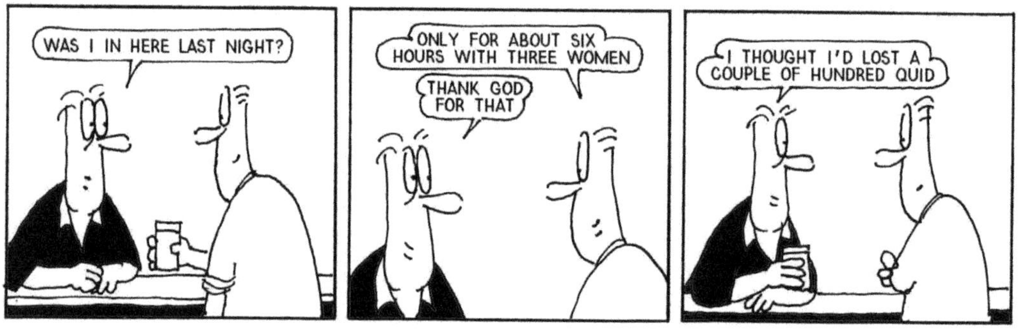
WAS I IN HERE LAST NIGHT?
ONLY FOR ABOUT SIX HOURS WITH THREE WOMEN
THANK GOD FOR THAT
I THOUGHT I'D LOST A COUPLE OF HUNDRED QUID

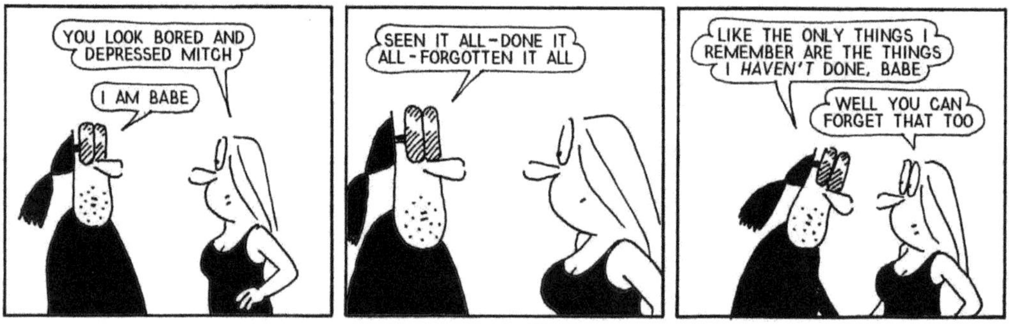
YOU LOOK BORED AND DEPRESSED MITCH
I AM BABE
SEEN IT ALL-DONE IT ALL-FORGOTTEN IT ALL
LIKE THE ONLY THINGS I REMEMBER ARE THE THINGS I *HAVEN'T* DONE, BABE
WELL YOU CAN FORGET THAT TOO

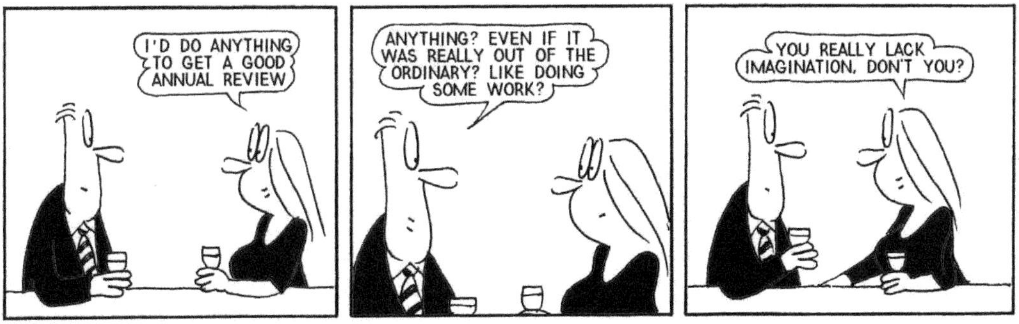
I'D DO ANYTHING TO GET A GOOD ANNUAL REVIEW
ANYTHING? EVEN IF IT WAS REALLY OUT OF THE ORDINARY? LIKE DOING SOME WORK?
YOU REALLY LACK IMAGINATION, DON'T YOU?

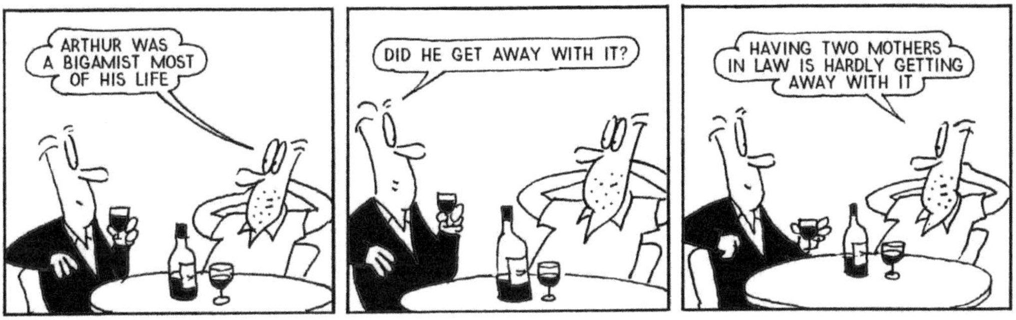
ARTHUR WAS A BIGAMIST MOST OF HIS LIFE
DID HE GET AWAY WITH IT?
HAVING TWO MOTHERS IN LAW IS HARDLY GETTING AWAY WITH IT

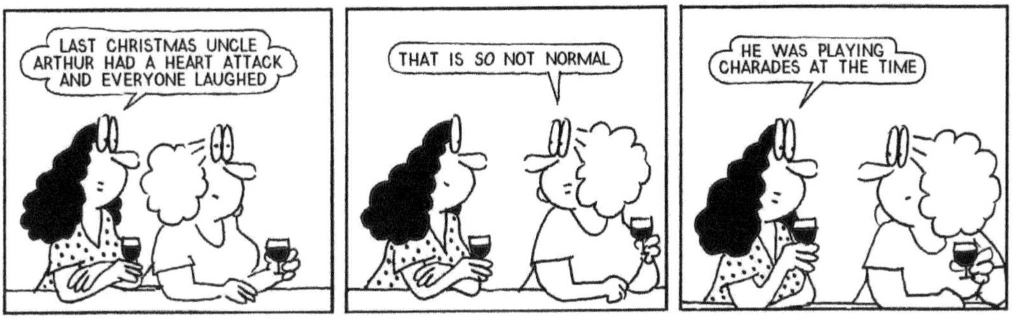
LAST CHRISTMAS UNCLE ARTHUR HAD A HEART ATTACK AND EVERYONE LAUGHED
THAT IS *SO* NOT NORMAL
HE WAS PLAYING CHARADES AT THE TIME

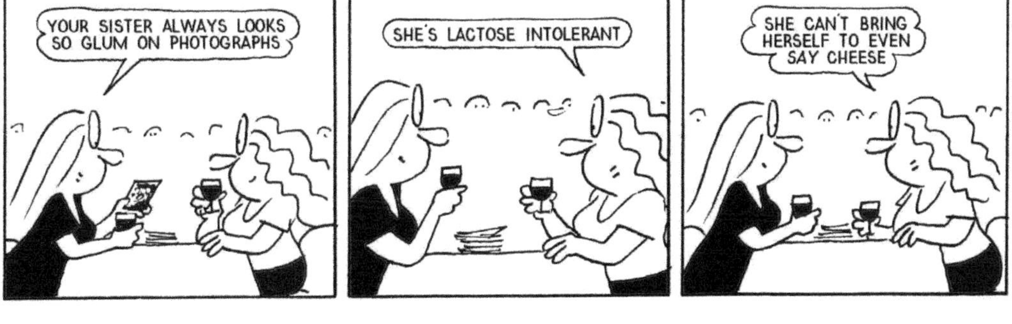
YOUR SISTER ALWAYS LOOKS SO GLUM ON PHOTOGRAPHS
SHE'S LACTOSE INTOLERANT
SHE CAN'T BRING HERSELF TO EVEN SAY CHEESE

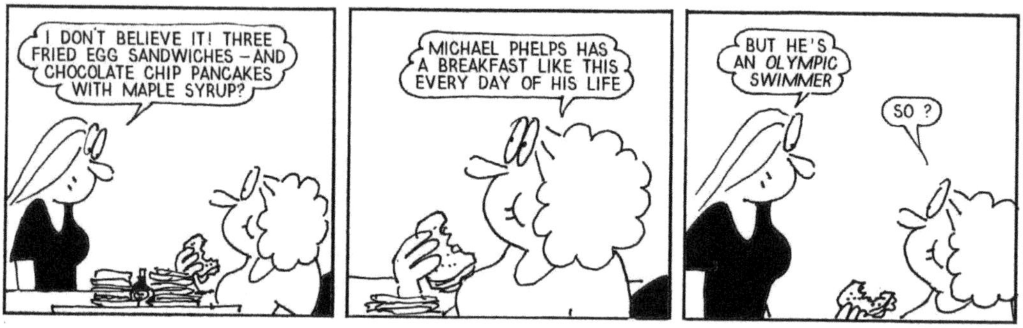
I DON'T BELIEVE IT! THREE FRIED EGG SANDWICHES – AND CHOCOLATE CHIP PANCAKES WITH MAPLE SYRUP?
MICHAEL PHELPS HAS A BREAKFAST LIKE THIS EVERY DAY OF HIS LIFE
BUT HE'S AN *OLYMPIC SWIMMER*
SO ?

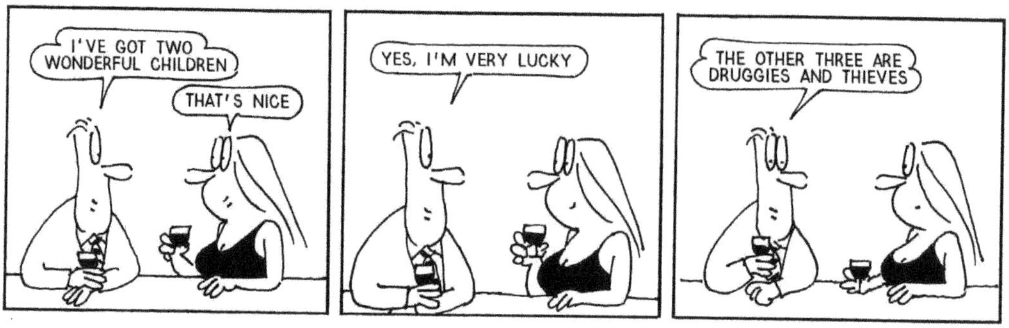
I'VE GOT TWO WONDERFUL CHILDREN
THAT'S NICE
YES, I'M VERY LUCKY
THE OTHER THREE ARE DRUGGIES AND THIEVES

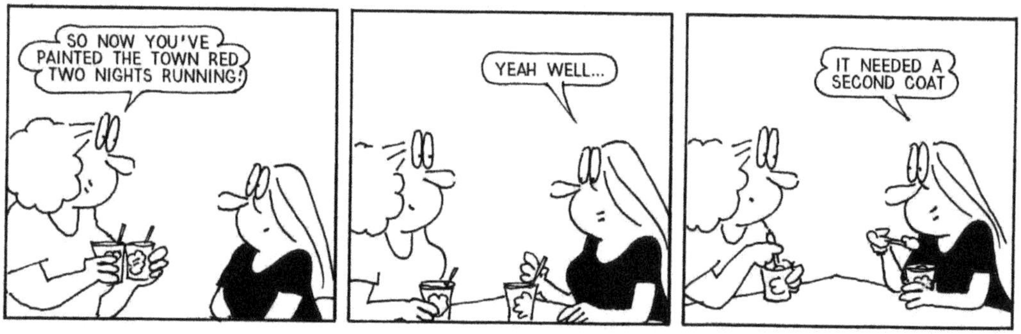
SO NOW YOU'VE PAINTED THE TOWN RED TWO NIGHTS RUNNING!
YEAH WELL...
IT NEEDED A SECOND COAT

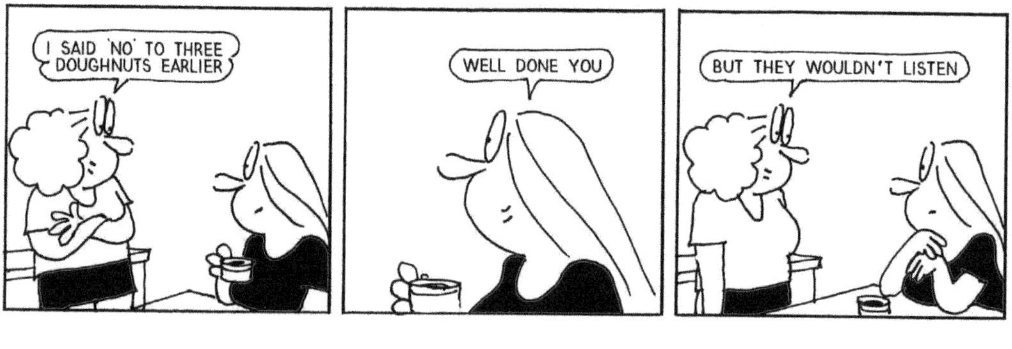
I SAID 'NO' TO THREE DOUGHNUTS EARLIER
WELL DONE YOU
BUT THEY WOULDN'T LISTEN

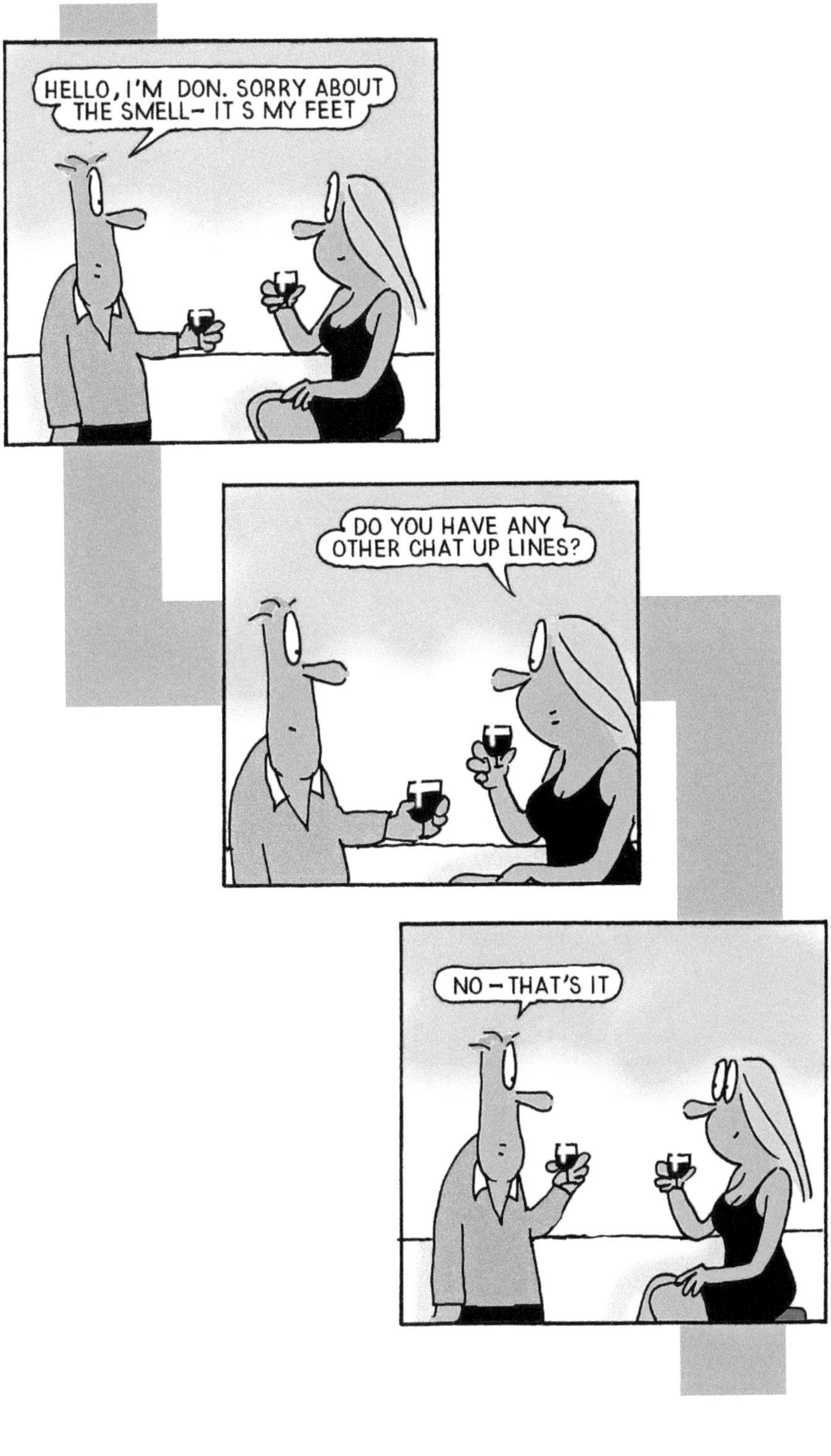
HELLO, I'M DON. SORRY ABOUT THE SMELL – IT S MY FEET
DO YOU HAVE ANY OTHER CHAT UP LINES?
NO – THAT'S IT

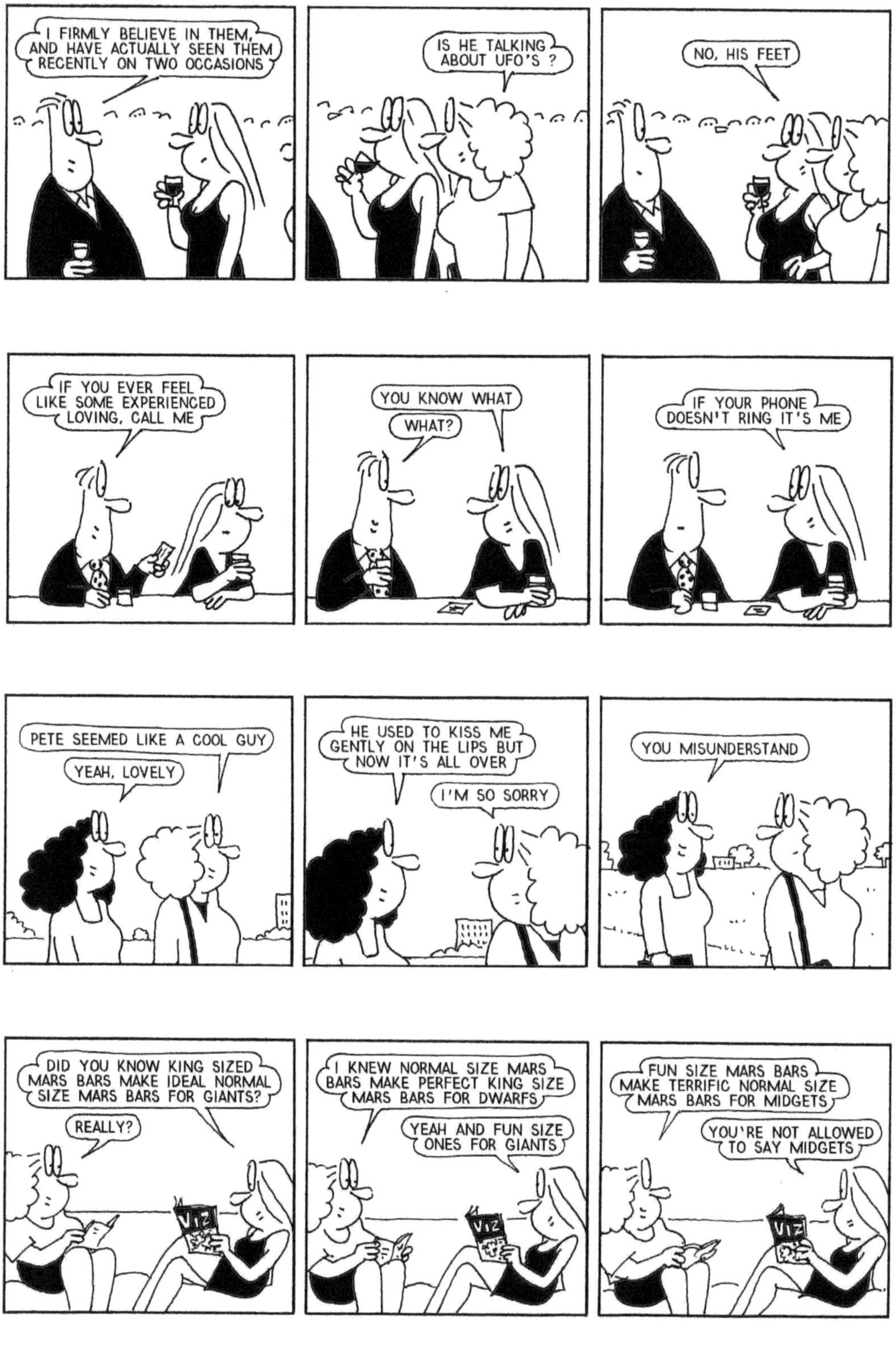
I FIRMLY BELIEVE IN THEM, AND HAVE ACTUALLY SEEN THEM RECENTLY ON TWO OCCASIONS
IS HE TALKING ABOUT UFO'S ?
NO, HIS FEET
IF YOU EVER FEEL LIKE SOME EXPERIENCED LOVING, CALL ME
YOU KNOW WHAT
WHAT?
IF YOUR PHONE DOESN'T RING IT'S ME
PETE SEEMED LIKE A COOL GUY
YEAH, LOVELY
HE USED TO KISS ME GENTLY ON THE LIPS BUT NOW IT'S ALL OVER
I'M SO SORRY
YOU MISUNDERSTAND
DID YOU KNOW KING SIZED MARS BARS MAKE IDEAL NORMAL SIZE MARS BARS FOR GIANTS?
REALLY?
VIZ
I KNEW NORMAL SIZE MARS BARS MAKE PERFECT KING SIZE MARS BARS FOR DWARFS
YEAH AND FUN SIZE ONES FOR GIANTS
VIZ
FUN SIZE MARS BARS MAKE TERRIFIC NORMAL SIZE MARS BARS FOR MIDGETS
YOU'RE NOT ALLOWED TO SAY MIDGETS
VIZ

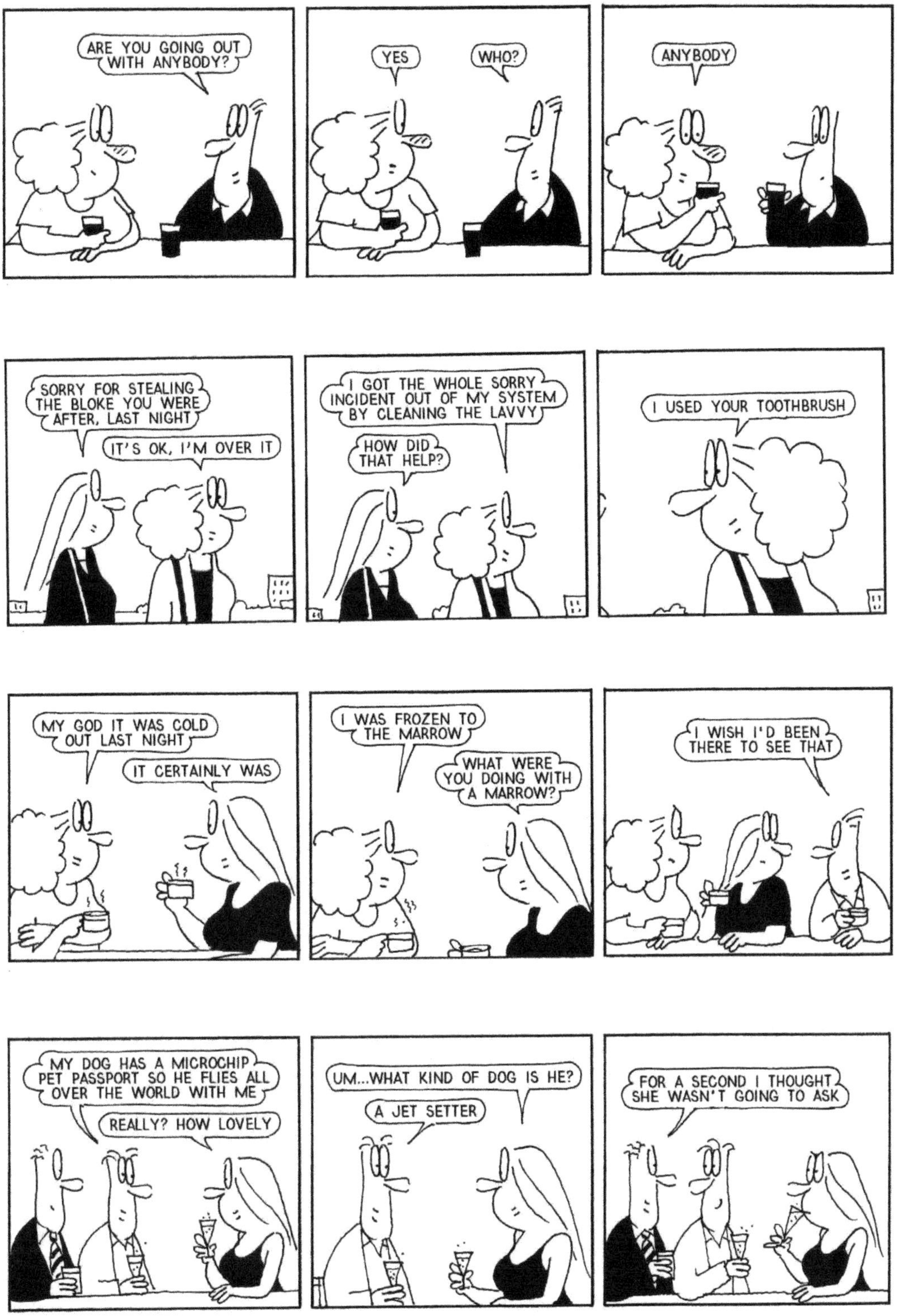
ARE YOU GOING OUT WITH ANYBODY?
YES
WHO?
ANYBODY
SORRY FOR STEALING THE BLOKE YOU WERE AFTER, LAST NIGHT
IT'S OK, I'M OVER IT
I GOT THE WHOLE SORRY INCIDENT OUT OF MY SYSTEM BY CLEANING THE LAVVY
HOW DID THAT HELP?
I USED YOUR TOOTHBRUSH
MY GOD IT WAS COLD OUT LAST NIGHT
IT CERTAINLY WAS
I WAS FROZEN TO THE MARROW
WHAT WERE YOU DOING WITH A MARROW?
I WISH I'D BEEN THERE TO SEE THAT
MY DOG HAS A MICROCHIP PET PASSPORT SO HE FLIES ALL OVER THE WORLD WITH ME
REALLY? HOW LOVELY
UM...WHAT KIND OF DOG IS HE?
A JET SETTER
FOR A SECOND I THOUGHT SHE WASN'T GOING TO ASK

RIGHT NOW I'M IN LOVE WITH KYLIE MINOGUE, PALOMA FAITH CHRISTINA HENDRICKS AND CHARLIZE THERON
AND JOANNA LUMLEY OF COURSE
BUT THAT'S JUST A PLATONIC THING

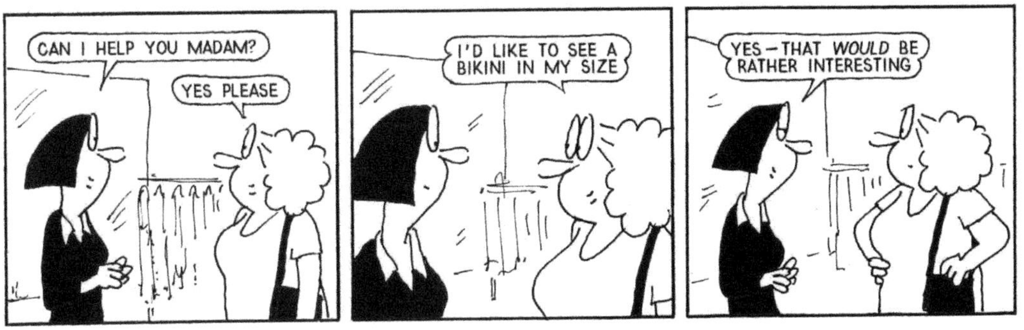
CAN I HELP YOU MADAM?
YES PLEASE
I'D LIKE TO SEE A BIKINI IN MY SIZE
YES—THAT *WOULD* BE RATHER INTERESTING

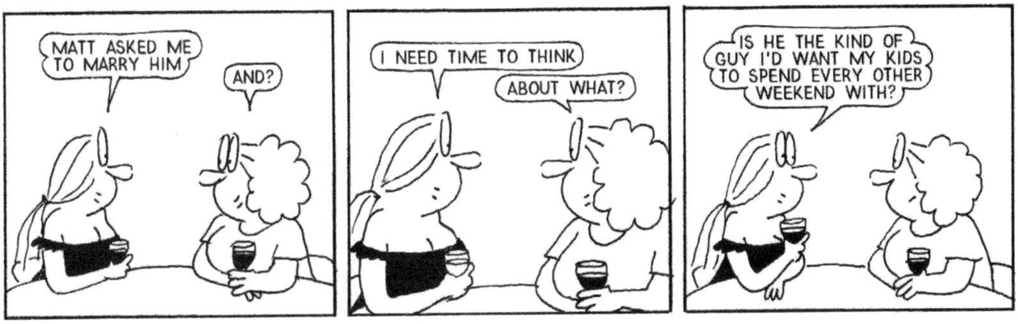
MATT ASKED ME TO MARRY HIM
AND?
I NEED TIME TO THINK
ABOUT WHAT?
IS HE THE KIND OF GUY I'D WANT MY KIDS TO SPEND EVERY OTHER WEEKEND WITH?

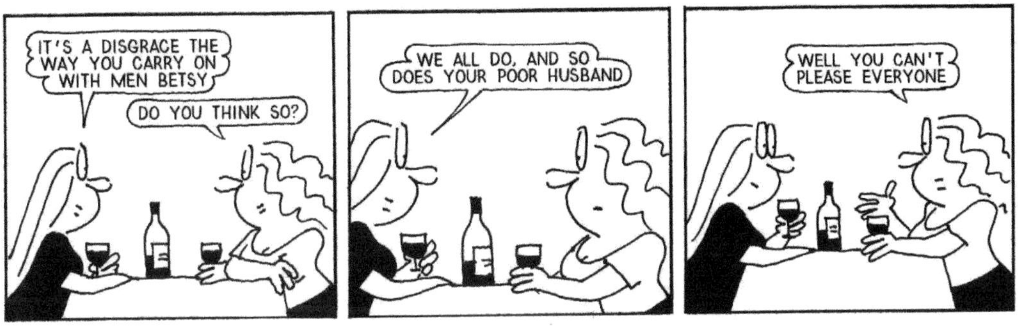
IT'S A DISGRACE THE WAY YOU CARRY ON WITH MEN BETSY
DO YOU THINK SO?
WE ALL DO, AND SO DOES YOUR POOR HUSBAND
WELL YOU CAN'T PLEASE EVERYONE

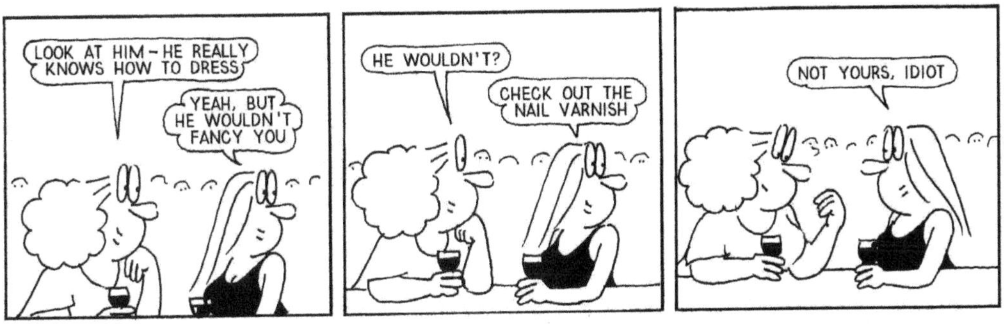
LOOK AT HIM—HE REALLY KNOWS HOW TO DRESS
YEAH, BUT HE WOULDN'T FANCY YOU
HE WOULDN'T?
CHECK OUT THE NAIL VARNISH
NOT YOURS, IDIOT

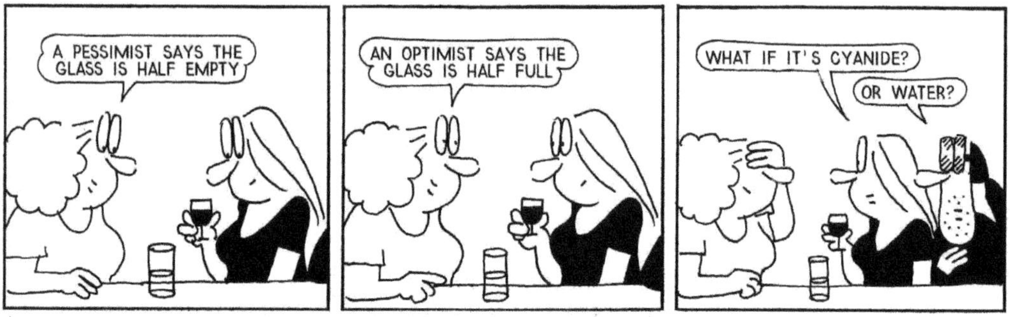
A PESSIMIST SAYS THE GLASS IS HALF EMPTY
AN OPTIMIST SAYS THE GLASS IS HALF FULL
WHAT IF IT'S CYANIDE?
OR WATER?

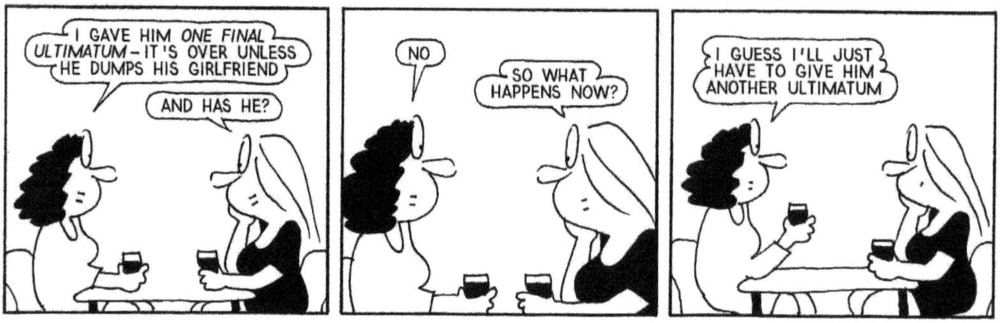
I GAVE HIM *ONE FINAL ULTIMATUM* – IT'S OVER UNLESS HE DUMPS HIS GIRLFRIEND
AND HAS HE?
NO
SO WHAT HAPPENS NOW?
I GUESS I'LL JUST HAVE TO GIVE HIM ANOTHER ULTIMATUM

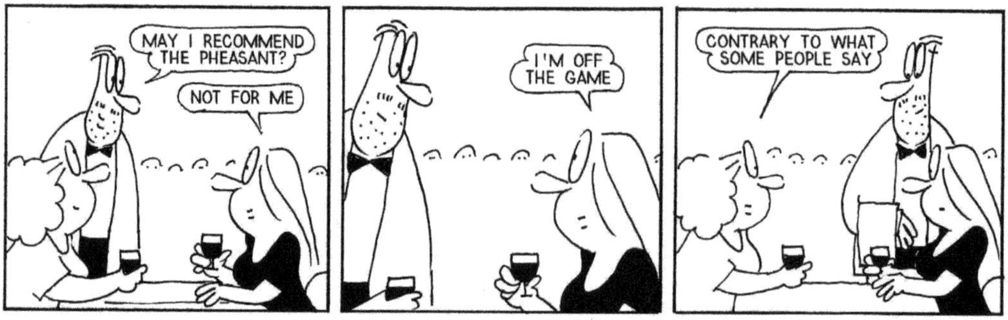
MAY I RECOMMEND THE PHEASANT?
NOT FOR ME
I'M OFF THE GAME
CONTRARY TO WHAT SOME PEOPLE SAY

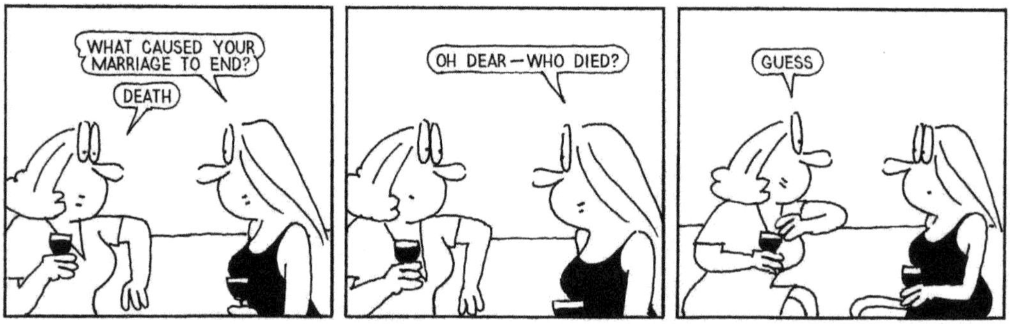
WHAT CAUSED YOUR MARRIAGE TO END?
DEATH
OH DEAR — WHO DIED?
GUESS

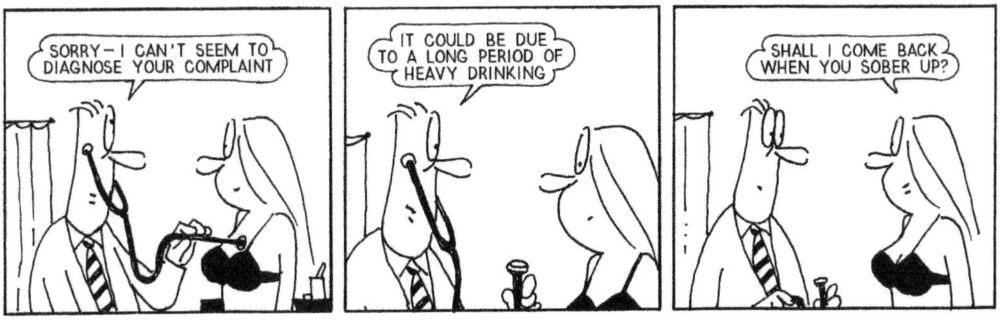
SORRY– I CAN'T SEEM TO DIAGNOSE YOUR COMPLAINT
IT COULD BE DUE TO A LONG PERIOD OF HEAVY DRINKING
SHALL I COME BACK WHEN YOU SOBER UP?

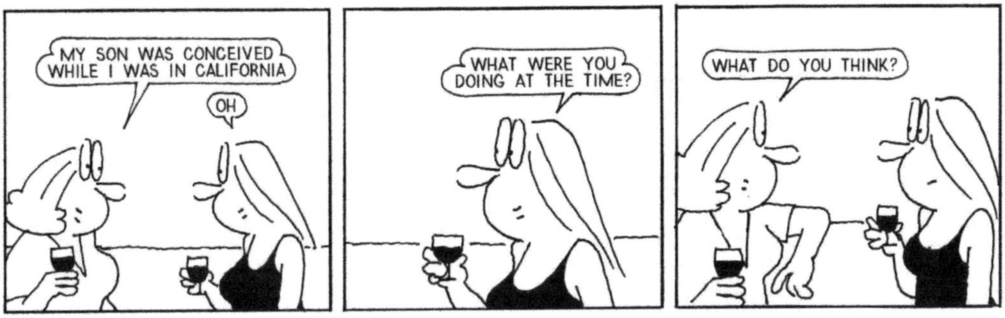
MY SON WAS CONCEIVED WHILE I WAS IN CALIFORNIA
OH
WHAT WERE YOU DOING AT THE TIME?
WHAT DO YOU THINK?

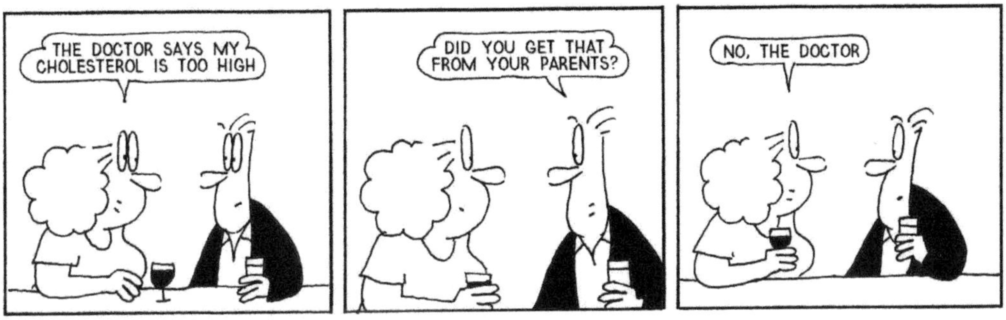
THE DOCTOR SAYS MY CHOLESTEROL IS TOO HIGH
DID YOU GET THAT FROM YOUR PARENTS?
NO, THE DOCTOR

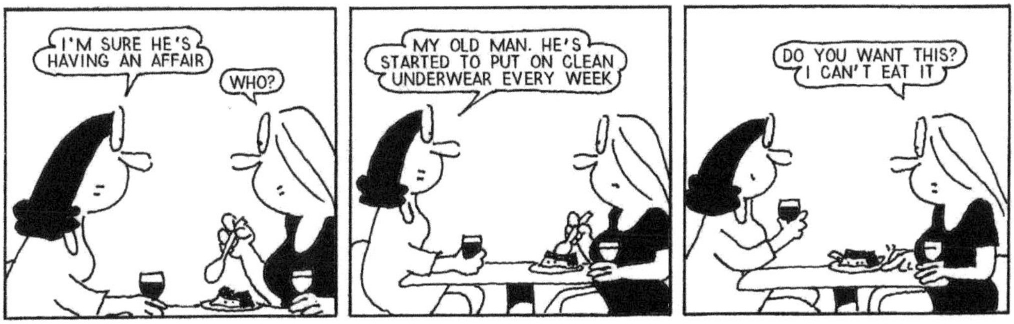
I'M SURE HE'S HAVING AN AFFAIR
WHO?
MY OLD MAN. HE'S STARTED TO PUT ON CLEAN UNDERWEAR EVERY WEEK
DO YOU WANT THIS? I CAN'T EAT IT

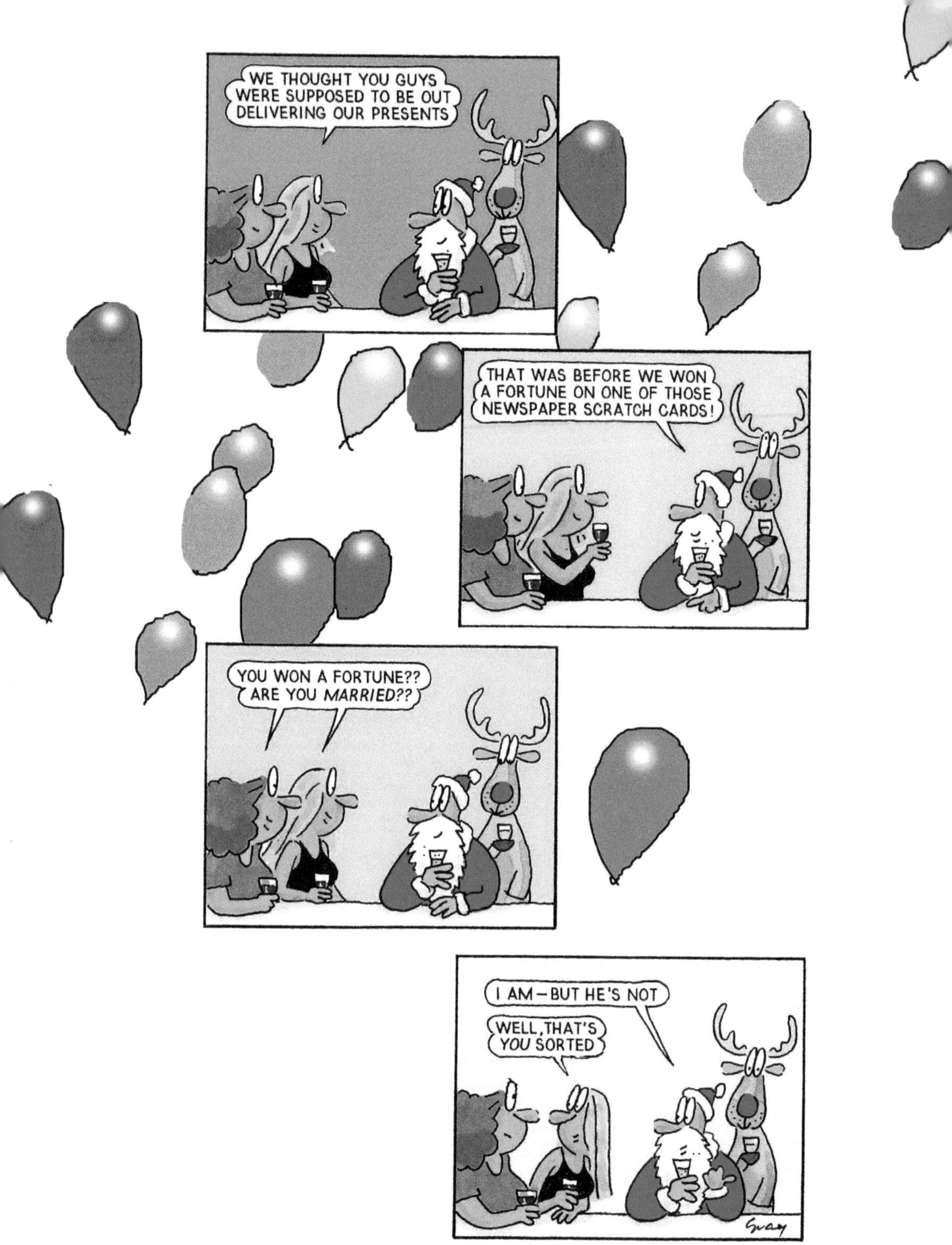
WE THOUGHT YOU GUYS WERE SUPPOSED TO BE OUT DELIVERING OUR PRESENTS
THAT WAS BEFORE WE WON A FORTUNE ON ONE OF THOSE NEWSPAPER SCRATCH CARDS!
YOU WON A FORTUNE?? ARE YOU *MARRIED??*
I AM—BUT HE'S NOT
WELL, THAT'S *YOU* SORTED